g. mai 2006.

New Crime in China

Since the collapse of communism throughout much of the world and the Tiananmen Square demonstrations in 1989, China has come under increasing pressure to reform its legal system and increase human rights protections. Yet the Chinese government's recent handling of issues such as crime within families, the Falungong sect, and the development of the internet demonstrates that despite significant criminal justice reform in 1996–7, the world's most populous country is encountering serious difficulties in incorporating the rule of law into its domestic policies.

This book examines the crimes which have recently been of the greatest concern in China and assesses the imbalance between public order and human rights in the way the Chinese legal system deals with them. These new crimes include the formation of cults, the intentional spread of infectious disease, domestic violence, sexual harassment, internet fraud and dissent, website pornography, terrorism and organized crime in the sex and drugs trades and in human trafficking. The issue of crime is of particular importance both because current social upheaval in China contributes a great deal to the increase of new crimes and because there is increasing international interest in Chinese law following the country's accession to the World Trade Organization.

A fascinating portrait of a society and legal system grappling with vast social change, *New Crime in China* will be of interest to scholars studying China and human rights as well as to legal experts with an interest in the developing countries of Asia.

Ronald C. Keith is a professor at the Griffith Business School, Griffith University. **Zhiqiu Lin** is a professor at Carleton University. Their publications include the jointly written *Law and Justice in China's New Marketplace* (Palgrave Macmillan, 2001).

Routledge Contemporary China Series

1 **Nationalism, Democracy and National Integration in China**
Leong Liew and Wang Shaoguang

2 **Hong Kong's Tortuous Democratization**
A comparative analysis
Ming Sing

3 **China's Business Reforms**
Institutional challenges in a globalised economy
Edited by Russell Smyth and Cherrie Zhu

4 **Challenges for China's Development**
An enterprise perspective
Edited by David H. Brown and Alasdair MacBean

5 **New Crime in China**
Public order and human rights
Ronald C. Keith and Zhiqiu Lin

6 **Non-Governmental Organizations in Contemporary China**
Paving the way to civil society?
Qiusha Ma

7 **Globalization and the Chinese City**
Fulong Wu

8 **The Politics of China's Accession to the World Trade Organization**
The dragon goes global
Hui Feng

9 **Narrating China**
Jia Pingwa and his fictional world
Yiyan Wang

10 **Sex, Science and Morality in China**
Joanna McMillan

New Crime in China

Public order and human rights

**Ronald C. Keith and
Zhiqiu Lin**

 Routledge
Taylor & Francis Group

LONDON AND NEW YORK

First published 2006
by Routledge
2 Park Square, Milton Park, Abingdon, Oxon OX14 4RN

Simultaneously published in the USA and Canada
by Routledge
270 Madison Ave, New York, NY 10016

Routledge is an imprint of the Taylor & Francis Group

© 2006 Ronald C. Keith and Zhiqiu Lin

Typeset in Palatino by
Newgen Imaging Systems (P) Ltd, Chennai, India
Printed and bound in Great Britain by
Biddles Ltd, King's Lynn

British Library Cataloguing in Publication Data
A catalogue record for this book is available from the British Library

Library of Congress Cataloging in Publication Data
A catalog record for this book has been requested

ISBN 0–415–31482–8

For Allisha, Amy, and Leia

Contents

Acknowledgements   ix
List of abbreviations   xi

1 New crime, human rights protection, and public order   1

2 The 'Falungong problem' and the prospects for criminal
  justice reform   37

3 The criminal justice response to violence in the modern
  Chinese family   63

4 'Organized crime', politics, and the law   90

5 Crime and human rights in cyber-space   117

6 Squaring the circles of criminal justice reform?   142

Select glossary of Chinese criminal justice terms   169
Notes   177
References   206
Index   215

Acknowledgements

The current volume is essentially the third volume in a series that deals with various aspects of legal reform and China's modern struggle for the rule of law. The continuous research funding of the Social Sciences and Humanities Research Council of Canada (SSHRC) made it possible to research and write these volumes. Additional funding was provided by the University of Calgary and Carleton University.

The present volume has greatly benefited from the ready and informative explanations of senior Beijing jurists, many of whom have been directly involved in the research and drafting of key legislation pertaining to criminal justice and the protection of human rights. The authors take responsibility for any of the interpretations that are offered in this volume; however, they would like to extend a special thanks to the following busy prominent jurists and law professors for their extensive and patient explanations, namely, Chen Mingxia, Chen Xingliang, Cui Min, Dan Wei, Huang Lie, Song Yinghui, Wang Minyuan, and Wang Zuofu. We are also indebted to the Chinese People's Association for Friendship with Foreign Countries for its help in arranging meetings with colleagues from the CASS Institute of Law, Peking University Law School, the People's University Law School, the Research Institute of Procuratorial Theory (Supreme People's Procuratorate), and the Procedural Law Research Center of the Chinese University of Politics and Law.

The authors have been particularly concerned to record and assess the progressive elements of legal reform in China. Indeed, in our view, Chinese successes have been underreported. However, the authors have also made some very direct criticisms that we hope our colleagues will take in the well meaning international spirit of 'criticism and self-criticism' (*piping, ziwo piping*).

Over the course of the preparation and writing of this book, Dr Keith enjoyed the academic hospitality provided through the good offices of President Charles Morrison of the East–West Center, Honolulu. The EWC provided essential respite from heavy administrative duties.

With appropriate permission, a significant part of a journal article was used as the basis for Chapter 2. The authors would like to thank the

Oxford University Press and *The China Quarterly* at the School for Oriental and African Studies, University of London, for permission relating to Ronald C. Keith and Zhiqiu Lin, 'The "Falungong Problem": Politics and the Struggle for the Rule of Law in China', *The China Quarterly*, no. 175, September 2003, pp. 623–42.

In the preparation of this volume, we were provided with excellent suggestions by an anonymous reviewer to whom we would like to extend our thanks. We are grateful for the research assistance of Xu Kai, University of Calgary PhD programme. Mr Xu also prepared the glossary of Chinese terms. Cathryn Kallwitz helped in compiling the English and Chinese bibliography. Last but certainly not least it was a pleasure to work with our editor at Routledge, Peter Sowden.

Ronald C. Keith and Zhiqiu Lin

Abbreviations

ACWF	All-China Women's Federation
AIDS	Acquired Immunodeficiency Syndrome
APEC	Association of Petroleum Exporting Countries
BR	*Beijing Review*
CASS	Chinese Academy of Social Sciences
CCP	Chinese Communist Party
CL79	1979 Criminal Law
CL97	1997 Criminal Law
COWTN	Criminal Organization with a Triad Nature
CPL79	1979 Criminal Procedure Law
CPL96	1996 Criminal Procedure Law
CPPCC	Chinese People's Political Consultative Conference
CQ	*The China Quarterly*
FBIS	Foreign Broadcast Information Service
FLG	Falungong
HIV	Human Immunodeficiency Virus
ISP	Internet Service Provider
NPC	National People's Congress
NPCSC	Standing Committee of the National People's Congress
PRC	People's Republic of China
SARS	Severe Acute Respiratory Syndrome
SEPA	State Environmental Protection Agency
SPC	Supreme People's Court
SPP	Supreme People's Procuratorate
WHO	World Health Organization
WTO	World Trade Organization

1 New crime, human rights protection, and public order

Invariably states monopolize the right to determine and to inflict criminal punishment.[1] Criminal justice is a jealously guarded prerogative as it is often the key to the state's control over society and public order. The 'rule of law' has a lot to do with the enjoyment of human rights, but, even in the Western liberal democratic context, it also is seen as a prerequisite to public order.[2] Especially in the post-9/11 context, there is among Western democracies, a new and growing concern with regard to public safety. Nevertheless, Western criminal justice has, for a long time, required a strong emphasis on the protection of human rights. This book will focus on the development of Chinese criminal justice reform since 1996–7, paying close attention to the balance or imbalance of public order and human rights in the reform context of the changing relationship between Chinese law and politics.

The People's Republic of China (PRC) is undergoing extraordinary social and economic change. It is no exaggeration to say that the direction and development of criminal justice has a direct bearing on both the legitimacy of the Party-State and the well-being of the Chinese people. As one Chinese observer noted, at the time of the passage of the amended 1997 Criminal Law (hereinafter, CL97), criminal law is a 'basic law' (*jiben falu*) that 'has a bearing on tens of thousands of households, [and] extensively attracts the attention of various sectors in any country with a legal system'.[3] Many of China's jurists have put the question as to how to achieve criminal justice reform, given China's rapidly changing and culturally distinctive social and economic environment. This question lies at the heart of the Chinese struggle to establish 'human rights' under a 'rule of law'.

China's jurists and legislators have undertaken unprecedented study of the international standards of criminal justice. Regardless of the Chinese Communist Party's (CCP) political interest in the 'Chinese characteristics' of the legal system, Western influence within this system has never been greater. China's jurists are students of criminal justice reform who are engaged in the self-conscious adaptation of international norms to local conditions. For them, such adaptation is a legitimate endeavour that cannot simply be dismissed as 'cultural relativism'.

While rejecting 'blind Westernization' as irrational, these jurists are interested in a practical working synthesis of 'globalization' (*guojihua*) and 'localization' (*bentuhua*). The latter supports a locally sensitive adaptation of external norms and experience to the underlying requirements of distinctive society and culture. The former, on the other hand, suggests an 'international developmental process in law in which the particular legal systems of each country in the world approximate more closely and come together in mutual interdependence and linkage'.[4] Pitnam Potter has recently described such synthesis as 'selective adaptation by which the forms of law borrowed from abroad are given meaning based on the norms of local legal culture'.[5]

China's jurists are responding to both international and domestic pressures to enhance protection of individual human rights. At the same time they are facing urgent demands to protect society from disturbing new criminal behaviour in what could be described as the raw context of compressed generational change, deep familial crisis, seemingly hopeless corruption, institutional challenge, and axiological despair. Those responsible for criminal justice legislation and the related reform of the justice and law enforcement systems are scrambling to define and apply a criminal justice strategy that can cope with wildly proliferating 'new crime'.

At the time of the National People's Congress' (NPC) approval of the CL97, official commentary hailed the emergence of a modern code that synthesized Chinese criminal law 'with the principle of a criminal law which is in keeping with international practice.' The Minister of Justice, Xiao Yang proudly proclaimed that the 1996 amendments to the criminal procedural and administrative punishment laws 'further established a good image of the legal system of our country'.[6]

The same optimism had been earlier expressed at the time of the 1996 revision to the Criminal Procedural Law (CPL96). There was an expectation that the CPL96 would facilitate a sea change in the application and implementation of new concepts of law. Wang Hanbin, the Vice-Chairman of the Standing Committee of the National People's Congress (NPCSC), reflected on the new balance between social control and the protection of rights and on the need to apply the CPL96 as against 'customary practices':

> The key to earnestly implementing the amended Criminal Procedural Law lies in changing our concepts, both in the ideological realm and in practical work; in conscientiously changing some customary practices and concepts inconsistent with the development of socialist democracy and legal institutions; in correctly applying legal means to punishing criminals and protecting citizens' rights; and in earnestly combining the efforts to fight and punish crime and to protect citizens' legitimate rights and interests.[7]

With the reforms of 1996–7 reformers also claimed that China's convergence with the International Covenant on Civil and Political Rights (*Gongmin he zhengzhi quanli guoji gongyue*) was underway with new domestic recognition of various norms concerning, for example, the presumption of innocence, the elimination of the official use of torture, *habeas corpus*, and the accused right to self-defence in a court of law. These reformers affirmed: 'The degree of importance attached to criminal procedural law directly indicates the degree of the rule of law in a country.'[8] This new priority has also involved a major structural shift in the justice system away from the Continental model of inquisitorial justice towards the Anglo-American adversarial system.

Reform jurists have repeatedly emphasized the fundamental conceptual shift in the CL97 that entrenched three key principles relating to the punishment that must fit the crime, equality before the law, and no crime without a law (*nullum crimen sine lege*). The last of these three maxims has sometimes been referred to as 'the principle of legality', and, in the Western context, the explanation of the general principles of criminal law often begins with the citation and explanation of 'no crime, without a law'.[9]

In order to ensure compliance with the three principles, China's legal reformers proposed a new strategy of comprehensive stipulation that would challenge past reliance on the principle of 'flexibility' (*luohuoxing*). The latter had been used to justify casual and unqualified, state-directed analogy in law and the opportunistic substitution of state policy for law. For a very long time, 'flexibility' had been recognized as a legitimate and key principle of Chinese jurisprudence, but in the 1997 context of reform, it came under direct challenge. For example, Zhang Fengge, Director, Criminal Office of the Supreme People's Procuratorate and Wang Zuofu, an eminent Peoples University criminal law expert, placed 'flexibility' in antithesis to rational modern legal development and hailed the 1997 strategy of comprehensive and specific stipulation as it

> is conducive to preventing the practice of determining crimes at one's discretion and has provided more effective legal protection for citizens' personal freedom, rights and interests .... This amendment will enable the criminal legal system ... to keep abreast of world trends.[10]

At the time of CL97 revision there was a euphoric optimism that the new emphasis on judicial justice and the protection of rights would be facilitated in the new strategy of comprehensive stipulation. A Xinhua commentary noted how, in the past, the criminal code had often failed to provide specific stipulation or had relied on very loose stipulation that offered little in terms of clear and specific language. The same commentary claimed in an effusive fashion:

> It is universally held that, compared with the old criminal law, the most significant characteristic of the new code is in its most detailed

possible and most comprehensive and concrete stipulations regarding each and every kind of criminal offense. It provides protection in an all-round way to a citizen's rights and interests. It strives to guarantee judicial justice and spares no effort to ensure the building of the socialist market economy will proceed smoothly.[11]

What was originally thought to be 'the most detailed possible' stipulation of 1997 was intended to deal with the fast-paced changes in China that had occurred since the start in late 1978 of the open door and the economic reform process. The question as to how many stipulations would be needed to make the law comprehensive was apparently moot. However, the 1979 Criminal Law (hereinafter, CL79) had 192 articles and only 103 Special Provisions. The CL97, on the other hand, included 452 articles that were intended to deal exhaustively and clearly with specifically stipulated crimes.

Much of the specific content of 1979 was carried over into the CL97, but for the advocates of revision, such as the Minister of Justice, Xiao Yang, the original CL79 had been outstripped by events. The criminal law needed 'to affix new criminal responsibility' in the face of rapidly developing 'new crime'. Moreover, the CL79 had still made room for analogy and for vaguely worded omnibus provisions. Reflecting on underlying assumptions of the CL79, reformers in 1997, for example, noted: '... the provisions on crimes of dereliction, hooligan[ism], profiteering were too sweeping and became three well-known "big baskets" '.[12]

The analysis in this book brings forward in time the 1997 strategy for criminal justice so as to discuss how well this strategy has stood up to the extraordinary, and often unanticipated, generation of new crime and fast changing political and social demands to affix new criminal liability, or criminal responsibility (*xingshi zeren*). The success or failure of the 1997 strategy is critical to the wider struggle to establish human rights under the rule of law in China. This study will ask how this new strategy that incorporates comprehensive stipulation, the new balance of values, and the new relation of criminal and criminal procedural law has withstood the exponential proliferation of new crime. It will also discuss the extent to which the new strategy has been able to cope with the so-called customary practices of the CCP's political–legal or *zhengfa* system.

Pitman Potter has elaborated on the integrated political, cultural, and institutional correlations of Chinese law and politics that characterize the *zhengfa* system. He concluded that the current reform approach to the rule of law is still 'fundamentally instrumentalist'. In 2001, Potter suggested contemporary legal reform 'remains confined to the discourse of "political–legal work" in which Party leadership continues as a dominant theme'.[13] However, Potter has also acknowledged that the 1996–7 CPL/CL revision did lay some new groundwork for legal reform: '... driven by principles of fairness (*gongzheng*) and process (*youxu*) the

[1996–7] revisions were to achieve a balance between punishing crime and safeguarding human rights by requiring greater attention to evidence of guilt'.[14] Indeed, many of China's own jurists saw in this reform a new and powerful statement on how the law's 'balance of values' (*jiazhi pingheng*) synthesizes public order and human rights protection.[15]

Post-1997 social conditions have not provided the law with any real respite to adjust to a new strategy for criminal justice. The post-1997 contents of new crime relate to a constantly proliferating range of very contentious political issues concerning, for example, membership in, and the organization of, 'evil cults', 'domestic violence', cyber dissent, internet fraud and website pornography, internationalized organized crime, terrorism and the sex and drug trades, illegal migration, and the trafficking in human beings.

The spread of new crime and related social instability threatens to compromise the Party struggle for legitimacy. The consolidation of a modern criminal justice system has, therefore, become a significant political priority. This consolidation, however, requires continuous consideration of the complex relationship between law, morality, and culture. Both the Party and the jurists are deeply involved in resolving the related contradictions between 'globalization' and 'localization'.

Most recently, the CCP has attempted to manage the contradictions of domestic institutional and societal change on the neo-traditional basis of combining the rule of law and rule of virtue (*fazhi yu dezhi*). This renewed emphasis on morality is grounded in ideological assumption that the rule of law, in and of itself, is inadequate unless it enters into a seamless and continuous relation to Chinese morality as it deliberately confronts negative foreign influence. The Party's correlation of law and morality reflects the Party's assertion of the importance of law responding to Chinese society, history, and culture as well as the Party's political need to counter the negative cultural affects of 'globalization' as 'blind Westernization'.[16]

Chinese politics is essentially conflicted in that there are competing trends that contemporaneously focus on the resuscitation of China's distinctive moral culture and on modern adaptation to international trends and norms. The political focus on morality has not stopped some of China's most senior jurists, and their patrons within the Party leadership, from advocating criminal justice reform as part of the wider struggle for the rule of law and human rights development. Law scholars, You Guanghui and Shi Yan'an, for example, argued that, while globalization is not identical with 'Westernization', modern criminal law development reflects not only the need to protect the rights and interests of law-abiding citizens, but also the human rights of those alleged to have committed crimes.[17]

Criminal justice reform has been justified in relation to the deepening of market reform. The CL97 revision dropped the special provisions on counterrevolutionary crime and featured 'new economic crime' as more important than the Cultural Revolutionary issues of class rule and struggle. China is now passing through World Trade Organization (WTO) induction and will be exposed, as never before, to the full impact of economic globalization. In 2001, the then Party chief, Jiang Zemin, instructed the CCP on the need for the development of a foreign-related system of law facilitating China's induction into the WTO's legal regimes: 'We should lose no time in sorting out, revising and improving relevant laws and regulations concerning the economy, establish a foreign-related law regime that conforms to the reality of our country and is in compliance with the rules of the WTO.'[18]

In 2003, reform jurists were claiming that, with 'cultural' and 'legal globalization', there would be much greater opportunity to create, in China, a 'rule of law in public security' (*gongan fazhi*). In effect, China's participation in the WTO provided domestic reformers with new political leverage to support the improvement of the quality of public security personnel and to promote human rights protection at the same time as controlling crime.[19] Similarly, reformers attempted to shine the WTO's spotlight on the domestic failure to define clearly 'procuratorial power'.[20]

Chinese society is experiencing increasingly serious insults to public order and morality. Jiang Zemin, in referring to the example of spreading pornography, once reflected on the paradox that characterizes China's modern predicament: 'Our skill at economic construction has been quite successful, and people are happy about it. This is our nation's success. But of what significance is economic success if morals decline?'[21]

Since 1996–7, criminal justice reform, while it has continued to develop its focus on economic crime, has evinced much greater interest in affixing 'criminal liabilities' that pertain more clearly to cultural and moral activities. The sex and drug trades, human trafficking, and illegal immigration are, for example, eating away at the basic foundations of society and morality. Contemporaneously, the Party panicked in the face of the rapid spread of 'heretical cults' (*xiejiao*) such as the Falungong (FLG). Also, 'black societies' (*hei shehui*) such as the 'Three Harmony Society' of Hong Kong, the Japanese Mountain Gate Organization, and the Zhulianbang from Taiwan are becoming more internationalized inside China.[22] This is all occurring at a time when the weak, new institutions of the justice system are adapting to a new strategy for criminal justice and are struggling to cope with the lack of trained professionals and persisting arbitrary patterns of public security behaviour in the justice system, itself. Moreover, debilitating and endemic corruption points to the Party-State's failure to provide even the most basic justice under the 'rule of law'. Corruption threatens to destroy any new modest capacity for judicial justice.

Drawing on both Chinese dynastic history as well as comparative international experience relating to the fall of East European and Soviet

Communist Parties, the electoral defeat of Mexico's Revolutionary System Party, and the declining political fortunes of Suharto and Fujimori, the CCP's former Party boss, Jiang Zemin candidly acknowledged that the CCP's survival is tied to 'public feeling':

> Whether the people are for or against is the basic factor deciding the rise and fall of a political party and a political power. An honest style of government has always been an important factor for popular support, good government, and the stability and prosperity of the society. This is an important lesson of the law of rise and fall. The collapse of every dynasty in Chinese history and ... the loss of power in contemporary world of the political parties which had been in power for a long time were all closely connected with the trend of public feeling.[23]

Jiang saw in what he touted as a distinctively Chinese combination of the rules of law and virtue an opportunity to placate 'public feeling'.

Criminal justice has been caught up in a socially troubled context of competing values. The party has emphasized morality in response to spreading 'blind Westernization' in Chinese society. The legal issues surrounding religious freedom and participation in spiritual movements have become especially contentious as the criminal justice system has responded to social ferment, challenge to the integrity of the Chinese family, and profound popular cynicism about the irrelevance of the Party's morality and ideology. The CCP's prestige and authority is on the line as corruption threatens to overwhelm the judicial process and law enforcement. Finally, add to this already volatile mix the affects of exponential technological and informational change. The management of political and legal change is increasingly influenced by technology. And the law has had to address new categories of electronic economic crime as well as the hugely sensitive human rights issues concerning the regulation of internet communication and cyber dissent.

Again to cite the former Party chief, Jiang Zemin, the internet represents not only an opportunity for the creation of a modern information network, but also an important 'new front' that informs the CCP's communications strategy for public order and social stability:

> We should also continue to enhance the appeal of our publicity work and spruce up its capacity to guide public opinion. We should attach due importance to opinion-making and publicity by using the internet. In general principle we should actively develop the internet, make full use of it, tighten up its management, maximize what is good and minimize what is bad, tap our strengths, take the initiative in our hands, constantly increase the influence and combat effectiveness of our internet publicity work and turn it into a new front in the ideological political work of the Party.[24]

This book examines the criminal justice system's response to new crime in China's complex transitional political context of deep economic and societal change. In 1996–7, Chinese law-making and jurisprudence formally endorsed a 'balance of values' modifying the traditional subordination of criminal procedure to criminal law so as to create a new balance between human rights protection and social control. The analysis in each of this book's chapters will identify and assess the direction of contemporary criminal justice reform by focusing, in depth, on specific areas of new crime, paying close attention as to whether specific law and enforcement are converging with or diverging from the principles and organizational requirements of the 1996–7 strategy for criminal justice reform.

Criminal justice reform in historical context

Contemporary Chinese criminal justice reform deliberately seeks to avoid the worst excesses of 'blind Westernization' and 'cultural relativism'. Chinese and Western legal scholarship, however, agree that one cannot overestimate the extent to which history has affected the course of contemporary reform. A thumbnail sketch of the broad outlines of relevant imperial legal history provides a useful set of benchmarks against which one can begin to evaluate post-1996–7 criminal justice reform and the related implications of the combined rules of law and virtue.

According to Xin Ren's analysis, the hallmark of the imperial legal tradition was its pervasive adaptation to 'familism'. Criminal law vigorously responded to violations of the essential moral ethos of society that threatened to disturb the cosmological order. The legitimacy of the dynastic house was closely tied to the stability of society as it reflected the cosmological order. Xin describes the values underlying imperial criminal law as follows:

> The fundamental values of familism, such as the authority and reverence associated with seniority, the absolute and unconditional duty of filial piety, and the superior status of group welfare over individual interest were an integral part of imperial law and served as guiding principles for the criminal penalty system.[25]

In this view, the imperial legal system was little more than a 'tool of authority for the purpose of social ordering'.[26]

With respect to this 'Confucianization of the law', the judge and ruler could draw directly on morality 'in dealing with situations for which there is no legal rule exactly in point'.[27] Herein one might find the beginnings of a historical explanation for the modern use of analogy as well as precedent for the inclination towards 'policy as the soul of law' and the contemporary attempt to combine the rules of law and virtue.

Also, the penal codes over the centuries directly incorporated prevailing morality into the statutes, especially with respect to the punishment of crime relating to the so-called ten abominations, such as plotting against the emperor or plotting against the family's patriarch. These crimes were considered so serious as to attract especially severe punishment. The law had to work especially hard to compensate for the related loss of harmony in society and the cosmos.

In more minor matters, however, the penal code might defer to customary law. As Geoffrey MacCormack suggests, this was inspired by an imperial calculation to the effect that the best way to achieve results from moral instruction in society was to defer to the clan: 'The government had probably always been in favour of the clan exercising, within certain limits, jurisdiction over the behaviour of its members.'[28]

Recent PRC historiography also cites the structural burdens of imperial legal history. Criminal procedural law, in its style and composition, utterly subordinated itself to the substantive requirements of the law as it related to prevailing values. The criminal law system was dominant within the legal system as a whole, and apparently this restricted the systematic development of other critical 'departments' of law that specifically addressed procedure as well as civil affairs, administration, the economy, and marriage and the family.[29] According to contemporary Chinese historiography, imperial criminal law was all about social control, achieved through severe punishment as deterrence against deviant thought and action. The legal tradition required uniformity on the part of the Emperor's subjects and helped foster a 'timid psychology of obedience' that has resisted the development of a modern legal consciousness of freedom, equality, and democracy.[30]

In 1949, New China inherited a penal tradition that focused on punishment as the means by which to maintain a uniform morality and social stability. This tradition subordinated matters of process to substantive moral purpose. Judicial justice was, in large measure, a dependent variable that existed only to service the substantive content of the criminal law. Prior to 1978, this content represented an exclusive focus on social control, public order, and class struggle. Criminal procedural law was merely a set of reinforcing secondary rules designed to insure the realization of the punitive stipulations of the criminal law. In short, Criminal procedural law was a cipher. It was 'form' (*xingshi*), as distinguished from the 'essence' (*ben*), of criminal law. In fact, its status was so low that, prior to 1996, only a few intrepid jurists had made it the focus of their research.

1979 as the starting point of criminal justice reform

The punitive dimensions of criminal law and the related subordination of form to essence have deep roots in Chinese history and society. However, if there was an available developed tradition of criminal law, the NPC was not able to codify the Criminal Procedural and Criminal Laws until 1979. Speaking at the 16 January 1980 meeting of the CCP Central Committee, Deng Xiaoping proudly characterized the fashioning of the CL79 and 1979 Criminal Procedure Law (CPL79) as a major historical achievement:

> For the 29 years since the founding of New China, we have had no criminal law. Though we started repeatedly to draw up such a code and it went through more than 30 drafts, nothing ever came of the project. Now a code of criminal law and a code of criminal procedure have been adopted and promulgated and are being implemented. The whole nation sees in them the hope for a strictly enforced socialist legal system.[31]

Deng put his own gloss on the importance of law and order. To secure public order, he said, meant that law must be used effectively as a 'weapon'. To serve the masses and to support the modernization drive, unity and stability were absolutely essential. Deng was not personally 'soft on criminals'. He was in tune with a criminal law tradition of 'heavy penalty-ism' (*zhongxingzhuyi*). He was the architect of a new strategy for institutionalization, and he was interested in dealing with hostile forces on the basis of 'socialist legality' rather than on the basis of uncontrolled and arbitrary political movements.[32] Initially, Deng's utilitarian commitment to 'legalization' was qualified in the following way:

> But the legal system will be improved only gradually in the course of practice, and we can't wait for that. When we fail to mete out stern punishment to so many criminals, can we even speak of having a legal system? All those who undermine stability and unity in any way must be dealt with sternly, according the merits of each case.[33]

In 1979–80, some Western experts treated the much touted and delayed codification as an important step forward, which recalled some of the more progressive features of the 1954 state constitution such as its explicit reference to 'equality before the law'. However, these experts were, not surprisingly, still conflicted about the scope and nature of Chinese criminal justice reform.

Leng Shao-chuan and Hung Dahchiu's path-breaking 1985 study of Chinese criminal justice placed the 1979 codification in the post-1949 context of cyclical historical differentiation between the 'formal, jural' and 'informal, societal models' of legal development.[34] The 'jural' model anticipated the steady stipulation and perfection of the law as well as its deliberately qualified separation from the disruptive vicissitudes of politics. The tentative 1954 jural model suffered greatly in the extra-legal politics and mass campaigns of the 1950s, and again in the extremes of 1960s and 1970s class struggle. The 1979 codification was, therefore, considered a long overdue correction to the 'societal model' in its unqualified integration of the law and politics, in its justification of 'taking policy as the substitute for law' (*yi zhengce daiti falu*) and in its extension of mass-line flexibility in local time and space.[35]

The legal history of the early 1980s was somewhat conflicted, but a new jural perspective did emerge. In 1986, Deng Xiaoping, who had only a few years earlier advised 'striking hard' at criminals, became concerned about instilling a new sense of legality in the Party and the population. He started to deal with some of the long-standing problems that informed the *zhengfa* system. Deng instructed the Party's Central Commission for Discipline Inspection to yield to law when it comes to criminal matters:

> It is not appropriate for the Party to concern itself with matters that fall within the scope of the law. If the Party intervenes in everything, the people will never acquire a sense of the rule of law. The Party should concern itself with inner-Party discipline, leaving problems that fall within the scope of the law to the state and government.[36]

Progressively, the law's codification and implementation was given new political priority as part of Deng Xiaoping's Post-Cultural Revolution institution-building strategy that sought to support the modernization drive and to pre-empt any future reoccurrence of open-ended, large-scale class violence. The development of Party perspective related to the CCP leaders' reflections on their own experience during the Cultural Revolution with kangaroo courts, arbitrary arrest, and trumped-up charges relating to 'counterrevolution' and 'capitalist restoration'.

Even the most senior leaders were denied the law's protection. Often their own families were torn apart by the extremes of class struggle. Subsequently, distressed and chastened senior leaders attacked 'leftist' viewpoint that had called for the 'smashing' of the justice system that allegedly served the 'rotten' purposes of the 'new bourgeoisie'. All of this was important tuition in Mao's school of 'hard knocks'. The leaders' personal political experience underscore the institutional importance of a 'rule of law'. China's leaders wanted some form of insurance against the horrors of 'legal nihilism'. Having suffered from indiscriminate political persecution and having stared into the fiery abyss of Cultural Revolutionary destruction, the Party leadership hoped to rebuild the law and the legal system as a hedge against future political extremism. The complete stipulation of the law became politically necessary to insure against any relapse into the unqualified excesses of class struggle.[37]

The post-Cultural Revolution 'legalization' (*faluhua*) and 'democratization' (*minzhuhua*) did not, however, entrench an unqualified new paradigm of 'jural' development. In the first place, as is typical of Chinese law-making, codification focused on resuscitating and building upon past legal experience. Codification, in 1979, did not presume to challenge the 'political-legal system' (*zhengfa xitong*). This system had always pushed the law and politics together, hence the formal application of law in the criminal justice system was part of a 'comprehensive' socio-jural approach that called for concurrent 'strike hard' political mobilization, prevention of crime, and the 'comprehensive management of public order' (*shehui zhi'an zonghe zhili*).

The political aspect of the criminal law was tied up with a persisting notion of law as a 'weapon' to be used to resist 'counterrevolution'. In 1979, the reformers in the Party and legal circles were not so strong that they could throw out the existing special provisions on counterrevolution. Codification was certainly affected by the internal attacks on 'class struggle as the key link' and debates concerning the law's content highlighted the woolly and unscientific nature of counterrevolutionary crime. The latter had imposed frequently changing subjective and arbitrary political assumptions on the law. Such perspective, however, did not then determine the outcome of codification. 'Counterrevolutionary crime' stayed in the criminal law in order to deal with the occasional handful of future class enemies.[38] In 1979, the reformers could go no farther than a more rigorous definition of 'counterrevolution'. The latter was not abolished; it was placed within the more narrowly circumscribed stipulations of law.

Second, while codification clarified crime and punishment in newly stipulated detail, the drafters of the CL79 and CPL79 genuflected before the Party-sanctioned mass-line principle of 'flexibility'. This principle, for example, was used to justify the continued application of Supreme People's Court (SPC)-endorsed analogy in areas of 'criminal activity' where the legislated stipulation of 'crime' was weak, if not entirely absent.

Current reform analysis explains that in 1979, there was only a grudging recognition of the related problem of analogy (*leitui*) whereby new criminal responsibility was devised by state authorities through the loose analogical extension of extant stipulated 'crime'. This was often achieved with simplistic reference to 'other' types of criminal activity that seemed to parallel specifically stipulated crimes. According to the following provision, analogy was explicitly sanctioned in the CL79 Article 70:

A crime that is not expressly stipulated in the Special Provisions of this Law may be determined and punished according to the most closely analogous article of the Special Provisions of this Law, but the matter shall be submitted to the Supreme People's Court for approval.[39]

Although the SPC was granted the power to sanction new constructions of 'criminal liability', or responsibility, analogy, endowed the law enforcement agencies with a great deal of powers to determine guilt at the expense of the individual's right to judicial justice. The gap between domestic and international criminal law trends was acknowledged, but the CL79 retained analogy, as it was politically necessary to the protection of society in the state authorities' fight against post-Cultural Revolution crime waves.[40] Moreover, despite Deng Xiaoping's call for a complete set of laws, comprehensive stipulation was still a matter of aspiration rather than reality.

Third, the CPL79 bowed before the august supremacy of the CL79. The former merely provided a convenient form through which the substance of the latter was to be expressed. The Party's new interest in law, as a buffer against runaway class struggle, did not immediately result in a newly stated equality between criminal and criminal procedural law.

In coming to terms with the Cultural Revolution, the Dengist leadership sponsored the law's development as part of a new institutional strategy that was designed to contain the 'spirit of the leader'. As was indicated in his 1978 sixteen-character policy, '*you fa keyi, you fa biyi, zhi fa biyan, wei fa bijiu*' (we need laws, these laws must be followed, their implementation must be strict, and violations of the law must be punished), Deng wanted the accelerated legislation of more and more law. He expected that even the Party would 'act according to law' (*yifa banshi*) but his strategy for post-Cultural Revolution institutionalization was still heavily qualified in the priority given to social control and public order.

Having experienced the trauma of the Cultural Revolution, Dengist leadership feared instability; it qualified class struggle; and it interdicted large-scale mobilizations in Chinese politics. This was all part of Deng's strategy to pre-empt two-line struggle and unproductive extremist debates over policy. At the same time the Party leadership praised the inherently 'scientific' nature of the mass-line work-style based upon 'seeking the truth from the facts'. At the onset of reform, the Party not only emphasized new institutionalization, but it also updated the mass line in public security work and social control.

The newly formulated mass-line strategy for public security was announced as 'comprehensive management of public order' (*shehui zhi'an zonghe zhili*). This omnidimensional socio-jural strategy pushed the law close to politics. At the time, the Party was rushing to rebuild its own organizations. Any steps towards the 'rule of law' were taken within the overall struggle to create 'socialist spiritual civilization'. Crime fighting and criminal justice strategy involved the close networking and interaction of community and legal agencies but it also included new 'jural' emphasis on the comprehensive stipulation and enforcement of criminal law.

Stipulation and enforcement were presumably complimentary aspects of the comprehensive 'societal' and educational strategy requiring the directed networking of official state agencies and mass associations. This strategy self-consciously linked law to Party ideological and organizational discipline. In other words, like the criminal law on counterrevolution, social control, based upon mass-line organizational strategy, survived the demise of 'class struggle as the key link'. Comprehensive control was predicated in what critics might call a recidivist mass-line approach. The legitimacy of the latter related to its 'Chinese characteristics'. At the same time, this 'comprehensive control' was somewhat inconsistently rationalized in a science and theory designed to meet reform demands concerning the open door and national economic development.[41]

From 1979 to this day, in fact, the work of public security agencies reflects a strategy for social control based upon 'comprehensive management of public order'. This 'comprehensiveness' is predicated in an extensive networking connecting families, public security agencies, educational institutions, street committees, etc.[42] This extensive networking of official agencies and social forces in a public security 'system' (*xitong*) is nationally directed to pre-empt and fight crime. On 12 May 1986, the NPC passed regulations governing the 'comprehensive management of public order', and these were later amended in May 1994.[43]

Subsequently, the 1999 national plan for 'the comprehensive management of public order' spelt out the Party's prioritized concerns over social instability. The plan explicitly addressed the key contradictions within society, highlighting, for example, six areas that were seriously affecting public security and social stability. The plan referenced the spreading activities of organized criminal gangs. It called for the strengthening of rural social order in light of the production of fake agricultural goods and the growing phenomena associated with banned cults and 'illegal' religious activity.

The plan also called for the strengthening of grass roots social order; mobilizing social forces to prevent and reduce juvenile delinquency and the 'management' of the floating population. Transience was generating more and more new crime. The plan also highlighted the settlement and training of those released from prison, the improvement of security along the rail lines, and the consolidation of the leadership responsibility system within the management of public order.[44]

Even today, the Party still tends to bring the law within a comprehensive strategy to respond to its view of society and its problems. On 12 April 2004, Luo Gan, a member of the Politbureau Standing Committee and Chairman of the Central Commission for the Comprehensive Management of Public Order, affirmed that the 'comprehensive management of public order' is both a 'scientific concept and a political process that supports long-term harmony and stability'. Luo, in fact, described such comprehensive management as 'an important component part of the socialist cause with Chinese characteristics as well as 'the concrete manifestation of practicing the important thinking of the 'Three Represents'.[45] Luo was especially concerned to build up such a management system at the grass roots level.

Hopefully the foregoing analysis provides some sense of the parameters within which criminal justice reform has had to operate.

Politics and post-1996–7 criminal justice reform

The traditional bias that for so long eviscerated procedural justice came under increasing challenge during the post-1979 period of economic reform and open door. During the mid-1980s, and on into the 1990s, there was a growing interest in the legal definition and the protection of newly emerging 'rights and interests' (*quanyi*) in society. At the same time there was a new national debate about the need to establish 'the rule of law' (*fazhi*) so as to protect human rights. This resulted in changing political perspective on the inner substance of criminal justice reform as a matter of balancing public order and the protection of human rights.

In 1992, Deng Xiaoping's 'southern tour theory' focused attention on 'the market economy is a rule of law economy' (*shichang jingji shi fazhi jingji*). This perspective was the key to understanding the 1996–7 revisions to both the criminal procedural and criminal law. The revision finally shifted attention away from the class struggle and 'counterrevolutionary crime' to emphasize the CL97's new supporting role in the 'socialist' market economy.

Beginning in 1994, the CCP leadership refocused its attention on 'rule of law' theory. In 1996 Party and jurist debate yielded a new constitutional law formulation, '*yifa zhi guo, jianshe sheuizhuyi fazhi guojia*' ('ruling the country relying on law and establishing a socialist legal system country').[46] This wordy formulation was subsequently entrenched in the state constitutional amendments of March 1999.

However, under the 1996–7 reforms, the procedural law was to enjoy a status equal to that of the criminal law. This was seen as consistent with the growing interest in the 'rule of law', and it was part of a new understanding of the purposes of criminal justice as these reflect the 'balance of values' concerning public order and human rights protection. Ideally, this widely acclaimed balance was to become manifest across substantive and procedural law in a newly synthesized effort to achieve both 'protection of society' (*shehui baohu*) and 'human rights protection' (*renquan baozhang*).[47]

Spreading new crime is seen in China as one of the most important political issues affecting social stability and the legitimacy and viability of the state, but the complexities of what will likely be a long and perhaps self-contradictory struggle for legal reform and human rights development cannot be underestimated. The substantive importance of procedural protection in criminal justice was highlighted for the first time in a self-conscious challenge to a criminal law tradition that had so rigorously supported severe criminal punishment as the means by which to achieve social control. This exclusive emphasis on the deterrence function of the law required explicit correction in revised criminal procedural and criminal laws that were supposed to balance judicial justice and human rights protection so as to facilitate social stability in a time of profound economic transition.

Since the revisions of 1996–7, however, social control has received renewed political emphasis in light of pressing emphasis on the need to combine the 'rule of law' with the 'rule of virtue'. This emphasis raises an important question as to how post-1996–7 criminal justice reform will survive the contemporary CCP assertion of Chinese morality.

In March 1999, the State Constitution may have incorporated the Party's new formulation on the rule of law; however, shortly, thereafter, the Party leadership was fixated on the political dangers of the so-called Falungong problem. Just at a critical juncture when the legal circles were attempting to build on the newly declared 'balance of values', the CCP launched a nationwide political-legal campaign against the FLG. The Party leaders readily politicized the justice system in order to strike at its sworn FLG enemies.

Party leaders frequently observed that just talking about the 'rule of law' was not enough to deal with China's problems. The rule of law would only work if people of high morality implemented the law. The renewed combination of law and morality was a product of changing Party politics. Jiang Zemin took the lead on this, fulminating on the 'absurd fallacies' of the FLG and on Western cultural and ideological sabotage:

> we should persistently strengthen the construction of a socialist legal system and govern the country according to law. It is equally important to govern the country with high morals and persistently strengthen social moral construction. Ruling the country according to law and governing the country with high morals complement and promote each other. Neither is dispensable, or should be overemphasized to the neglect of the other.[48]

As the 'Falungong problem' took over the Party leadership's agenda, renewed emphasis was placed on the original assumptions of the *zhengfa* system. There was a greater ideological emphasis on morality and social control calling for a renewed mass-line subscription to 'comprehensive management of public order' (*shehui zhi'an zonghe zhili*). Even as the legal community debated the new content of human rights legislation, they had to deal with the resurging politics of Chinese morality. The latter seemingly provided a remedy for the growing spiritual malaise characterized by generational and familial crisis, societal instability, and spreading anomie.

In the mid-1980s, the 'rule of law' was advanced by legal reformers as the solution to the problems associated with the Cultural Revolutionary 'rule of man'. At the March 2001 NPC, Party leaders called for a 'rule of virtue' that would be coeval with the 'rule of law' in the difficult societal transition to a socialist market economy. This invoked traditional 'good person politics' (*xianren zhengzhi*), whereby the law sought to reinforce '*li*', as the ritual or decorum governing human behaviour and thinking.

The Party's interest in morality was hardly new, but did this interest imply anything more than an emphasis on citizenship as a prerequisite to a 'rule of law' consciousness. Deng Xiaoping had issued repeated warnings about 'blind Westernization'. Throughout the reform period, the Party had generalized about the 'rule of law' as part of China's 'socialist spiritual civilization'. The latter's content, for example, included the 'four beautifuls' (*si mei*): beautiful thought, language, behaviour, and environment. While the citizens of socialist China contemplated the law's new importance, they were expected to embody the 'four haves' (*si you*) or to have consciousness, morality, culture, and discipline.

The NPC adoption of the combined rules of law and virtue reflected the CCP's reaction to the apparent non-performance of the rule of law in its response to the corruption that was threatening to engulf the entire judicial system. By this time, the horrible consequences of the 'rule of man' and the headlong Cultural Revolutionary assault on the legal system seemed less immediate than the threat of venal corruption and its potential for destroying Party legitimacy.

Some jurists, however, understood the underlying implications of the combined rule of law and virtue. They resisted its neo-traditional nature. Wen Xiaoli, for example, argued that the separation of law from morality and the separation of the rule of law from the rule of virtue are the necessary prerequisites of 'modernity'. Indeed, the comparative prioritization of law and morality has been a key issue in Chinese politics. Wen conceded that morality might play some sort of positive role in the management of the state, but he warned that an excessive emphasis on morality might again foster the 'rule of man' syndrome and that, at any rate, morality is inferior to the rule of law.[49]

Other jurists were more circumspect. Zhang Chunsheng and A Xi responded to Jiang Zemin's combining of the rules of law virtue. They elaborated: 'Laws must be supported by the power of morality. Without the support by morality, laws cannot be effective.... Laws are external rules of behaviour...while morals are internal standards of behaviour.[50] Those who immediately accepted the CCP's cue emphasized that profound change in contemporary society and economy requires the entwined efficiencies of the combined rules of law and virtue.

The renewed underlying concern for 'Chinese characteristics' looks very much like a re-statement of a mid-1980s minority view that resisted the exclusive focus on the 'rule of law' in favour of a deliberately 'sinified', or 'localized' law, as part of an organic understanding of human society in China. This earlier view, however, had extolled a self-conscious synthesis of the 'rule of law' with the 'rule of man'. The latter was disassociated from the excesses of Cultural Revolutionary personality cult and positively imbued with an assumed goodness in the application of the law by humane magistrates.[51]

A neo-traditional synthesis of the 'rule of law' with the 'rule of virtue' now informs post-1999 interpretation of the rule-of-law amendment to the 1982 State Constitution, and it has a bearing on criminal justice reform as it was originally cast in the 1996–7 revisions. The synthesis of law and virtue is once again recommended as especially appropriate to the specific nature of Chinese society. Ostensibly, law and virtue are to compensate for each other's limitations. While the Party has issued warnings against the twin dangers of 'feudalism' and 'blind Westernization', some reform jurists have warned against the law's close proximity to morality. Some have even cautioned against 'the negative influence of the abnormal combination of traditional autocratic Chinese legal culture and the western postmodern trend of thought in legal science'.[52]

There is a continuing, and, given the focus on 'Chinese characteristics', possibly an overly sanguine, political expectation of reconciliation between international legal standards and Chinese culture and morality. The modern history of Chinese law and jurisprudence reflects reoccurring syntheses of *fa*, as law, and *li*, as moral decorum; however, Chinese criminal justice has been caught between an activist state's political agenda stressing the need for public order in a time of deepening societal and economic transition and the need for law, which self-consciously qualifies the arbitrary position of the state *vis-à-vis* society, and which places the formation and protection of rights and interests beyond the reach of power and privilege.

Each of the following chapters in this book explores several specific areas of stipulated new 'criminal liability' so that we can begin to construct a ledger of success and failure in the formation of law and institutional response to the requirements of human rights protection and public order. This ledger, however, requires a chronological overview of the interpretations of recent criminal law and criminal procedural law development.

Interpreting the trend of criminal justice reform

Chinese criminal law has long been a focal point of Western criticisms of 'state instrumentalism'.[53] Moreover, China's own criminal law experts have conceded that criminal law was historically the most developed department of imperial law and that it was almost exclusively punitive in nature. Severe criminal law punishment was purposefully Draconian; it sanctioned deterrence as the basis for social stability and public order.

Some qualification is needed here as neo-traditionalism has had to compete with the synthesis of 'internationalization' and 'localization'. Moreover, it is important to remember that the long-term trend of criminal justice change has not been exclusively captured in conservative, revitalized mass-line strategies. At the same time as the regime emphasized 'comprehensive management of public order', there was a growing 'jural' emphasis in the 1980s and 1990s on the procedural protection of citizen's rights. Keith and Lin have detailed elsewhere how the Chinese legal circles moved from 'independent purposes theory' (*duli jiazhi shuo*) to 'dual purposes theory' (*shuangchong jiazhi shuo*).[54] The unqualified prioritization of substantive over procedural criminal law was challenged in the context of the 1996–7 debates over the amended contents of the criminal and criminal procedural laws.

In the 1990s, with rising internal discourse on the need for internal human rights legislation criminal procedural law became more than a technical guide for insuring the enforcement of criminal law. With the CPL96, judicial justice gained new status. The CPL96 was to be used in conjunction with the CL97 to guarantee a new substantive goal of rights protection. This goal, in turn, was partly justified as necessary to social stability, and thus, social control and human rights protection informed a new 'balance of values' in institutionalized criminal justice.

At the same time, some of China's leading criminal law jurists noted that the new emphasis on human rights protection was important because the state is in such a strong position *vis-à-vis* the individual citizen. They also noted that administrative punishment without reference to the court system and due process diminishes the rule of law. The determination and punishment of crime was no longer placed on an exclusive basis of procedural efficiency. Procedure, itself, acquired new substantive significance as judicial justice that protects the rights of citizens. This represented a critical conceptual breakthrough; however, the new emphasis on rights protection avoided any frontal challenge to 'Chinese characteristics', and it was never placed in a zero-sum relation to the protection of society.[55]

The CL97 assimilated many of the provisions of the CL79, but the former incorporated a newly revised theoretical base for the justification of a criminal justice strategy that optimized a comprehensive stipulation of new crime. The criminal law on counterrevolution, although it was replaced by less extensive provisions on crimes against the security of the state, was finally eliminated as 'unscientific'. Analogy, as it was premised in the principle of 'flexibility', was de-legitimized and the new strategy for criminal justice alternatively featured the comprehensive stipulation of all types of crime. This strategy conformed to a new international principle of legality, 'no crime without a law'. Also, there was a corresponding jurisprudential shift from 'punishment and no stipulation' (*li er buyan*) towards '*yan er buli*' (stipulation and less punishment).[56]

Criminal liability and the limits of 'social harm'

Perhaps the most important of the four components of 'crime' was the extent to which it incorporated a specifically Chinese understanding of the 'social harm' (*shehui weihai*) caused by 'criminal action'. Some reform jurists have attacked this concept, highlighting the need for less politics and more science. The hard-line interpretation of social harm had apparently resulted in a 'Chinese exceptionalism' that overemphasizes the harmful societal consequences of specific 'criminal' behaviour at the expense of legally scientific definitions of 'crime'.[57]

Flying in the face of very strong opinion favouring the retention of the 'social harm' concept, some outlying reformers directly challenged the established definition of 'crime': 'A crime is the behaviour which is harmful to society at a certain level and is in violation of the Criminal Law and should be punished with criminal penalty.' Indeed the clear definition of what is 'a certain level' has often been problematic. These critics wanted to delete reference not only to criminal penalty as it is extraneous to the defined components of 'crime', itself, but they were also prepared to delete 'harmful to the society' as they considered this terminology as too elastic and indefinite.

Apparently, such harm related to criterion set by legislators at the time when criminal legislation had been passed, and apparently, the criminal law would loose some of its authority if it was to be too flexibly interpreted by judges and the public. Reformers then offered the following alternative definition: 'A crime is a behaviour within the definition of the provisions of the Criminal Law and should be subject to criminal penalty.'[58] Herein is an emphasis on the strict adherence to, and comprehensive stipulation of, the law, as opposed to the flexible reliance on human interpretation of the law as would almost certainly be the case under the Party's combination of the rules of law and virtue.

While Communist dialectical analysis often formally highlighted the need for both severity and leniency in a self-conscious response to the feelings of the masses who suffered social harm, it, nonetheless, highlighted the primary purpose of criminal law as providing social control in the wider interests of the masses. The latter, of course, is very much a matter of self-conscious political decision and has resulted in cyclical 'cracking down', or 'striking hard' (*yanda*).

Reference to the importance of determining 'social harm' has also been used by more conservative jurists to qualify the principle, 'the punishment fits the crime'. Zhao Tingguan, for example, placed an interesting gloss on this principle. Claiming that the Western notion is much too 'metaphysical', he insisted that the application of criminal punishment must be equal to the extent of 'social harm'. The CL97 Article 5 reference to this principle must, therefore, be understood alternatively in terms of the Chinese notion of 'balance of crime, criminal liability, and criminal punishment'. This balance may, however, have a diminishing effect on the reform emphasis on the state's past tendency to resort too quickly to severe punishment.[59]

One could argue that the purpose of this particular 'balance' was to insure a continuing emphasis on the importance of gauging 'criminal liability' in an exact proportionate correlation with 'social harm'. The use of illegally collected evidence to insure criminal liability is a case in point. Given the persistence of traditional thinking, it has been difficult to separate substantive and procedural justice. For many jurists these two concepts necessarily belong in synthesis.[60]

Critics of the proposed use of American evidentiary principles in China point out that such principles conflict with the national psychology and culture. Indeed, if they are forced to choose between efficiency and justice, China's jurists deliberately lean to justice in so far as it supports society and the collective good. Allowing for the court's consideration of illegally acquired evidence is seen as more appropriate in China where there is a tradition emphasizing the societal importance of substantive justice and where there is a cultural predisposition that insists that punishment must effectively deal with the social harm to the collective interest. Simply, the US idea of 'emphasizing protection and ignoring punishment' would not work in China.[61]

Indeed, the state's arbitrary deployment of severe punishment is an open subject of contemporary jurist debate. The senior criminal law expert, Gao Mingxuan, emphasized the importance of the CL97's subscription to the 'punishment must fit the crime' in order to deal with the harmful nature of neo-traditional 'heavy penalty-ism' (*zhongxing zhuyi*).[62] Gao warned of the persistence of 'feudal criminal law' even in the minds of judges. Also, while the CL97 did little to restrict the expanding categories of crime requiring the death penalty, there has been rising dissatisfaction within the legal circles with the extension of the death penalty to new areas of economic crime.[63] Even making some allowance for the Chinese balance, that includes emphasis on criminal liability, execution for 'economic crime' seriously distorts the principle, 'the punishment must fit the crime'.

There is also reform interest in how to interpret '*qingqing zhongzhong, yi zhong wei zhu*' (as for leniency and severity, take severity as primary) in light of the implications of the international trend towards 'non-penalization' (*feixingfahua*).[64] Yu Wei and Cheng Jianhong, in their recent review of Chinese policy and law relating to '*congzhong chufa*' (severe punishment), urged review of criminal policy based on the traditional principle, 'leniency to those who confess, and severity to those who refuse'. They wanted the definitional components of 'severe punishment' to be understood in strict accordance with the criminal law's emphasis on the graduated severity of the circumstances relating to the crime. These authors stressed that the latter be interpreted strictly in accordance with the stipulated provisions of law and that they not be loosely or creatively interpreted by judges.[65] In the latter case, judges too easily become part of the law's problem with the politics of morality. More generally, contemporary reform has pitted the strict construction of the law, based upon comprehensive stipulation of crime and punishment, against the politically casual expansion and loose analogical interpretation of the law's provisions.

The threat to the reform strategy of comprehensive stipulation not only relates to the persistence of analogy as an aspect of 'flexibility' but more recently flexibility has also become manifest in the SPC and Supreme People's Procuratorate's (SPP) misuse of their powers to expand rather than to interpret the content of law. Since the approval of the CL97, there have been more than eighty judicial explanations and some of these that have been applied in areas of new crime concerning heretical cults, organized crime, and the internet have overstepped the proper boundaries separating the judicial and legislative powers.

'Extended judicial interpretation' (*kuodajieshi*) has attracted public criticism. The jurist, Liu Yanhong, for example, notes a growing trend whereby judicial explanation is substituted for the making of new criminal law provisions to deal with the problems of new crime. Liu noted that the upshot is that the penal code is not developed in practice and that the 'practice of judicial explanation' is substituted for the application of the CL97. In other words, the judiciary, itself, does not always recognize the importance of the scientific objectivity that originates in comprehensive stipulation. In short, judges have, at times, exceeded their responsibilities at the expense of the legislative power, and they have done so because they have not entirely transcended the behaviour associated with the old 'political–legal system' (*zhengfa xitong*).[66]

Western and Chinese views on criminal justice reform

Western scholarship remains conflicted on the nature and substance of contemporary legal reform. In their 1995 article on criminal law, Clarke and Feinerman referred to the ongoing dilemma associated with the 'political–legal system' (*zhengfa xitong*) that characterizes the Chinese administration of justice.[67] The latter organizationally ties together the law and politics, and obstructs rule-of-law making, predicated in judicial independence and the supremacy of law in China. Western critics have even questioned the utility of any study of formal legal change in China. In 1994, Stanley Lubman noted with some exasperation: '...exegesis of legislation is arid and formalistic, and close observation of institutions at work by foreigners is downright impossible.'[68] Carlos Lo's 1995 book, *China's Legal Awakening* highlighted new internal Chinese debate on the 'rule of law', but Pitman Potter criticized it as 'deeply flawed' in its failure to challenge directly the Chinese government's claim to the 'rule of law'.[69]

The major 1996 revision to China's criminal procedural law occasioned new division between Western scholarly experts. Jonathan Hecht, in his 1996 report to the US Lawyers Committee for Human Rights, expressed a number of misgivings about internal reform, but he also saw important movement towards 'the greater protection of the rights of suspected criminals'.[70] David Lanham was less qualified. He hailed the CPL96, as a remarkable piece of legislation, which could in some sense stand up to comparison with Australian criminal regulations.[71] Adopting a cautious tone of reserved optimism, Pamella Seay found a rough comparability between American and Chinese principles of judicial justice.[72] Linda Chelan Li, while recognizing China's 'under-institutionalized political system' contended in her study of the 'rule of law' in Guangdong that it would be 'over-simplistic...to resign the law to an entirely instrumental position at the disposal of political leaders'.[73]

The successful passage of the CL97 generated a new round of controversy. Stanley Lubman, in his 1999 book, *Bird in a Cage: Legal Reform in China after Mao*, again cast doubt on the basic relevance of Chinese criminal law reform: 'Because the criminal process is still in the grip of CCP authoritarianism, I do not study criminal law and procedure closely, although in noting reforms I do address some of the principal defects in the criminal process, that reforms have not remedied...'[74]

The present authors, however, would argue that, despite the practical difficulties of achieving criminal justice reform from within China's *zhengfa* system, new concepts in law are necessary to create legislative benchmarks for new practice, which can hopefully support a rational correlation of substantive and procedural law. The study of the domestic efforts to stipulate new crime from within the shifting parameters of control and protection is important to the understanding of progress and failure in the Chinese struggle for the rule of law. However, there is no shortage of international, and for that matter internal criticism of the exclusively punitive dimensions of Chinese criminal justice.

Criminal justice reform and the system for administrative detention

Administrative detention has become a huge matter of human rights controversy. Some contemporary Chinese reform analysis has pointed out that the relation between arrest and human rights is dialectical and that the deprivation through arrest of an individual's human rights requires serious study. Much of this analysis stresses the need to control the state's arbitrary use of detention, but it also highlights the protection of society.[75] The 'balance of values' is at issue in this controversy.

While some Western observers, such as Keith and Lin, emphasized the new 1996–7 criminal justice strategy highlighting comprehensive stipulation, based upon no crime and no punishment without law, there was a great deal of criticism of the revision's failure to deal with outstanding issues of extra-legal detention as in the case of 'custody for investigation' (*shourong shencha*) which was carried out on the basis of the extrajudicial authority of public security agencies.

The CPL79 had addressed the specific excesses of the Cultural Revolution by placing new stipulated emphasis on personal freedom,[76] and it had attempted to delimit the public security powers of arrest. At that time, jurists argued that the administrative regulations allowing the detention of individual citizens up to three months were inappropriate to the law, even if the related regulations had been passed by the State Council.

At least two schools of thought contended. Some scholars argued that there were already coercive measures in the criminal law and that, therefore, extra-Criminal Law administrative measures could be eliminated without any cost to law enforcement. Those supporting the Ministry of Public Security countered with a law-and-order theme. They believed that the administrative measures were especially efficient in the maintenance of public order and that, in particular, there was no alternative when dealing with suspected criminals who refused to identify themselves.[77]

In response to the 1979 attempt to delimit the legal conditions of arrest, public security subsequently circumvented this new emphasis by resorting to a previously widespread administrative coercive measure, 'custody for investigation' (*shourong shencha*). The latter was predictably justified on a renewed basis of 'flexibility'.

In fact, 'custody for investigation' was never part of the codified CPL79, and there was no related amendment to the stipulated clauses of the CPL96. It was, nonetheless, the stated subject of political compromise. Accompanying NPC documents clearly stated that 'custody for investigation' was no longer acceptable as it conflicted with 'no punishment without a law'. On the other hand, in response to the Ministry of Public Security's grave concern lest social control be jeopardized, the new CPL96 Articles 60 and 61 were reworked so as to lower the CPL79 standards of arrest. Revision to Article 61 in particular updated the description of two categories of person who were of special interest to public security, namely, those who refuse to provide identification to the authorities, and those suspected of going 'from place to place committing crimes, or who repeatedly committed crimes'.

In his critique of the 1996 revision, Jonathan Hecht welcomed the elimination of 'custody for investigation', but he regretted the CPL96 weakened restrictions on the use and length of pre-trial detention.[78] US State Department reporting in 1998 hammered away on the short-comings of the 1996–7 criminal justice reform. In 1999, the US State Department reported that, even if one were to accept the CPL96 as 'an improvement over past practice', it still falls well 'short of international standards in many respects' and its implementation is 'uneven and far from complete'.[79] Subsequent 2000 State Department reporting also focused on issues of detention and supervision as well as on the new implications for the rule of law originating in the banning and nationwide FLG crackdown. The State Department zeroed in on administrative coercive measures used against the FLG and specifically condemned the extra-legal nature of the Chinese 'system of re-education through labor' (*laodong jiaoyang zhidu*).

As discussed in Chapter 2, many FLG members were subjected to the administrative discipline of re-education through labour. Domestic Chinese legal reform has by and large fallen silent on the exact legal implications of the 'Falungong problem'; however, at the abstract level of legal principle, there has been some convergence between domestic reform opinion and Western human rights criticism of administrative law-based detention and labour re-education.

Domestic reformers who favour the retention and reform of the existing administrative system of detention and labour education have stressed that it is a rational response to the serious problems of social control that China faces in the current transition to the market economy. They have argued that the scope of 'crime' in China concentrates on serious crime and is more narrow than is the case in Western jurisdictions. Apparently, the existing Chinese system is designed to handle misdemeanours in a way that very roughly compares to the English system of summary conviction by a justice of the peace. However, in dealing with 'minor crime' in China, there is no clear legal procedure to insure the legal basis for conviction and punishment.[80]

The system of re-education through labour also reflects the underlying assumptions of a Chinese socio-legal approach to crime that lies at the heart of the *zhengfa* system. The August 1992 State Council white paper, 'Criminal Law Reform' reiterated the theme of reform within the two separate administrative and criminal law systems: 'Reforming criminals is mainly the responsibility of state organs in charge of reform-through-labour programmes and is carried out at prisons and reform-through-labour institutions.'[81] This policy approach to reforming re-education through labour suggests the difficulties in establishing judicial justice, or due process, and deliberately invokes the explicit relation between law and morality that characterizes the *zhengfa* system:

> The legal and moral education of criminals in reform-through-labor institutions emphasizes the need to plead guilty, abide by the law, improve moral values and better one's outlook on life. The purpose is to help criminals know, abide by and accept the law and to improve their moral standards.[82]

Some Chinese jurists have more specifically pointed to the success of administrative coercive measures and re-education in dealing with the rehabilitation of serious drug users and recidivist prostitutes.[83] Mainstream opinion argues for reform rather than abolition of the system, and related reform is often cast in terms of the administrative system's adaptation to the procedural standards set out in the criminal justice system. In effect, the preferred solution is to make the two systems converge in the development of formal procedural protection; for example, the administrative decision to detain someone could be made conditional on a judge's approval.

Some domestic critics have gone so far as to support abolition, suggesting that this system was devised in response to the priorities of a different era when social control was informed by frequent large-scale class struggles and that its extra-legal status outside the specific requirements of criminal justice is not rationally compatible with the contemporary economic reform and the 'criminal law's rule of law' (*xingshi fazhi*).[84] In an interesting example of e-governance, law and social science professors as well as newspaper editors recently proposed a motion to the Guangdong Provincial Committee of the Chinese People's Political Consultative Conference (CPPCC) to abolish the entire system of re-education through labour. 'Establishment' critics responded emphasizing the system's 'Chinese characteristics'. They also contended that any such move on the part of a provincial CPPCC would be *ultra vires*.[85]

One might compare this minority domestic view with that of University of California, Los Angeles (UCLA) Professor Randall Peerenboom, who has argued for a better understanding of China's societal and administrative realities. Peerenboom disagrees with Western human rights activists who claim that the re-education through labour system is focused on 'political offenders', and he is concerned lest the alternative criminalization of behaviours, that are currently dealt with from within the administrative system, might serve to exacerbate poor human rights conditions.[86] Peerenboom concludes that 'abolishment will hurt more than it will help the majority of those currently subject to administrative detention'.[87]

In 1996–7, reformers did succeed in eliminating a specific category of administration, known as 'custody for investigation', but the revisions failed to address several other major categories of administrative detention. Of special significance to international human rights reporting is 'custody for repatriation' (*shourong qiansong*). This particular system was originally designed to deal with the difficult demographic realities of economic reform. Specifically such custody targeted rural migrants who were flooding into the cities. Supporters of such detention have argued that the Western human rights critics have failed to understand the serious implications of the extraordinary population movements that have come with the deepening of reform in China.

Indeed, China does face an extraordinary problem of vagrancy. The authorities, in the past years of state planning, were able to control closely the migration of people from the rural to the urban areas. While in the West there has been comparatively little problem regarding the free movement of large numbers of people, China, with a population of more than 1.3 billion, has had to deal with wholesale changes in the state's control over the movements of unemployed rural population. As the 'floating population' has grown to what some observers believe is more than 100 million people, city services have been overtaxed and there has been a marked increase in crime on the part of jobless migrants.

Under these aggravated social circumstances, 'custody for repatriation' has provided an administrative means by which the cities can attempt to control enormous social pressures.[88] Those who moved into the cities and would not provide their identity could be administratively detained without reference to the courts. Once their identities were established they were subject to repatriation back to their native place. Public Security agencies could jail without cause anyone on the street who failed to produce proper identification. The Ministry of Civil Affairs and the Public Security authorities jointly oversaw approximately 700 detention centres across the country.

'Custody for repatriation', however, was suddenly discredited in the recent transition to a new Party leadership under Hu Jintao. The media had been allowed to cover the gruesome beating to death of Sun Zhigang, a graphic designer, who had been detained in Guangzhou in March 2003. The new Party leadership responded to the protests of the legal circles and abolished the twenty-year old regulation on vagrancy.[89] Responsibility for the voluntary accommodation of homeless beggars in the urban areas was turned over to the Ministry of Civil Affairs. The elimination of 'custody for repatriation' reflected the surprising strength of legal reform even in the politically sensitive context of the 'Falungong problem'. No doubt, domestic leadership conflict and concerns over China's 'good image' informed this event.

Although Amnesty International and other international human rights organization praised this particular reform, they immediately refocused on the persistence of the rest of the re-education through labour system. Moreover, the elimination of detention for repatriation did not solve the ongoing problems of 'heavy penalty-ism'. Amnesty disclaimed the results of a subsequent trial of those involved in the Sun Zhigang case.[90] The nurse's aide, who was allegedly Sun's principal antagonist, was sentenced to death. Eleven police officers and detention inmates received prison sentences and twenty-three officials including senior Guangzhou police officers were either fired, or censured.

Administrative detention is the subject of serious and ongoing research and debate among China's jurists, but there is a strong domestic sentiment that it is a mechanism with 'Chinese characteristics' that is rationally justified given the extraordinary depth of China's social problems and the related need for social control in a stressful time of accelerated economic change.[91] The reform of the entire system of administrative detention obviously has far-reaching domestic policy consequences. On the one hand, the elimination of 'custody for repatriation' has shown that occasionally reformers, drawing on international norms and criticism, have been able to reassert the importance of procedural justice and the protection of the rights of the innocent. On the other hand, the larger issue of administrative detention is not exclusively a matter of satisfying external human rights agendas that focus on procedural justice and ignore social justice.

Social control and *'Ren fa tong zhi'* (combined rule of law and virtue)

Continuity and discontinuity within the recent history of Chinese legal reform reflects a transitional politics and a changing, if not self-contradictory, ledger of competing trends in state–society relations. There is obviously concern as to the fact that 'rule-of-law making', or what some Chinese observes have sometimes referred to as 'nomocracy',[92] and related human rights formation are essentially state-led phenomena in China.[93] The modern history of the CCP has demonstrated considerable focus on a government based on 'teaching by personal example' (*shenjiao*), and the power of personal demonstration of morality which was once so wildly denounced by Cultural Revolution 'leftists' as 'self-cultivation' (*xiuyang*).

Some reformers, who support the balancing of human rights and public order, are concerned lest in combining the rule of law and rule of virtue the focus on social protection, as the foremost aspect of the new balance of values, becomes too exclusive. The squeezing together of law and virtue might possibly result in a culturally acceptable adaptation to 'rule-of-law making' and human rights formation, or it might degenerate into 'cultural relativism' that fosters the unity of state and society in such a way as to challenge autonomous civil society development.[94] The balance of law and virtue has been significantly affected by Party politics relating to both the threat of 'evil cults' and the criminal dimensions of the post-9/11 struggle against 'terrorism' as 'organized crime'.

While one might argue that the rule of law needs to be grounded in public ethics, combining the rules of law and virtue could have negative consequences, giving the judicial and administrative institutions a new excuse to persist in punishment without law. Punishment outside the law in turn might satisfy inflamed opinion about public order and immorality and might justify local failure to uphold the laws of the central government, but the logical effect of all of this would be to denigrate the law's authority.[95]

Since the mid-1980s, there have been cycles of national debates concerning the importance and meaning of the 'rule of law'. At the same time, there have been a number of national educational campaigns centering on legal education in society and the fostering of new attitudes towards law as an impartial mediator of disputes. While Dengist theory supported 'comprehensive management of public order' on the basis of entwined 'democratization' and 'legalization', this same theory has also called for citizenship based upon 'modern legal concept of equal rights and obligations'.

The Propaganda Department of the CCP Central Committee and the Ministry of Justice recently provided the following gloss on the conceptual basis of the Fourth Five-Year Plan for Giving Publicity to and Conducting Education in the Legal System:

> Attention should be paid to fostering citizen's modern legal concept of equal rights and obligations and strengthening their sense of abiding by the law and discipline, protecting their own legitimate rights and interests, and engaging in democratic participation and supervision. Attention should be paid to raising the theoretical level of the socialist legal system among large numbers of cadres, especially among the leading cadres, and increasing their ability to make decisions, perform their official duties, and exercise management according to law.[96]

Attention is drawn to the importance of improving everyone's knowledge of the law. The top Party leaders are included in this, but the strategy herein tentatively reaches beyond a crudely exclusive state instrumentalism as there is also an emphasis on citizen's knowing and protecting 'their own legitimate rights and interests'.

But the above also clearly reveals the attempt to fuse the rule of law and Chinese morality. After so many years of emphasizing the importance of law, the Party now seems to have concluded that the law alone is insufficient to the tasks of contemporary society and it needs to connect with revived morality in Chinese society.

The modern 'rule of virtue' presumably still includes the early to mid-1980s Dengist emphasis on 'acting according to law', but the current strategy focuses attention on the comprehensive application of law at all levels of society and organization as 'institutionalized management' (*fazhihua guanli*):

> We should persist in combining education in the legal system with the practice of law and continue to promote exercising management according to law. Exercising management according to law is an internal requirement of giving publicity to and conducting education in the legal system. It is necessary to properly handle the relationship between the study of law and the use of it and to step up the efforts to exercise management according to law and to expedite the process of doing so by putting stress on performing official duties in accordance with the law and administering justice impartially and trying to achieve the target of legally exercising institutionalized management.[97]

The above strategy synthesizes law and morality and reflects deliberately updated mass-line thinking: 'It is necessary to combine education in the legal system closely with ideological and moral education, to integrate governing the country by law with running the country by virtue, and to promote the development of democracy and the legal system and the building of the spiritual civilization.'

This strategy of 'institutionalized management' is considered omni-dimensional in that it is designed to deal with whatever comes up in the new context of modern social development including, for example, law specifically designed to help develop China's western regions, law related to China's accession to the WTO, law concerning the maintenance of social stability, etc. The contemporary strategy suggests but a new variant on a combined 'jural' and 'societal' approach, and it parallels the 1990s human rights legislation on the rights and interests of women, children, workers, handicapped, and the elderly which required a comprehensive *social and legal protection* of rights and the related coordination of official governmental agencies with officially recognized popular organization and social forces.[98]

From within the dialectical dualism synthesizing law and morality, reformers are struggling to establish a new approach to criminal justice so as to give self-conscious precedence to procedural law and human rights protection. The modernization of the legal system towards rule-of-law making is burdened with an updated notion of the Party's mass line as it relates to the self-conscious synthesis of 'jural' and 'societal' models. Arguably, this context will complicate the future relationship of procedural and substantive criminal law, and it may make it more difficult to extend and develop the post-1996–7 trend in favour of comprehensive stipulation based upon no crime without law and no punishment without law.

Current leadership statements have stressed that the law is now more or less complete and political attention is now focusing on law enforce-ment and the discrepancy between formally declared law and practice or 'institutionalized practice'. Over the last few years, it has been widely rec-ognized that there are major problems in the application of the CPL96 as the law governing the standardization of judicial proceedings in the various parts of the country.

In December 2000, the NPC appointed a criminal procedural law enforcement team to inspect the implementation of the CPL96 in six provinces, autonomous regions, and cities. Hou Zongbin, Chairman of the NPC Committee for Internal and Judicial Affairs, indicated that, while the team was encouraged by improvements in the law's implemen-tation, there were 'problems' that could not be overlooked:

> First, the problem of extended detention is still quite conspicuous in some localities. A number of cases in which the persons concerned have been detained for years remain unresolved. Moreover, after old cases of extended detention are straightened out, new ones have emerged, and cases of extended detention in disguised form have also increased. Second the phenomena of extorting confessions by torture still exist in varying degree. In some localities, they are quite serious

and exert a baneful influence. With regard to guaranteeing lawyers for the fulfillment of their duties in accordance with the law, there are still three kinds of difficulties. Due to numerous restrictions, it is difficult for lawyers to meet with criminal suspects in the investigation state; it is difficult for lawyers to look through the files, because the time given to lawyers to consult, make extracts from, and reproduce case litigation documents and technical reports, as well as facts and materials about the accused crime, is short and, in some cases, only partial materials are provided; and it is difficult for lawyers to review and obtain evidence.[99]

Hou regretted the extent to which erroneous law enforcement concepts still inhabit the minds of public security officers who continue to subscribe to 'valuing a substantive law more than a procedural law'.[100] The focused and consistent creation of new substantive concepts of criminal justice in order to capture the rational synthesis of public order and human rights protection is already a very difficult proposition, given the combined rules of law and virtue, but, then on top of this, there are significant systemic problems that are adversely affecting the appropriate enforcement of judicial justice.

A note on the structure of this book

The issues surrounding criminal justice reform are, indeed, complex. Chinese criminal justice has become involved in the contradictions of 'globalization' and 'localization'. The pitfalls of 'cultural relativism' are well known to international human rights organizations, but Chinese jurists still insist that human rights protection under a rule of law requires a legitimate adaptation of criminal justice strategy to the particular characteristics of Chinese society as it undergoes unprecedented socio-economic change. Some sense of the range of contemporary Chinese criminal justice thinking and strategy may be gleaned from an overview of post-1996–7 developments relating to new crime in several pre-selected areas of leading controversy. Analysis within each of these areas can then focus on the extent to which the 1996–7 criminal justice strategy has succeeded, or failed.

Chapter 2, 'The "Falungong problem" and the prospects for criminal justice reform', examines the impact of the Party's 'Falungong problem' on the prospect for post-1996–7 criminal justice reform. This is potentially one of the saddest chapters in China's modern struggle to achieve the rule of law. This impact reveals a number of internal inconsistencies, which threaten the post-1996–7 effort to entrench 'no crime without law and no punishment without law' and which draw attention to the negative repercussions of combining the 'rule of law' and 'rule of virtue'.

In the FLG case, the focus on social control and public order has compromised the 'balance of values' that includes new emphasis on the protection of human rights, especially as these relate to freedoms of religious belief and conscience. In dealing with 'heresy' as distinguished from 'official religion', the state is trying to exercise its moral leadership deep inside society; and the legal treatment of 'evil cults' constitutes a parallel with the past treatment of counterrevolutionaries under pre-1997 criminal law. Moreover, the state's contrived resort to judicial interpretation in order to fill in the blanks left by stipulated law suggests a disingenuous trend towards 'crime without law'.

With respect to the new emphasis on the legal protection of the human rights of individual family members, Chapter 3, 'The criminal justice response to violence in the modern Chinese family', plumbs criminal law debate and legislation concerning adultery, 'domestic violence' and the 'maltreatment' of and indecent assault on women, 'sexual harassment' versus 'hooliganism, prostitution, the trafficking in women and children, and the abuse of family members.

The CL79's chapter 7 stipulated a range of crime relating to the disruption of marriage and the family. This range included third-party violent interference with the relations of husband and wife, bigamy, having sex with the spouse of a military personnel, the abuse of family members, for example, the abandonment of dependent minors and the elderly. These crimes relating to marriage and the family were subsequently incorporated into the CL97 chapter 15: 'Crimes Infringing Upon the Rights of the Person and the Democratic Rights of Citizens' so as to give new emphasis to human rights protection.[101] The latter also re-visited the importance of gender equality and the 'statutory principle of monogamy'.

Regardless of the 1997 reference to human rights, there is an underlying paradoxical tendency to state institutionalized morality. The state's active intervention to insure the integrity of traditional family values is in contradiction with a tradition that delimited the state's involvement with sensitive family matters. The extent to which family values ought to be sustained in law became a matter of more recent political controversy in the 2001 revision to the Marriage Law. At the time of the drafting of the 1979 Criminal Law, there was contention over whether to criminalize adultery and the issue re-surfaced in debates running up to the 2001 revision of the Marriage Law.

A June 2000 Guangdong opinion survey conducted by the All-China Women's Federation (ACWF) indicated that 54.8 per cent of respondents believed that an adulterer should face criminal charges. On another question, 30 per cent believed that the law should forbid the keeping of concubines.[102] Ultimately, concubinage was placed together with provisions on 'domestic violence' in a newly revised Marriage Law. Conservative opposition to 'illicit sex' with 'third parties' did not, however, result in new provisions, and the reasons for not declaring adultery a 'crime' will be covered within this chapter's wider analysis of those areas where the gap has or has not closed between political reinforced morality and the legal definition of crime in the present day era of new market relations in society.

The new crime of 'domestic violence' emerged as the result of debates concerning marriage law and the relation between this and the existing criminal provisions regarding the 'maltreatment' and 'sexual assault' of women requires explanation with reference to the domestic debates and perspectives of China's jurists as they have interacted with legislators to find a solution to what was fast becoming an epidemic of physical abuse against women. Jurists and lawmakers are under political pressure to insure new human rights protection while at the same time there is an emphasis on the protection of Chinese values and the criminalization of immoral behaviour.

The making and selling of pornography is regarded as a multifaceted crime, as these activities are associated with tax evasion, giving and taking bribes, the forging of official documentation and seals, and organized crime and human smuggling. For China's political leaders the spreading of pornography is an especially vivid challenge to the socio-economic order. It is regarded as a serious threat to the morals of the young, and the related issue of freedom of publication has received comparatively little political attention. The CL79 only briefly referred to pornography as a crime in its Article 170. The latter was incorporated into a broader set of stipulated provisions in the CL97 Articles 363–67. Already, the latter are seen as insufficiently comprehensive, and pornography as 'illegal publication' has received special attention in SPC judicial interpretation.

While there is no immediate legislation planned for criminalizing 'sexual harassment', this issue has been the subject of jurist debate since the holding of the Fourth World Women's Conference in Beijing in 1995. Professor Chen Guizun, a member of the NPCSC suggested, in the summer of 1998, that China now needs a law to punish sexual harassment that includes assaulting a woman with obscenities or taking liberty with the opposite sex by using one's position and power.[103] Apparently, this was the first time that sexual harassment got the attention of China's legislators, and Chapter 3 will review the internal debates of China's jurists on this issue, particularly as it relates to the place of law in Chinese society and culture.

Chapter 4, ' "Organized crime," politics, and the law' reviews the political and legal problems associated with the protracted and cumbersome definition of 'organized crime' and discusses the development of China's criminal justice response to the changing organizational structure and content of 'crime' in areas, which, according to China's leaders, profoundly influence social stability and public order. The need for severe punishment, including the death penalty, to deal with public anxiety over 'social harm' is almost tangible in this area.

Chinese jurists started to consider the dilemma of 'organized crime' and related escalation of criminal violence only in the early 1990s when triad-like organization in Guangdong and Hainan started to spread into the inland provinces. Wang Hanbin, the Vice-Chairman of the NPCSC, in the context of debate concerning the newly revised CL97 spoke of the spread of 'criminal organization with a triad nature'. CL97 Article 294 stipulated the three categories of crime relating to organizing, leading, and participating in triad organization, crossing borders to develop triad organization, and the crime of shielding triad criminal organization from the law.[104]

The newly defined components of triad crime were fourfold. First of all, there was a horizontal variation in the types of triad criminal activity which ranged across smuggling, drug trafficking, the production and sale of fake goods, kidnapping for extortion, killing and plundering, organizing illegal smuggling of people, prostitution, gambling, etc.

The second component focused on the scope and nature of triad organization. The latter was characterized by internal rules, regulations, and ceremonial rituals such as that for the induction of new members and also such organization was assumed to be multi-tiered. Third, triad organization had to have extensive geographical spread so that its activities crossed over various localities. The fourth component stressed the degree of social harm in that the extensiveness of organized criminal activity threatens the integrity of judicial process and constitutes grave damage to society.

The spread of organized crime into the sex and drug trades and into the illegal trafficking of human beings may have, at least in theory, sparked new interest in the protection of human rights of individual victims, but the political issue in the justice system was one of widening the scope of 'social harm' and the related need for increasingly severe punishment. With the development of organized crime, the law not only had to make new provisions regarding the identification of criminal responsibility, but jurists had to consider new crime relating to membership in criminal organization and crime by association.

Interestingly, 'prostitution' *per se* is not 'criminal' in the context of the CL79 and the CL97 and the 1992 NPCSC Decision on the Prohibition of Prostitution and related SPC and SPP judicial interpretation. The onus of the law, however, falls on the organization of prostitution as a criminal activity. This is with the important exception of the CL97 Article 360, which targets prostitutes who have caused social harm by sexually transmitted disease. A similar balance of calibrated leniency and severity on the aforementioned basis of *'qingqing zhongzhong, yi zhong wei zhu'*, was apparent in the CL97 regarding illegal immigration. Those who paid 'snake-heads' to abet their illegal immigration faced under one year imprisonment, whereas those involved in the organizing of illegal immigration operations faced severe punishment under the March 1994 NPCSC decision, 'Severe Punishment for Organizing and Transporting People Across State Borders' and the 1997 Criminal Law. The degree of severity was then tied in degrees to the organizational scope of criminal activity.

Drug smuggling and trafficking is the area of greatest political concern in terms of social harm broadly construed as harm to China's economic development and social life. The stipulation of crime in this area is somewhat more developed than elsewhere. The criminal law's punitive dimensions, including the application of the death penalty, are especially conspicuous in comprehensive campaigns against drug-related crime. Narcotics control is a key issue area within the 'comprehensive management of public order', but the principal focus has been on criminalization, based upon severe punishment, and compulsory re-education based upon administrative regulation. Herein, there is an imbalance of values that responds to 'social harm' in such a way as to highlight the protection of society rather than the procedural protection of the accused.

Cyber-crime is the fastest growing area of criminal activity in the world, and some commentators have speculated that within the next fifteen years half of China's population will have access to the internet. Chapter 5, 'Crime and human rights in cyberspace', reviews the balance or imbalance of rights protection and public order within the technologically fast and politically sensitive context of new information technology. Through the 1980s and 1990s, pendulum of reform swung away from the criminal law of 'counterrevolution'. In the 1980s the regime claimed that there was no such thing as 'political crime' and that just thinking about 'counterrevolution' could not be construed as a crime, *per se*. In 1989, the legal circles publicly challenged the scientific and legal quality of 'counterrevolutionary crime'. Their arguments eventually prevailed with the deletion of the 'special provisions on counterrevolution'. These provisions were replaced by an apparently more narrowly defined category of 'crimes endangering state security' (*weihai guojia anquan zui*).[105]

China's political leadership is determined to exploit fully new information technology in the cause of national economic development. While addressing the new technological dimensions of economic crime, the regime seems supinely confident that proper social control can be achieved over the internet as 'uncontrollable media' (*bu kekongxing meijie*). On the one hand, the government has claimed that the internet will provide a new basis for citizen participation in the making of decisions and laws so as to create 'dialogue with government'.[106] Such dialogue, however, has to reckon with surviving 'customary practices' and the expanded 'flexibility' of the *zhengfa* system. Chinese criminal courts are beginning to implement tough internet law against dissidents for posting articles on democracy and political reform on the bulletin boards of overseas websites.[107] Criminal law development in these new areas is still tentative, but it is likely to have a significant impact on the balance of rights protection and social control, and hence Chapter 5 will review embryonic criminal law and related jurisprudence and judicial interpretation concerning the nature and range of both 'pure computer crime' and 'computer-related conventional crime'.

Chapter 6, 'Squaring the circles of criminal justice reform', will sift and aggregate the specific legal and political controversies concerning the new crimes, identified and assessed at length, in Chapters 2–5. This chapter reviews the tensions between neo-traditionalism and the reform attempts to promote legal reform on the basis of a new synthesis of 'international-ization' and 'localization'. Even more importantly, it places the contradic-tions of criminal justice reform within the wider context of Chinese rule-of-law making, human rights formation, and state–society relations. This chapter considers the extraordinary need for public order and the protection of human rights in the context of national emergency such as that of Severe Acute Respiratory Syndrome (SARS), and it provides the opportunity to review a wide range of newly legislated crime, judicial interpretation, and related jurisprudence for the purposes of assessing the successes and failures of post-1996–7 criminal justice reform in balancing human rights protection and public order.

2 The 'Falungong problem' and the prospects for criminal justice reform

This chapter examines the relation between the criminal justice treatment of the FLG and the struggle for the 'rule of law' in China. CCP's political handling of its so-called Falungong problem has had a largely negative impact on criminal justice reform, particularly as it was originally envisaged in the major revisions to the CPL96 and the CL97. The following analysis parses the formal criminal justice response to the FLG, paying particular attention to whether or not the syntax of this response respects the 1996–7 reform synthesis of public order and human rights protection.[1] Unfortunately, the FLG issue has not been a happy chapter in the struggle to create a 'rule of law' in China. The treatment of the FLG serves as a distressing reminder of the complicated paradox of legal reform and state power under the CCP's *zhengfa* system.[2]

The case against FLG 'heresy' has raised a number of familiar substantive and procedural human rights issues. The struggle to maintain key rule-of-law principles such as the supremacy of law, all are equal before the law, and judicial independence is highly relevant to the enjoyment of human rights. It is an ongoing struggle in any jurisdiction, but it is especially problematic in the Chinese *zhengfa* context that so deliberately overlaps the political and legal worlds. The *zhengfa* system has often accepted the 'spirit of the leader', and it touts its very own jurisprudential doctrine of 'flexibility' (*linghuoxing*). The latter casually assumes that policy, as interpreted by Party leaders, can, in the absence of comprehensive stipulation, be substituted for law, passed by the NPC.[3] This accorded with the pre-reform implications of the Party's notion of 'policy is the soul of law' (*zhengce shi falude linghun*).

From 1949 to 1997, heretical cults were an ideologically construed matter of 'counterrevolutionary crime'. Although the latter category of 'crime' was formally replaced by new crime concerning state security in the CL97, the contemporary treatment of the FLG both politically and legally harks back to the underlying *zhengfa* dynamic and the pre-1997 conventional treatment of secret societies as 'counterrevolutionary'. At least in the FLG case, the 'flexible' revival of past form and practice has had a disturbing impact on the manifest applications of the post-1996–7 'balance of values' and its related operational strategy for the comprehensive stipulation of the law, based upon the twin principles of 'no crime, without a law; no punishment, without a law'.

Secret societies, politics, and 'evil cults' in historical legal perspective

Why is there so much political concern over apparently innocuous meditation exercises in China? A review of post-1949 history on the law's response to secret societies suggests that the CCP's response to the FLG as a 'heretical cult' is rooted in a historical preference for an 'instrumentalist approach' to the criminal law as the state's preferred 'weapon' of choice in dealing with threats to the regime. The 'Falungong problem' has complicated market-related focus on human rights protection under the rule of law. It has raised difficult questions about freedoms of assembly, demonstration, religious belief, and conscience. The regime's harsh and uncompromising approach to its 'problem' has had a chilling impact on the normally robust internal jurist debates concerning the importance of judicial independence and related problems concerning the substitution of 'extended judicial interpretation' for legislative responsibility in the criminal justice system. Moreover, the response to the FLG may well suggest the extent to which the modern Marxist–Leninist regime has been caught up in the contradiction between its policies and planning for the development of a 'rule of law' and the prerogatives of Party leadership within the *zhengfa* system.

By going deep into Chinese history, one might extrapolate at least a partial explanation of what appears to be the CCP's obsessive contemporary anxiety over the influence of 'evil cults' in modern Chinese society. Throughout the centuries of imperial history, superstitious sects and secret societies (*huidaomen*) were believed to have played a pivotal role in the rise and fall of China's dynasties. The uncontrolled development of these societies often heralded a change in the 'Mandate of Heaven'.

The Qing legal codes did not offer a fully developed law that clearly distinguished between orthodox and heterodox sects. This ambiguity may, in fact, have been a matter of political convenience. Local imperial officials had to weigh very carefully the repercussions of reporting to the capital that certain sects had crossed the line into anti-dynastic activity.[4] This was a serious matter of directly challenging the virtuous legitimacy of the reigning dynasty. It was an especially serious matter of the timely elimination of heinous abomination, or *danibudao*, implying the pollution of the most fundamental moral principles underlying Han civilization. The allegedly heretical violation of the 'way' generally attracted the most brutal and indiscriminate criminal law punishments available.

On the other hand, at least at the level of an abstract reading of modern Chinese history, the CCP claimed that through time anti-dynastic struggles of the secret societies reflected the beginnings of the modern struggle of the Chinese people against 'feudalism' and 'imperialism'. This hagiography, however, has been forgotten in the recent Party focus on the 'heretical' nature of secret society activities and the related social cost to China's modern development. Within the contemporary framework, if the FLG has not been branded as 'counterrevolutionary', it has, nevertheless, been persecuted as a 'feudal' heresy that allegedly challenges the 'socialist' essence of modern Chinese 'spiritual civilization'.

In fact, the CCP's actual political experience with the secret societies significantly conflicted with Mao Zedong's formal celebration of secret society revolt in Chinese history. Such inchoate revolt was supposed to serve as precursor to Mao's modern revolution. The CCP's nationalism had developed within the context of peasant war, and this nationalism sought validation through the combing of Chinese history for redeeming examples of rebellious peasant opposition to oppressive 'feudalism'. Historical exercises of this sort confirmed China's place within the mainstream of modern revolutionary development.

In his December 1939 *classicus locus* on the subject, Mao Zedong rambled on about the 'unparalleled' scope of peasant revolt in Chinese history:

> There were hundreds of uprisings, great and small, all of them peasant revolts or peasant revolutionary wars – from the uprisings of Chen Sheng, Wu Kuang, Hsiang Yu and Liu Pang in the Chin Dynasty, those of Hsinshi, Pinglin, the Red Eyebrows, the Bronze Horses and the Yellow Turbans in the Han Dynasty, those of Li Mi and Tou Chien-teh in the Sui Dynasty, those of Wang Hsien-chih and Huang Chao in the Tang Dynasty, those of Sung Chiang and Fang La in the Sung Dynasty, that of Chu Yuan-chang in the Yuan Dynasty, and that of Li Tzu-cheng in the Ming, down to the uprising known as the War of the Taiping Heavenly Kingdom in the Ching Dynasty. The scale of peasant uprisings and peasant wars in Chinese history has no parallel anywhere else.[5]

Notwithstanding these 'hundreds of uprisings', Mao failed to mention how the secret societies had banded together with Chiang Kai-shek to slaughter Party stalwarts in the bloody April 1927 'Shanghai massacre'. He also neglected to cite the merciless attacks by religious and ethic groups on the retreating Red Army during the Long March.

The most senior architect of the CL79, Gao Mingxuan, has traced the development of criminal law concerning the organization of superstitious sects in light of what was actually a checkered political experience with secret societies. Gao cited the tentatively 'revolutionary', and sometimes vacillating role of several secret societies such as the White Lotus sects that fed the Boxer movement as well as societies that helped overthrow the Qing dynasty, but he also acknowledged how most of the superstitious sects and secret societies in the 1930s and 1940s formed an inglorious alliance with 'counterrevolutionary forces'. Secret society members, who had served under the northern warlord governments, were recruited into the secret services of the Japanese controlled Manchukuo regime as well as into the Nationalist government services in the effort to exterminate the Communists.[6]

Related new CCP law has had more to do with practical political experience rather than Party hagiography. In 1949, the CCP was not about to tolerate any suspect form of alternative political organization. All secret societies were immediately outlawed under the new public security regulations. Apparently, economic crime and political subversion went hand in hand. Ezra Vogel, in his informative description of the Guangzhou area in the autumn of 1951, described how the CCP initially concentrated on the suppression or elimination of high-ranking Kuomintang (Guomindang) counterrevolutionaries before moving to target the underground leaderships of tightly organized secret societies which were controlling the vice rackets and transport gangs in the Guangzhou area. Rather than making direct attacks on the secret societies, which might strengthen their unity, the CCP practiced a classic united front divide-and-rule-tactic separating out the ringleaders from the followers for severe punishment.[7]

The initial PRC law on counterrevolution, the 20 February 1951 'Regulations for the Suppression of Counterrevolutionaries', reflected the Party's urgent concern for state security in light of the unfinished business of liberation in the vast 'newly liberated areas', where there had been a steady diet of anti-Communist propaganda, and where the new CCP government had to rely on the personnel of the past regime in order to deal with widespread sabotage by Kuomintang forces that had been driven underground. This concern was heightened in the Korean War context. The CCP was very concerned that it not loose control of vital rear areas while prosecuting a volunteer's war against the world's strongest military power in Korea.

Article 6 of the 1951 regulations made it criminal to '*use*' secret societies for the political 'purpose' (*mudi*) of 'counterrevolution', hence it stipulated: 'Those who use feudalistic sects and societies to carry on counterrevolutionary activities shall be sentenced to death or life imprisonment. A minimum of three years' imprisonment will be meted out to less serious offenders.'[8] The early 1950s represented a tumultuous time when extremes were often justified as politically necessary to the consolidation of the new regime; however, the 'people's democratic dictatorship' did not go so far as to make it illegal '*to organize*' superstitious cults and secret societies. Article 3 of the 27 June 1952 'Measures for the Control of Counterrevolutionaries' empowered the Ministry of Public Security to subject 'leaders of reactionary secret societies' to invoke supervisory control usually for a period of three years in order to pre-empt 'counterrevolution'.[9]

In the early 1950s, the cognate issue of religious freedom was ideologically tied to China's 'colonial' history explicitly entwining foreign missionization with 'imperialism'. The issue came to head in the Protestant 'three-selfs movement' and the establishment of a national Catholic Church, which was ordered to defy the authority of the Vatican. The CCP targeted the political dependence of domestic religious organization on parent Church organizations outside China. The Party preferred that its own membership subscribe to atheism, but religion that respected Chinese policy was not automatically dismissed as 'the opiate of the masses'. The CCP, in its united front calculations, claimed to uphold the people's freedom of religious belief and over time the laws have largely reflected a politically convenient distinction between 'official religious organization' and secret-society based 'feudal cults'.

In a separate Article 88, the 1954 State Constitution offered all citizens 'freedom of religious belief'. Later, Article 28 of the radically truncated, left-wing State Constitution of 1975[10] downgraded religious freedom by running it together with a number of other freedoms relating to strikes, procession, demonstration, etc., and by juxtaposing religious freedom with an explicit Party preference for the 'freedom not to believe in religion' and 'to propagate atheism'. The separate Article 46 of the subsequent 1978 state constitution[11] reiterated the same 1975 qualification.

The latter was also carried forward into the much longer separate Article 36 in the current 1982 State Constitution, which includes the following caveat concerning the protection of 'normal religious activities':

> The state protects normal religious activities. No one may make use of religion to engage in activities that disrupt public order, impair the health of citizens or interfere with the educational system of the state. Religious bodies and religious affairs are not subject to any foreign domination.[12]

Over the course of denouncing the FLG, in 1999, the CCP's religious affairs establishment reiterated the subscription to atheism as equal in force to the parallel constitutionally guaranteed right of religious freedom. Atheism and officially sanctioned religious belief are considered mutually respectful and equally guaranteed under the law. However, if the CCP endorsed the right to participate in 'official religion', it has had no political tolerance for any 'feudal' challenge to public order and social stability.

In his 1954 report on the new constitution, President Liu Shaoqi, prematurely as it turned out, announced the elimination of 'the age-old grip of feudalism'. Subsequently, whenever the Party relaxed and receded from the economy, superstition and secret society organization came back in full bloom. Invariably, the CCP responded with more restrictive political and social control.

In the early 1960s' Socialist Education Campaign, class struggle was re-emphasized against 'spontaneous capitalism' and the concomitant rise of 'feudal superstition'. The 20 May 1963 'Draft Resolution of the Central Committee of the Chinese Communist Party on Some Problems in Current Rural Work' (often referred to as the 'first ten points') described the class situation in the countryside in terms of nine points of description, including the following third and fourth points:

> 3) In some places landlords and rich peasants are carrying out activities for the restoration of feudalistic patriarchal rule, putting out counter-revolutionary propaganda, and developing counter-revolutionary organizations. 4) Landlords, rich peasants, and counter-revolutionaries are making use of religion and the reactionary hui-tao-men [secret, religious, and welfare societies] to deceive the masses and carry out criminal activities.[13]

More importantly, the Party's later 1980s' post-mortem on the Cultural Revolution featured 'feudalism' as an even more dangerous threat to political stability and unity than bourgeoisie liberalism, which had freely entered society through China's new 'open door'. This 'feudalism' had been explicit in the scary ritualistic behaviour of the Red Guards and in the ecstatic patriarchal adulation of Mao as the 'red sun' at the centre of the universe.

There was, however, some backlash among some Party leaders against the notion of 'counterrevolution' in law. The charge of 'counterrevolution' had been wildly bandied about in Red Guard kangaroo courts. At the height of Mao's personality cult, even the most senior leaders in the Party had been gratuitously accused of 'capitalist restoration' and 'counter-revolution', but, if the Cultural Revolution represented an explosion of pent-up 'feudalism', the Party, in 1979, still preferred to restrict, rather than to scrap the criminal law's special provisions on counterrevolution.[14]

In 1979, the criminal law was codified for the first time. Article 6 of the 1951 regulations referring to 'use' of superstitious sects and secret societies was folded into CL79 Article 99. This same article newly criminalized the *organization* of secret societies bent upon 'counterrevolutionary activities'. The drafters of the CL79 may have sought to balance controlling 'feudalism' and 'counterrevolution' with new policy on the protection of official religious freedom in the context of converging legal and open door policies, but Article 99 greatly expanded the terms of reference allowing for more state control over society in the name of public order.

On the other hand, Party conservatives, who had attempted to press their advantage, failed to entrench stipulations concerning the 'use' of religion for 'counterrevolutionary purpose'. Reformers successfully argued that such proposed stipulation would confuse the lawful and constitutionally endorsed religious activities with those of superstitious sects and secret societies.[15] Whether or not this was of any comfort at all to those practicing religion, the reformers also failed to fully press their advantage. Instead, they conceded that those who might have 'used' religion for the purpose of instigating sabotage could still be dealt with under the specific criminalization of espionage in Article 97 or sabotage in Article 102.

Moreover, CL79 Article 165 focused on 'crimes' involving the use of superstition and witchcraft to swindle China's good citizens out of their property. According to Gao Mingxuan, this article responded to the new emphasis on the law and the economy and increasing cases in Southern China where 'sorcerers or witches' were defrauding citizens of their property. Gao distinguished between the political issue of counterrevolution in Article 99 and the specific property issue in Article 165.

In response to a post-CL79 surge in 'counterrevolutionary crime', the NPCSC incorporated into its now discredited 1982 decision on severe criminal law punishment,[16] the death penalty for severe crime relating to Article 99. This entire decision on public security was later critiqued during the debates that inspired the 1997 revision of the Criminal Law. The Decision was widely condemned on a number of counts. It had generally violated 'no crime without a law; and no punishment without a law'. It had also confounded the proportionate relation between the nature of a crime and the related severity of criminal punishment.

A subsequent 1985 circular jointly issued by the SPC, SPP, and the Ministries of Justice and Public Security warned of the rapid revival in the rural areas of previously suppressed superstitious sects and secret societies, which were allegedly undermining public order. The circular treated all of these revived sects and societies as 'counterrevolutionary' regardless of the specific nature of their current activity. Local government was ordered to dismantle such organization. The circular, however, attempted to respect a number of points of conventional principle including the careful differentiation of lawful religious activity from the counterrevolutionary activities of the sects and societies, the differentiation of ringleaders from followers, and the assignment of severe punishment to the former and education to the latter.[17]

At a 17 January 1986 meeting of the Politbureau, Deng Xiaoping spoke about the need for extended severe punishment that relied on both the conventional stress on punishment, as a matter of societal education and deterrence against spreading crime, and the political targeting of an increasing criminal recidivism in society. His statement reflected the Party's growing alarm over new economic crime, the trafficking in women and children, and the organization of reactionary secret societies:

> I understand there are a great many habitual criminals who, on being released after a few years' remolding through forced labor, resume

their criminal activities.... Why don't we have some of them executed according to law? Why don't we punish severely, according to law, some of those people who traffick in women and children, who make a living by playing on people's superstitions or who organize reactionary secret societies and some of those habitual criminals who refuse to reform despite repeated attempts to educate them.[18]

While emphasizing entwined democratization and legalization for the sake of economic development, Deng also reminded the Party of the ongoing need to apply the people's democratic dictatorship in light of spreading feudalism and bourgeoisie liberalism.

Deng did not acknowledge any contradiction between his emphasis on dictatorship and the new emphasis on legalization and institution building. Moreover, for Deng, the rule of law was quite compatible with capital punishment. He referred to capital punishment and severe punishment as 'in accordance with law', but several months later on 28 June 1986 he referred to the importance of judicial independence. He informed the Standing Committee of the Politbureau: 'It is not appropriate for the Party to concern itself with matters that fall within the scope of the law. If the Party intervenes in everything, the people will never acquire a sense of the rule of law.'[19]

But as we have seen in the history of the law's response to secret societies, the CCP has often exercised its prerogative to prosecute counter-revolutionaries. The CCP's 1989 reaction against 'counterrevolutionary turmoil' did not in the long run silence China's legal circles. The latter reiterated that 'counterrevolutionary crime' was too political and conflicted with the scientific nature of the law. Legal reformers cleverly placed such anachronistic 'crime' in antithesis to Deng Xiaoping's 'open door' policy and his goals of institution building and 'political restructuring'.[20]

In the several years leading up to the 1996–7 criminal justice reform, official and scholarly arguments coincided to the effect that the law on counterrevolution had involved tortured and slippery interpretation of 'purpose' (*mudi*). The latter had originally been consigned to a category separate from *mens rea* so as to underscore its essential political implications.[21] The CL97 revision, eliminating the law on counterrevolution, was predicated in a new judgement that the law, in the period of reform, had been irrationally burdened with the woolly and uncertain political nature of 'counterrevolution'. With the passage of the CL97, the special provisions on counterrevolution were, therefore, challenged as essentially 'unscientific'. This formal progress ought to be placed in context. For more than a decade, China's jurists had vetted 'human rights protection' *vis-à-vis* the state's reflexive resort to flexibility and analogy, and they had gained a new measure of Party support for emphasis on the rule of law and human rights as these were seen as part of a process contributing to social stability in a time of rapid socio-economic change.

At any rate, in the CL97, the CL79 Articles 99 and 165 were folded into a new omnibus Article 300 and re-allocated to chapter 6, 'The Crimes of Disturbing the Order of Social Administration'. This had conceptual and symbolic significance in light of the 1997 elimination of 'counterrevolutionary crime' in favour of a new focus on economic crime and the criminal law's relation to the market economy. With the 1997 revision, the FLG was seemingly spared the charge of 'counterrevolution' in 1999.

In some sense, however, the notion of 'heresy' simply replaced the earlier notion of 'counterrevolution'. What makes the FLG case so interesting is the level and extent of Party intervention and the preferred strategy for the *ex post facto* criminalization of the Falungong as an illegal heretical cult. The FLG leaders were accused of having organized a 'heretical cult, opposed to science and modern principles of civilized governance based upon the "rule of law"'. In the attempt to make the charge of 'heresy' stick, the CCP resorted to expanded notions of 'flexibility'. Sources within the judicial system have suggested that the CCP usurped the provincial high courts and municipal middle-level courts in determining crime and punishment particularly in the two key areas, namely those relating to the 'Falungong problem' and senior-level official corruption.

Many of the recent cases relating to FLG members have not made it into court. The Ministry of Justice asserted its right to approve PRC lawyers seeking to represent FLG members and admonished them to interpret the law in such a way as to conform to the spirit of the government's decrees on the 'Falungong problem'.[22] Moreover, the SPC instructed the lower courts to focus on social stability and the authority of the state. While judges were reminded of the importance of the rules of evidence, they were also told to pre-empt FLG attempts to use the courtroom as a public platform. Moreover, in a politically interesting move, the SPC required that the lower courts not accept FLG practitioners' civil suits against Li Hongzhi ostensibly for fear that this would politicize the judicial process.[23]

In many of the cases against FLG organizers, the government resorted to administrative discipline. The accused were given hard labour in the Public Security Administration's re-education through labour system. US State Department reporting claimed that as many as 5,000 were sentenced up to three years of 're-education'. The same human rights reporting pointed to the growing number of deaths of FLG members while in the custody of public security. The FLG case was also featured in a more broadly conceived critique of the CPL96, which was faulted for no law of evidence and for having failed to address 'custody for repatriation', inappropriate extension of detention for 'further investigation', re-education through labour and the lack of provisions concerning the right to remain silent, and double jeopardy.[24] The US State Department cited Chinese re-education through labour as one of the key areas of default in criminal code reform. While this specific issue and its impact on the 'rule of law' is the subject of open jurist debate, the specific legal implications of the 'Falungong problem' as they relate to religious freedom, freedom of expression, and demonstration have not been directly explored by China's jurists.

Not surprisingly, China's 'Falungong problem' has been internationalized in human rights diplomacy. The US House of Representatives, in 18 November 1999, for example, passed a motion chastising the Chinese government and calling for the freedom to practice FLG spiritual exercises. While the Chinese have been criticized for an inappropriate banning of 'cults', they criticized the Americans for their rude interference in China's attempts to restore public order. Chinese reaction has countered that the FLG is an 'evil cult' and not a 'religion', and that Li Hongzhi, the 'criminal founder' of the FLG, long ago treacherously 'exposed his horse's hoof beneath his unicorn skin'.[25] Ironically, the CCP spontaneously resorted to 'feudal' metaphor to attack 'feudal superstition'.

For its part, the FLG rejected the CCP's attack on 'superstition' as unscientific, political labelling,[26] and insisted that its 'cultivation practice' is neither religious nor political in nature. Apparently, as early as 3 September 1996, Li Hongzhi had disavowed those practitioners who took advantage of Dafa to get involved in politics. Such action was 'born of a filthy mentality', which corrupts the process of cultivation, itself. Li instructed: 'A cultivator does not need to mind the affairs of the human world, let alone get involved in political struggles.'

Li did not want the FLG to come under existing state law on official religion, hence the following conclusion of Professor Julie Ching: 'The Falun Gong was careful not to make itself into a religion. In China, it had no temple, no official headquarters, no formal rituals, and it exacted no fees from its followers. Its gatherings were always in public.'[27] Prior to 1999, the FLG had only managed to achieve a very loose affiliation with the State Sports Administration. Paradoxically, its own interdiction against religion made it more attractive to CCP members who were generally careful not to get involved in religious groups.[28] When in 25 April 1999 FLG members mobilized in front of Zhongnanhai, they did not demand recognition as a patriotic religious organization, but they did request that the government recognize the FLG as an independent state-sanctioned organization, distinguished by its 'cultivation system' or its 'spiritual belief system'.[29]

Although the CCP and FLG have agreed that the latter is not a religion, over the last several years, the US Secretary of State has named China as a 'country of particular concern' under the International Religious Freedom Act of 1998. The US State Department's 2001 report on international religious freedom focused on increasing domestic suppression of unregistered religious groups as well as of 'spiritual movements'. The report claimed that the crackdown on the FLG's spiritual movement was having 'a spillover effect on unregistered churches, temples, and mosques'.[30] Subsequently, the US Commission on International Religious Freedom made a series of recommendations in its 13 February 2002 report on China that included a call on the Chinese government to reform its 'repressive legal framework' as it relates to religious and spiritual organization.[31]

Since the mid-1980s, there have been several stages of debate concerning the nature, scope, and content of the 'rule of law', and the contemporary 'Falungong problem' is but one of these stages; however, it offers an opportunity to place the legal and political issues of religious freedom and assembly within the wider frame of human rights formation and protection in an advanced context of accelerated economic reform.

The 'Falungong problem' became apparent even as the state constitution was revised in March 1999 to incorporate reference to China's new socialist 'rule of law'. Moreover, the 'Falungong problem' filliped a Conservative tendency within the CCP leadership to give *equal* weight to the 'rule of law' (*fazhi*) and 'rule of virtue' (*dezhi*). In the CCP's view the 'Falungong problem' was connected with the US strategy of 'Westernization' and 'disintegration'. Party Conservatives responded with a call for state-led morality.

In the mid to late 1980s, the 'rule of law' (*fazhi*) had been articulated in political opposition to the 'rule of man' (*renzhi*). The reaction against the Cultural Revolution and personality cult provided the legal circles with an unprecedented opportunity to make a convincing political case against the 'rule of man'. Those who attempted to preserve the latter defensively highlighted its positive and especially Chinese connotations of a principled human application of law. Unqualified jurist opposition, however, countered that 'rule of man' was a serious ongoing matter of 'personality cult' that had to be resolutely and without qualification opposed with the 'rule of law'.[32] Even in the aftermath of the Tiananmen Square, Jiang Zemin was said to have grasped and endorsed the 'rule of law' as distinct from 'rule by man'.[33]

Jiang Zemin subsequently supported the March 1999 revision to the state constitution regarding 'running the country according to the rule of law'.[34] However, in a speech of 10 January 2001, he resurrected the mid-1980s combined 'rule of law' and 'rule of man' (*fazhi he renzhi*):

> we should persistently strengthen the construction of a socialist legal system and govern the country according to law. It is equally important to govern the country with high morals...Ruling the country according to law and governing the country with high morals complement and promote each other. Neither is dispensable, or should be overemphasized to the neglect of the other.[35]

In explaining the importance of 'rule of virtue' (*dezhi*) Jiang decried the 'strong impact' of the 'absurd fallacies' of the FLG, as well as that of 'Western capitalist theories and corruptive ideologies'.[36] Apparently, the CCP leadership considers the utility of official religious affiliation and belief as a benign aspect of the 'rule of virtue'. While CCP members were disciplined for participation in the FLG they were still allowed to join in 'normal religious activities'.[37]

Jiang's leadership role in the FLG crackdown has been at the centre of Western media speculation. In April 1989, Shanghai, under Jiang, was the first to express its support for Deng Xiaoping's actions in Tiananmen Square. In 1999, the FLG gave Jiang the political opportunity to recall his strong and unflinching leadership in 1989. According to FLG sources, in April 1999, the Party Secretary General disagreed with Premier Zhu Rongji who wanted a more measured approach to the 'Falungong problem'.[38] Peerenboom's interpretation in fact suggests that Zhu's approach would have involved more open and fair trials:

> Although it might strike some as naïve to expect that the ruling regime would have responded to 10,000 people surrounding Zhongnanhai in a measured way, Zhu Rongji and other leaders apparently did favor a more measured response. Unfortunately, the regime appears to have missed a chance to gain legitimacy and strengthen the role of law, and to begin to articulate a long-term policy on just what kind of social activity will be tolerated.[39]

The difference between 'normal religious activity' and the practice of feudal superstition has a collateral bearing on the enjoyment of freedom of assembly and religious belief in China. There is an estimated total of 200 million religious adherents in China,[40] and the issues of assembly and religious freedom form part of a much larger puzzle concerning the potential for cognate rule-of-law making and human rights formation and protection.

Educational campaigns of the 1980s and 1990s emphasized that the law, as a 'supreme authority', was to have its own legitimacy. The balancing of public safety and the protection of individual rights, particularly in terms of the practice of religious belief and freedoms of expression and demonstration, is becoming more complicated as it involves the weighing of differently conceived rights across constitutional and national legal and political cultural settings. Lobbyists for new international human rights instruments have considered placing lawful limits on states so that they do not unduly restrict the freedom to engage in religion; however, international law and organization has yet to define the concepts of 'sect' and 'new religious movement' as they relate to the changing post-9/11 priorities concerning public safety.[41]

The FLG issue has become part of an international consideration of the issues of state sovereignty and cults in criminal law. Any particular balancing of individual and collective rights is likely informed by prevailing social values and political cultural understandings of these competing rights. While US diplomacy on religious freedom has reiterated that terrorism must not be used as an excuse to suppress religious freedom, new legislation in Western democracies concerning 'terrorism' reflect changing viewpoint on the relative balance of civil liberties and public order. Certainly, the Chinese were quick to criticize the 'serious infringements on judicial rights' that characterized the US Anti-Terrorism Law.[42]

With reference to the 1996–7 'balance of values', it is not easy to decide when such balancing is appropriate for legitimate reasons of modern institutional development and when such balancing becomes *ex post facto* political rationalization, or 'cultural relativism'. Also, the conception and the institutionalization of the 'rule of law' may vary from one constitutional setting to the next, and as was indicated in Chapter 1, there is ongoing disagreement as to the degree to which China has made progress towards the 'rule of law'.

The law and issues of public order and social stability

Li Hongzhi, the founder of FLG, freely compared the 25 April 1999 Zhongnanhai passive demonstration to the 4 June 1989 event.[43] And the FLG also explicitly compared Jiang's role in 1999 to his role in 1989. The CCP leaders were greatly alarmed by this new threat against their regime, but they had assented, in 1997, to the elimination of the law on counter-revolution and, in 1999, to a state constitutional amendment endorsing a socialist 'rule of law'. Was there any difference in the law's relationship with politics in 1999 as compared to 1989? To what extent does the post-1997 issue of heresy represent a surrogate political and legal form of 'counterrevolution'?

In 1989, the Party elders denounced student activists for 'complete [or blind] Westernization'; however, there was also an important domestic side to the 'Falungong problem'. The CCP had to counter an unsettling misappropriation of a popular indigenous Chinese culture as a messy legal and political matter of public order versus the contagious spread of socially harmful 'superstition'. Regardless of the law's preference for science, it was compelled to deal with the subjective issue of 'superstition'. As for the Party, as the custodian of Chinese nationalism and culture, it had to find a way to target the FLG without placing itself in direct opposition to a popular Chinese recreational activity, while preserving established policy on 'religious freedom' and the policies of the open door and economic reform. At a time when the regime was experiencing a 'crisis of faith', favourable internal Party member perception of the innocuous semi-Buddhist nature of the FLG made the FLG all the more threatening to the survival of the regime.

In the Party's view, the FLG was deliberately sowing socially harmful confusion. Ye Xiaowen, the Director of the State Bureau of Religious Affairs, for example, explained the confusion associated with 'Falun' as

Buddha Law organization as follows:

> How is the common practitioner supposed to know that his or her
> 'Master' has so many motives, and how is the practitioner supposed
> to know that his or her organization has so many characteristics like
> an evil cult? They are also unclear that the 'Falun' Buddha Law
> organization has already created great harm towards society and the
> people. The practitioners have all had the wool pulled over their eyes,
> and have been deceived. Even more pitiful is that their psyche is
> under the control of others.[44]

The issue of 'social harm' has been generally debated over the course of
criminal law reform. While some reformers accepted social harm as an
appropriately rational concept that assists the law in making a determination as to whether any act constituted a 'crime', some critics protested
that it serves as an irrational Chinese exceptionalism. Add to this, however, the history of CCP policy on the political difference between 'normal
religious activities' and 'feudal' superstition. As we have seen, policy had
for a very long time distinguished between constitutionally recognized
religious affiliation and freedom and the organization and use of secret
cults for 'counterrevolutionary' purposes.

Li Hongzhi sidestepped the whole issue of religion, insisting that his
association was an innocuous spiritual expression of local culture. While
Li attempted to depoliticize his breathing exercises, the CCP politicized
the collective exercise of such breathing as an aspect of 'heretical cult
organization' (*xiejiao zuzhi*).[45] The emphasis on 'heresy' burdened the law
with the state's moral judgement as to whether the act of organizing an
alleged heretical cult and whether cult membership actually constitute
'social harm'. Officially sanctioned religion, on the other hand, was still
thought to make a legitimate contribution to society and public order. The
1997 reforms had formally left behind the old political issue of counterrevolutionary 'purpose' (*mudi*), but the new issue of heresy invoked
similar political notions concerning the state's role in protecting Chinese
culture and morality.

What is the nature of the state's legal prosecution of the FLG in light of
the transition from the law on counterrevolution to the newly revised
criminal law? Is there discernible progress, or is there backsliding with
respect to the evolving relation between law and politics in China? What
are the explicit legal implications of 'heresy' for the freedoms of religious
affiliation, assembly, and demonstration? The 'Falungong problem' came
to a head within an inflamed context, and the subsequent disposition of
this case revealed continuing tensions within the Party leadership over
the political consequences and costs of accelerated economic reform.
Moreover, media condemnation of the FLG was roughly contemporaneous
with the latest stage in the rule-of-law debate.

Official viewpoint drew on familiar, if not debased, Marxist–Leninist argument so as to place the FLG's 'feudal' superstitions in contradiction to the 'rule of law' in China. State and Party officials unabashedly asserted that the lawful treatment of the FLG has confirmed China's new commitment to rule-of-law making, and that the FLG, as a heretical 'evil cult', acted in such a way as to denigrate China's state constitutional and criminal laws.

Foreign Ministry spokeswoman, Zhang Qiyue, for example, dismissed US State Department criticisms of China's handling of the FLG case claiming that it was dealt with 'according to law' (*yifa banshi*) and that the related legal process protected 'the basic human rights and freedoms of citizens and safeguarded the China's constitution and laws'.[46] Whether the domestic proponents of legal reform will ultimately accept this internal gloss on relation between the FLG and the fifteenth NPC gloss on the rule of law is a matter of speculation. Western human rights critics, however, generally do not accept the CCP's antithesis between the rule of law and the FLG. Conceivably, the treatment of this case could reinforce a renewed tendency towards state-led morality, and the latter could potentially distort the 1996–7 balance of rights protection and public order in favour of 'state instrumentalism'.

Specifically applying the law to the FLG

Even though the CCP had agreed to the 1997 elimination of the criminal law, special provisions on counterrevolution, the regulations on public security, and the CL97 provisions provided a working basis for the state's post-1997 hard-line response to the FLG's 'feudal superstition' threatening the security of the state and its provision of social administration.

The CCP did not view the FLG as a religion. The FLG was an 'evil cult' that had defied the law's authority on a number of specific grounds. Also, in a manner reminiscent of the charge of 'peaceful evolution' in the repudiation of 1989 Tiananmen dissidents' affiliations with the West, Party leaders claimed that the FLG was supported by foreign organization. To a certain extent this conflicted with the thrust of the Document 19 policy that attempted to accommodate friendly relations with foreign religious groups while maintaining CCP strictures regarding the independence of domestic religious organization.[47]

Allegedly, the FLG's own 'great wheel of law' had less to do with religious doctrine and more to do with the malicious spread of feudal superstition so as to 'corrode the people's thinking' for the purpose of undermining the regime and its socialist spiritual civilization.[48] In summing up the extent and nature of FLG 'illegal activities', the *Renmin Ribao* addressed the question of 'social harm':

> In recent years the organizations of this cult have rapidly developed and have conducted large numbers of acts of violation of law and

criminal activities. They frequently gathered people to besiege and charge state organs, enterprises and institutions, disrupted normal social order, and illegally held assemblies and demonstrations; instigated, deceived and organized its members to undermine the enforcement of state laws and regulations; poisoned people's minds; and deceived its believers 'to go to heaven,' commit suicide and inflict wounds on themselves. The 'Falungong' organizations have done serious harm to society.[49]

The Chinese media also linked such domestic social harm with the backlash to globalization. It justified the necessity of state intervention with reference to the new international dimensions of post-Cold War cult terrorism. The FLG was compared to socially disruptive 'end-of-the-world' *terroristic* cults such as the 'People's Temple' and the Davidians in the United States, the Solar Temple in Europe and Canada, and the Japanese Aum Shinrikyo.[50] Evil cults in various parts of the world apparently shared three astonishing similarities, namely, they prophesized the end of the world and the destruction of humankind, they unconditionally worshipped a cult founder, and followed methods and taboos that militate against the human community.[51]

While breathing exercises hardly constitute the same category of threat to public order as the release of a lethal gas in a crowded urban subway, Chinese commentary, nevertheless, stressed the FLG's potential for bloody violence and the responsibility of government to protect social administration and public order. Official Chinese analysis has found the Japanese case to be worthy of emulation:

> First of all, applying the weapon of law to restrict and ban cults. In view of the 'sarin' terror incident caused by the 'Aum Shinrikyo' cult, the Japanese authorities concerned took sanctions against the cult and arrested its leader Shao Asahara and a large number of backbone elements; they applied the 'Law on Prevention of Sabotage' and the 'Law on Religious Legal Identities' to disband the cult and cancel its qualifications as a religious legal entity; they froze all its assets in line with the 'Bankruptcy Law'.[52]

Chinese commentators applauded the Japanese government's vigorous approach. Moreover, Chinese allegations against the FLG included extensive references to the 'criminal' use of superstition against the cult's own practitioners; for example, Xia Yong of the CASS Institute of Law contended:

> the 'Falungong' organization and its activities have harmed the physical and psychological well-being, lives and the security of property of 'Falungong' practitioners. Firstly, they have used such heresies as 'the end of the world' and 'global explosion' to confuse practitioners,

thus causing some practitioners to lose the ability to think, judge, and discriminate things normally; they become distraught; behave in an eccentric and unreasonable manner, and even cripple themselves, commit suicides, or cruelly injure or kill other people. Secondly, they have asked believers not to visit the doctors when they are sick.[53]

This particular argument invited an open-ended extension of the notion of the purpose and object of criminal behaviour. There is no clear distinction in law here as to the harm done and the supposedly scientifically determined criminal nature of 'anti-social' activity. How does the law identify and deal with 'anti-social' behaviour, as it is explained, for example, by the Director of the State Bureau of Religious Affairs, Ye Xiaowen?

> Anti-social tendencies have two extreme modes: One mode is from a passive shielding against the world to hate of the world and suicidal tendencies. The other mode is a repugnance with society moving toward an insane anti-social bent. 'Falun' Buddha Law is also irresistibly moving toward an anti-social perspective, continuously inciting the masses; at one moment they are surrounding this, then they are surrounding that, believing that when the situation is ripe they can begin surrounding Zhongnanhai. Actually, they are trying to display power.... The core elements of the 'Falun' Buddha Law organization, in propagating the 'canon' of Li Hongzhi, have openly stated that 'shedding blood is alright'.[54]

Obviously, the CCP never wanted to face another Tiananmen Square, and the collective breathing exercises just outside the leadership compounds at Zhongnanhai were, in the CCP's view, a politically brazen act of defiance that deliberately conjured up the tumult in Tiananmen Square in 1989. Despite the passive and quiet nature of FLG activities, the media and the CCP still insisted on focusing on the potentially bloody consequences of the FLG's assault on China's social stability. There was free and easy cross-reference to cult violence elsewhere in the world. Ironically, the media, for example, approved of the US government's application of force in the 1993 Davidian case. Such commentary did not deal with the First Amendment of the US Constitution. It focused instead on the necessary dispatch of military and police personnel, tanks, and helicopters to attack the headquarters of the 'Branch Davidians'.[55]

The CCP had wanted to establish the credibility of rule-of-law making in Chinese while at the same time it did not wish to be constrained in its legal and political attacks on the FLG. The March state constitutional amendment was passed just before the 25 April FLG Zhongnanhai 'demonstration'. The CCP tried to square the new constitutional guarantee of the 'rule of law' with its condemnation of Li Hongzhi's 'theory on the uselessness of the law'. Li was accused of having attempted to sabotage public order and social stability based upon the 'rule of law'. Official commentary repeatedly referred to Li's statement: 'Human law is mechanically restricting and blocking men.... Men, like animals, are governed and have no way out.'

Apparently, Li had an 'insatiable appetite' for spiritual authority, which waged war on civilization and legitimate governance. Li purportedly touted his own spiritual authority at the expense of the supremacy of law as it reflects a community bound by rules.[56] Li was condemned for seeking total ideological control over his followers through a tight discipline based on his teachings and instructions. Li's acolytes were quoted as saying, 'We were told that what he said was law, and whoever opposed his statements would be committing a felony.'[57] The parallel here to the CCP's own historical problem of 'substituting the [CCP leader's] words for law' (*yiyan dai fa*) was not pursued.

However, it was argued that the FLG was not a 'religion' because its activities did not take place in regular places of worship. In the FLG case, the law followed very closely in the track of prevailing politics. Government analysis offered a monolithic political judgement as to the nature of FLG organization and belief. While in the 1990s legal reformers had generally weakened the relation between law and class struggle and had disposed of the law on counterrevolution as essentially unscientific, the FLG case provided fodder for Party conservatives who used this new enemy to affirm the use of the law as a 'weapon' to support the people's democratic dictatorship.

If the Party no longer had the benefit of 'counterrevolutionary purpose', it still had a number of legal weapons in its arsenal. The FLG was accused of breaking a wide range of specific laws on publication, associational registration, the law on demonstration, the illegal misappropriation of confidential state materials, various sections of the 'Regulations on Governing Public Order and Security' and related criminal law provisions with regard to disturbing 'social administration order', specific crimes dealing with illicit sexual relations and cult practices resulting in personal injury or death.[58]

Curiously, The Party had hesitated for a long time. There was a conspicuous hiatus between the 25 April Zhongnanhai 'demonstration' and the first legal decision regarding the banning of the FLG. On 22 July 1999, the Ministry of Civil Affairs finally declared that the FLG was an illegal organization that had failed to register itself under Article 7 of the November 1989 'Regulations Governing the Registration and Administration of Public Organization'. Apparently, the FLG had also violated Article 19 (3) of these same regulations, which forbade the creation of regional subsidiaries. Moreover, the FLG, in conducting its activities without the benefit of registration, had violated the companion Article 24 (6) of the 'Regulations on Administrative Penalties for Public Security'.[59]

Together with the 31 October 1989 regulations on assembly and demonstration, the regulations on registration had originally been cast in the post-1989 aftermath of Tiananmen Square as a purportedly enlightened revision to the September 1950 'Interim Provisions on the Registration of Public Organization'. These regulations had been drafted with reference to foreign legal experience. They had already been under consideration for ten years, but in 1989 there was some concern lest either the public or the lawmakers might be biased and would, therefore, rush to pass flawed legislation designed to deal with the Tiananmen Square aftermath.[60] The NPC lawmakers, nevertheless, forged ahead to pass the regulations in light of the law's 'prolonged state of stagnation and lax administration' and so as to proceed with Deng's agenda for legal reform in the face of great changes in society and the economy.

These permanent regulations were hailed as significant in a new period of reform during which there was an expected proliferation of all kinds of popular organization. The regulations were designed to operationalize the 1982 State Constitution's provision on freedom of association, and they were characterized as part of Deng Xiaoping's reform entwining democratization and legalization in that they represented a dialectical unity of the citizen's right of association and the legal administration of public organization.[61] The Deputy Minister of Civil Affairs, Li Baoku, defended the July 1999 ban affirming that the Falun Dafa Research Society had not registered with the various levels of civil affairs organization and that Article 26 of the 1982 State Constitution regarding the freedom of religious practice did not apply to the FLG as it was not a religion, *per se*. The Deputy Minister quickly offered immediate reassurances to the effect that the ban would not infringe upon the lawful practice of *qigong*.[62]

The 'PRC Law Governing Assemblies, Parades and Demonstrations' had also evolved over years of the Chinese comparative study of international legal experience and had been passed in the immediate context of post-Tiananmen Square events. Like the law on registration, it was introduced with formal reference to the need to balance the protection of citizen's rights with the state's need for public order. However, there was nothing therein that specifically addressed the problem of 'evil cult' activities.

This law dealt with the very slippery distinction between 'legitimate' and 'illegitimate' protest in light of the prevailing Dengist focus on democracy and the legal system as 'twin sisters'.[63] However, the new law was particularly interested in excluding non-residents from participating in locally approved demonstrations. As has been noted, one of the political issues surrounding the FLG case had to do with the 'unlawful' extent of its organizational discipline across the various cities and regions of China.[64]

In facing the 'Falungong problem', the authorities were dealing with what they saw as an inherently wicked, large-scale, non-verbal, passive aggressive behaviour. Collective meditation did not quite fit the mould of law circles' post-Tiananmen Square discussion of what constitutes legally defined protest. Moreover, in Article 2 cultural and sports activities are expressly excluded from the parameters of the law on demonstration:

> Demonstrations in this law refer to activities held in public areas or roads and carried out in the forms of assemblies, parades, or sit-ins to voice demands, lodge protests, or express support and other common wishes. This law does not apply to cultural, recreational, or sports activities; normal religious activities; nor traditional, nongovernmental activities among the people.[65]

However, Li Hongzhi's tentative affiliation of his *qigong* practices with sports ultimately failed to offer any genuine shelter from the coming political storm.[66]

In the summer of 1999, the Ministry of Civil Affairs relied heavily on the law of registration, as distinct from the law on assembly, and it issued on 22 July a public notice banning specific FLG activities in accordance with CL provisions and the 'Regulations Governing Public Order and Security'. These forbade, for example, the display of FLG scrolls and symbols, the distribution of FLG books and videos, demonstrations, etc. Also, between 24 July 1996 and July 1999, the Information and Publications Office issued five notices requiring the confiscation of FLG publications, which were alleged to have spread superstition.[67]

On 29 July, the Ministry of Public Security issued an arrest warrant for Li Hongzhi for spreading superstition and heresy resulting in death and the illegal organization of assemblies for the purpose of disturbing public order. The CCP treated the organization of heresy as a criminal act under the law, and this opened up the possibility of pursuing a new generation of heretics as latter-day 'counterrevolutionaries'.

Prior to April 1999, there was very little relevant experience with the application of related provisions of the CL97. Li was accused of violating the key Article 300 of the CL97, which, unlike Articles 99 and 165 of the CL79, did pay specific attention to 'evil cults'. The CL97 Article 300 dropped the CL79 Article 99 reference to 'counterrevolutionary purpose', but criminalized 'organization' that is purposefully designed to undermine the implementation of law and administrative regulation. At the time of revision, several SPP legal experts had alternatively stressed that organization, in and of itself, was not to be construed as criminal in nature. In this more 'scientific' view, the commission of actual specific crimes was necessary to prove that such organization had actually undermined state law and regulation.[68]

Also, the law offered a typical distinction in sentencing that reflected the degrees of 'severity' characterizing such criminal liabilities. Zhou Daoluan and his SPC colleagues, Shan Changzhong and Zhang Shihan, suggested that the related 'serious circumstances' could be interpreted in terms of six categories relating to the recruitment of followers across the country, namely, the involvement of large numbers of people, collusion with superstitious sects, secret societies and cults in other countries, leadership and organization, the instigation of the masses to resist state law and the related injury of state officials, deception resulting in suicide and causing social disorder, and the stoppage of production.[69] The first three categories highlighted the existence of organization, *per se*, whereas the last three tied extant organization to actual criminal activity resulting in disruption to the administration of social order.

Recruitment *per se* had not been widely seen as inherently 'criminal', nor for that matter was organizational size. The Party, however, accused the FLG of widespread disinformation through the manipulation of classified state documents. The *Renmin Ribao*, for example, reported on how the Ministry of Public Security put together a relevant case in October 1999:

> [The FLG] intended to create a situation in which the practitioners were antagonistic to the party and government, and the law could not lay blame on the masses. In addition, they tampered with and distorted some of the meanings in the internal documents, and disseminated extensively through the internet, and incited the masses who were unaware of the truth to be discontent[ed] with the party and government.[70]

Published 'truth' has always been a sensitive political issue in China. The CL79 had incorporated a stipulation in its Article 102 concerning the distribution of scrolls and pamphlets for 'counterrevolutionary purposes' and Article 170 had dealt with pornography. The CL79 Article 102 was simply deleted from the CL97. Article 170, however, was re-stated in the CL97 Article 363. The November 1999 joint interpretation in its criminalization of publication and distribution of cult materials and its prescription of 'severity' in relation to the widespread publication and distribution of such materials as constituting 'severe circumstances' seemed to stretch the original legislative intent of Article 300. CL97 Article 300 roughly parallels CL79 Article 102. The latter, in fact, had been eliminated together with all of the criminal law references to 'counterrevolutionary purpose'. Article 102 had been specifically rejected for obscuring the predictability and clarity of law.

In actual fact, the criminality of organization relies on the extent to which a cult or secret society is proven to have misappropriated religion in order to propagate heresy and superstition at the state's expense. Such an open-ended and possibly tautological determination of 'heresy' could well place any 'religious' activity in legal jeopardy. Li Chun and Wang Shangxin, criminal law experts at the powerful Legal Work Committee of the NPCSC, had tried to offer reassurances that an 'evil cult', unlike official religious organization, does not have a permanent place for worship; and it recruits followers through so-called anti-social propaganda.[71]

Indeed, Article 2 of the 31 January 1994 'Regulations Governing Venues for Religious Purposes' subsequently clarified that 'venues for religious activities' would include monasteries, temples, mosques, churches, and 'other fixed venues', and it required formal registration to establish such venues.[72] However, within the FLG context, the law was burdened with the question of determining 'heresy' as it relates to membership in, and the use of, organization.

Judicial versus legislative interpretation

While there was in place some law for dealing with the 'Falungong problem', it was not enough. It had to be reinforced in either NPC decision or judicial interpretation. On 30 October 1999, the NPCSC passed an unusual decision to eliminate FLG activities. The decision announced policies to eliminate evil cult organization, to combine education and punishment in dealing with the deceived masses, to launch an educational movement to reveal the true essence of the FLG challenge to society and civilization, and to mobilize against the FLG through the 'comprehensive management of public order'.[73]

As was explained in Chapter 1, the latter anticipates a coordinated state–society approach to public order, encompassing the judicial determination of crime and sentencing as well as various types of political initiative in the organization of related crime prevention, propaganda, and education throughout the Chinese society and state. Even at the level of the State Council, for example, government officials were exhorted to accept 'three stresses' of theoretical study, political consciousness, and healthy trends so as to arrest the spread of the 'evil cult' into state agencies.[74]

As for the law's specific response, the CL97 Article 300 contained new reference to 'evil cults' but it had not clarified the degrees of severity of related 'crime'. This understanding was subsequently provided in the specific joint formal interpretation of the SPC and the SPP on 1 November 1999. The latter defined 'evil cult' with reference to specified patterns of behaviour, and its effect was to expand the field of punishable behaviour under Article 300 and to increase the range of severe criminal, rather than administrative, law punishment with reference to other cognate articles in the criminal law.[75]

Such interpretation highlighted the relative interpretative powers of the legislature and judiciary. It has often been the practice to develop the detailed regulations for the application of national law subsequent to the latter's passage; however, in such a sensitive political case, one has to wonder whether the SPC and SPP were under stiff political pressure to make an *ex post facto* determination of criminal law liability that was specific to the FLG. This form of 'flexibility' conveniently saved the NPCSC from having once again to go the notorious route of 'legislative interpretation' at the expense of the principle of non-retroactivity. The new emphasis on 'running the country according to law and building a socialist rule of law' had partly originated with a critique of early 1980s NPCSC decisions, which were seen to be retroactive and in contradiction with 'no crime, and no punishment without law'.

Had the NPCSC exercised its own power of legislative interpretation, legally it would not have applied to the FLG case, as its leaders were already under arrest. For decades, there has been a lack of consensus in legal circles as to what specific authorities have the right to interpret the criminal law, and, for Western human rights critics, this raises the serious problem of the law's impartial independence from state institutions. The Chinese legal system is peculiar to the Western observer in its extension of the powers of judicial interpretation to a confusing array of key state agencies.

Actually, NPCSC interpretation has been very rare. Between 1981 and 1990, over two-thirds of 'interpretations' originated with the joint pronouncements of the SPC and SPP, whereas the rest mainly involved the State Council, and the Ministries of Justice, Public Security, Health, and Finance. While the NPCSC had violated the principles of no crime and no punishment without law in the early 1980s, it had at the same time attempted to regularize the process of judicial interpretation. In the FLG case, the resort to SPC–SPP joint interpretation offered a way round the NPC retroactivity, but, at the same time, it threatened to confuse judicial interpretation with law-making.

The unlimited power of the NPCSC to interpret legislation was entrenched in the 1982 State Constitution, but this sharply contrasted with the lack of a clear definition of the sources of judicial interpretation. Chinese rule-of-law making has been complicated if not compromised within the *zhengfa* system that has often asserted the CCP's mass-line principles of state organization.

The NPCSC's 10 June 1981 'Decision Strengthening the Work of Legal Interpretation' favoured interpretation by both the SPC and SPP. At the time there was also interesting reform objection to the inclusion of the SPP as a law enforcement agency rather than a judicial agency responsible for the legal determination of crime and the imposition of punishment.[76]

Also, there was sharp criticism of the scope of judicial interpretation and the related potential for the judiciary's misappropriation of legislative responsibility. In 1998, Chen Sixi, a legal expert at the NPC's Legal Work Committee, had pointed to the need for a clear distinction between the legislative and judicial interpretations of law. The former embodied the abstract creation of law while the latter featured an understanding or interpretation of concrete points of law with reference to specific cases. By limiting judicial interpretation to specific cases, should any errors occur, the negative consequences of these would be limited to specific cases and would not necessarily undermine the inner logic of law as it relates to the rule of law versus non-retroactivity. The latter, however, could be sacrificed should judicial interpretation freely extend beyond the specifics of a particular case to supplement the provisions of NPC legislation.[77]

Chen's view has been voiced a number of times, but it is not yet widely accepted. Expert opinion is frequently divided over the issue of interpretation. Even in the traditional terms of mass organizational imperative, extended judicial interpretation might be construed as seriously undermining the separation and combination of functions between different governmental agencies.[78] But the same *zhengfa* tradition gave priority to 'flexibility' and alternatively reinforced argument to the effect that the powers of interpretation ought to be widely shared so that, at a wider variety of institutional points, the law can become more extensively engaged with changing social conditions.[79] This viewpoint conflicted with the reform interest in the principle of legality, 'no crime and no punishment without law', and the newly conceptualized balance between emphases on public order and the procedural protection of human rights.

The interpretation of the first section of Article 300 is important in light of such controversy. Article 300 identified six categories of criminal behaviour, which have to do with political action and purpose designed to undermine the social administration of public order: the gathering of the masses to attack and to disrupt the activities of state organs, enterprises, and social organizations; illegal assembly, demonstration, occupation or the disturbing of public places and normal religious activities; the revival of cult organization previously dismantled by state order or the creation of new cult organization; instigating or deceiving others to disobey the law; the printing, publication, and copying of illicit cult materials; and finally a standard catchall with a long history of association with the nefarious principle of 'flexibility', namely, 'other conduct violating state law and regulation'.

The state's political and legal response to the 'Falungong problem' has revealed the competing political and institutional influences affecting contemporary rule-of-law making in China as well as the serious definitional problems associated with the law's treatment of religious freedom and assembly. Certainly, the issue of law on 'heresy' and the related issues surrounding the criminality of organization, as distinct from the criminal use of organization, have highlighted the potential abuse of the rule of law within the Party's updated mass-line traditions. These trends conflict with the 1996–7 effort to enhance criminal justice, based upon the 'balance of values'.

Conclusion

One could argue that in any given place the struggle for the 'rule of law' is not only 'open-textured', it is multifaceted, unremitting, and never ending.[80] China in transition, however, is a place of 10,000 contradictions, and correspondingly the struggle for the rule of law is uneven and episodic, if not spasmodic. While Western scholars have been generally mixed in their view of the CPL96 and CL97 revisions, most would accept that these revisions represented to some degree a progressive qualification of the pre-reform *zhengfa* dynamic which subordinated law to policy and which vetted the principles of flexibility and analogy. 'State instrumentalism' was formally challenged in 1996–7. Unfortunately, the subsequent response to the FLG suggested that this challenge was not carried forward in legal practice and that the 'balance of values' was overtaken in the *zhengfa* applications of 'flexibility'. The law was threatened with politicization as the CCP leadership succumbed to its own worst instincts in its rush to crackdown on the FLG.

Since 1985, the progressive conceptualization of the 'rule of law' came about in domestic response to (a) the self-consciously articulated need for law and stable government in light of the tragic political extremes of the Cultural Revolution, (b) the need for law as a predictable predicate facilitating the business of a modern economy, (c) the attempt to guarantee, in law, new rights and interests in a society undergoing profound value change, and (d) the need to arrest deepening corruption, which is so serious that it threatens to engulf the judicial process, itself. In this volatile context, policy exigency can be used wilfully to rationalize 'state instrumentalism', but it may also point to the importance of qualifying the arbitrary character of the Party-State and to furthering the legitimate mediating role of law in a fast-changing society experiencing unprecedented competition.

The CCP response to the 'Falungong problem' points to the dangers of recidivist state instrumentalism in the context of a deep transition in China's society and economy. In the FLG context, the 'rule of law' was saddled with the 'rule of virtue'. Contention that the regime's legal treatment of the FLG supports the struggle for the rule of law is hardly compelling. In the modern era of economic reform, the Party is using law for the political purpose of insuring state-led morality against heresy!

Moreover, the Party co-opted the SPC to deal with 'heresy', and 'extended interpretation' has challenged reform argument for narrowly constructed judicial interpretation that focuses on the need for the comprehensive stipulation of new crime and on the specifics of criminal cases so as to avoid trenching on the legislature's role to make law. This co-optation represents yet another form of 'flexibility' that has challenged judicial independence in the post-1996–7 period of criminal justice reform. At the same time, Party policy has also muddied the issue of 'criminality' as it has highlighted mere membership in organization as new crime. By tying the 'rule of law' to 'heresy', the CCP reinforced anachronistic mass-line arguments favouring the socio-jural approach to the 'comprehensive management of public order' and the need for a variety of state institutions to interpret the law in an overt ideological way so as to consolidate 'socialist spiritual civilization' as against 'feudal superstition'. Judicial independence is thus demeaned as the state acts as the custodial parent of preconceived mass morality rather than as the champion of individual rights protection.

And finally, while the Chinese leaders have treated the FLG as a heretical cult rather than as a religion, their preferred political–legal approach may well expose religious and cultural organizations to more threatening state scrutiny at the expense of improved human rights performance. The charge of 'heresy' will always be out there lurking in changing Party politics. Moreover, the state's approach to heresy has challenged the rule of law. 'Flexible' judicial interpretation circumvented the proper role of the legislature as it is based upon comprehensive stipulation and 'no crime, nor punishment without law'. The ballooning of the content of Article 300 of the CL97, through inappropriate resort to SPC–SPP interpretation, appears to have been inspired by the same political tendencies that sanctioned 'policy is the soul of law'. This trend tends to elevate widely defined 'flexibility' and to subordinate the law within the wider political framework of the 'comprehensive management of public order', calling into question the 'supremacy of law', and thwarting the efforts of jurists who for many years have struggled to articulate the new balance of values synthesizing concern for both public order and human rights protection in law.

3   The criminal justice response to violence in the modern Chinese family

The time has come to review the relation between the state and family in evolving Chinese criminal justice. Tradition focused on the importance of the family unit as a whole and often worked against the imperial state's consistent and intimate involvement in highly sensitive family matters. A more recent trend, however, has witnessed increasing state intervention within the family to insure the protection of individual family members against newly acknowledged violence in the family, itself. The past tendency in law to insure the integrity of the family as a whole at the expense of the suffering of the individual family member is now under challenge. Economic reform is having a major impact on traditional family values and the integrity of the family unit. Post-1996–7 criminal justice reform has marked a new stage in the attempt to use the law so as to insure more protection of individual family members.

In light of the current politics emphasizing the convergence of the 'rule of law' with the 'rule of virtue', what new areas of familial and societal behaviour are to be criminalized? To what extent is the contemporary political correlation of law and morality consistent with the 1996–7 strategy of judicial reform that focused on both the protection of society (*shehui baohu*) and the protection of human rights (*renquan baozhang*)? In short, how has criminal justice responded to the growing patterns of violence within the modern Chinese family?

Plumbing the relevance of tradition

The history of Chinese imperial law reveals a strong emphasis on the severely punitive dimensions of criminal justice so as to reinforce familial values and to insure the prevailing social order on a basis of deterrence. The state established order on the formal basis of a strategy synthesizing decorum and law (*lifa jiehe*).[1] If there were philosophical tensions between Confucianism and Legalism, the principles underlying Chinese culture, familism and morality were continuously incorporated into law through time, and this imperial tradition rationalized and facilitated the hierarchical convergence of state and society. The latter convergence has for many years been the subject of Sinological interpretation of 'organic naturalism', which places the state in the moral continuum of a society that above all else valued familial harmony as the basis of public order and peace under heaven.[2]

Also, the punitive dimensions of imperial criminal law were often imposed on the collective basis of *baojia* (one hundred households). The latter was essentially a system of registration whereby the government and local gentry used the family system for police purposes.[3] The legal consequences of individual criminal behaviour often became the shared responsibility of family members who then had collectively to bear the brunt of the state's insistence on morality and public order.

However, the Confucian tradition, in particular, presumed that the best means of upholding the moral order was to encourage moral development within the family as the basic unit of society. Confucian respect for the autonomous moral sanctity of the family often qualified the way in which the state only cautiously intervened to deal with instances of family violence.

Intervention was more likely in politically sensitive cases where officials were greatly concerned about 'abominations' that threatened to disrupt the cosmos and imperial rule. Even plotting to kill, let alone actually killing the family patriarch was considered as one such gross violation of the Chinese 'way'. On the other hand, the husband who seriously beat his wife often managed to escape criminal law punishment. The Qing penal code reflected a core gender bias that was predicated in hierarchical familism.

To establish the crime of 'rape', for example, required that a woman resist during the entire commission of the act. It seems that the protestation of chastity was more important than a women's enjoyment of life, itself. Moreover, if an aroused man, upon seeing a woman in intercourse with another man, subsequently proceeded to rape the same woman he was subject, not to the charge of rape, *per se*, but to the lesser charge of having illicit sexual intercourse. Women were more likely to experience severe criminal punishment than men. At times the imperial penal code even demanded the immediate strangulation of any women who accidentally killed her husband. A 1783 statue also required immediate strangulation in cases where a woman was alleged to have driven her husband to suicide.[4]

Also, customary law, as understood by the clan, was more likely to be applied than criminal law when it came to the nitty-gritty of family decorum and dispute. Magistrates preferred not to challenge directly the responsibility of the *pater familias* and were wary of becoming too deeply involved in family matters, to take sides, and to assign blame, hence the common saying 'Even an upright official finds it hard to settle a family quarrel' (*jingguan nanduan jia wushi*). Furthermore, even when the law contained stipulated rules relating to familial relationships, these rules were not always enforced. Indeed, these 'rules' were often treated only as 'ideals' to which the members of society should collectively aspire.[5]

Although the penal code gave priority to severe punishment for crimes against the state, the philosophy that underscored the law's particular rationality gave extraordinary precedence to filial piety, righteousness, and the reciprocal moral obligations owed to family members. In the event of a clash of values, familial values even took precedence over the civic virtues requiring loyalty to the state. Confucius was often cited for admonishing the Duke of She, who mistakenly believed that uprighteousness required a son to report his father's crimes. Confucius reportedly admonished the Duke for his muddled thinking saying: 'In my part of the country, the upright are different from this. The father conceals the misconduct of his son and the son conceals the misconduct of his father. It is in this that uprighteousness lies.'[6]

There is also the hoary story of the Emperor, who, on the revelation of his father's criminal acts, was morally obliged out of filial piety to carry his father on his back out of the reach of his own officials. 'Sageliness within' was not only integral to, but also prior to 'kingliness without'. Whereas persons who concealed the offences of a relative were often exempted from punishment, an unfilial son who revealed his father's crime to authorities could, himself, become liable to criminal punishment.[7]

Deference to familial values personalized and skewed the fit between crime and punishment. The law's application reflected a personalized particularism rather than any likely principle of equality before the law. A person, for example, who confessed to a crime on behalf of a relative, was treated comparatively leniently out of respect for such a selfless act that supported the family. Such confession was allowed as if it was a confession by the actual perpetrator of the crime, and often it resulted in immunity or reduced punishment.[8]

The imperial criminal law legacy was such that the law was integral with state-imposed morality. Equality before the law was not even an issue as the law sought to legitimate the patriarchical hierarchy that characterized family relations. The law only respected gender distinctions in so far as they were predicated in the superiority of men over women. The 'traditional ideas of family integration' emphasized 'the interest of the family as a whole' without regard for the rights of individual family members.[9] Even now in urban, let alone rural China, the happiness of the individual is to be found outside the individual, in fulfilling the 'responsibility' associated with 'establishing a family'. James Farrar and Sun Zhongxin have elaborated on this very same point:

> 'Responsibility' to the family, rather than 'communication' between spouses is the primary language for describing the effort of keeping this relationship working. Moreover, the referent of these responsibilities is not the couple, but the family, especially the child. Responsibility signifies practical mutual help that maintains the well-being of family members (including sexual attention to the spouse). Romance is never used as an account of marital relations.[10]

Modern law and the persistence of traditional culture

Historically, it was only very recently in law, such as the 20 December 1993 'Declaration on the Elimination of Violence Against Women' that international, let alone domestic Chinese law, bridged the divide between public and private behaviour to treat domestic violence against women as a breach of human rights requiring the intervention of the state's criminal justice system. In the Chinese legal tradition, violence against women was often deliberately relegated to a 'private' realm of familial relations and morality. Male offenders often escaped criminal punishment for the law's intervention was regarded in society as an inappropriate intrusion into family life.[11] Drawing on Chinese history and culture, some contemporary conservative observers have even now expressed doubt about the state's current strategy for human rights development, suggesting that if judicial organs too often interfere against violence in the family they might de-stabilize the family unit.[12]

In the modern legal context of human rights protection, reformers have argued that Confucian ethics left the male, who resorted to violence, with nothing to fear from the law, whereas the victims were often socially compelled to suffer in silence for the sake of the family as a whole.[13] However, since the early 1990s, there is a new discourse on rights and the state's related obligation to define more rigorously 'criminal liability', based upon gender inequality, and to intervene within the family so as to insure the lawful protection of individual family members. Reformers often advocate that the state take 'countermeasures' (*duice*) to intervene in society to insure the individual against violence. It remains to be seen how this new emphasis on the activist state's protective role will play out in the current context requiring the convergence of the 'rule of law' with the 'rule of virtue'. State functionaries, in their quest for the 'comprehensive management of public order', might still err on the side of virtue that resists the new focus on human rights ostensibly for the sake of protecting the family.

Domestic advocates of reform have, nevertheless, sought the state's active involvement in human rights protection. They have urged the state to deploy legal and social 'countermeasures' against the new crime of 'domestic violence' (*jiating baoli*). Some reformers have justified state activism in light of a perceived loss of social interest in correcting the problem. The Peking University's Centre for Women's Law Studies and Legal Services, for example, described this problem of 'social environment' in the following manner:

> For a long time, people consider domestic violence as family business and non-family members should not interfere. Neighbors usually stand by when seeing husbands beating their wives and parents beating their children; at most they simply try to persuade and play the role as

mediator. Added with the fact that the whole society is undergoing transition and heated economic competition makes people suffer from great pressure, people now can hardly spare their time on the 'domestic affairs' – domestic violence of other people. In other words, the social net's ability to cope with family disputes decreases; lack of public condemnation allows [the] abuser to be free from any psychological pressure and consequently causes repeated occurrence of domestic violence.[14]

For some reformers the dilemma highlighted the need to redouble their efforts in fostering community-based social action. This argument may, however, have placed a greater onus on the state to take a proactive position on human rights in light of social disinterest and the decline of community interventions.

Formal 1990s Chinese human rights strategy concerning women, children, handicapped, and the aged sought an improvement in human rights performance highlighting the comprehensive coordination of state and society. Ideally, both rights protection and social control, required a broadly conceived division of labour encompassing the family, mass associations, and state administrative and legal organization.

The continuous division of labour between state and society so as to guarantee the legal and social protection of rights was, for example, outlined in the following *Renmin Ribao* explanation of the 1992 'Law on the Protection of the Rights and Interests of Women':

> The work of protecting women's rights and interests involves various social aspects, and its progress depends on the endeavours of the entire society. Hence, it calls for society to show concern for and give support and help to the implementation of the Law on Protecting Women's Rights and Interests, and create a favourable social environment... According to their own limits of authority, various departments in society must perform their obligations of protecting the rights and interests as stipulated by the law; have a division of labour with individual responsibilities; co-ordinate with each other; and employ various administrative, economic and legal means to bring their activities into line and exercise an overall control so as to ensure the implementation of the Law on Protecting Women's Rights and Interests.[15]

Article 3 of this women's law highlighted shared overlapping social and legal responsibilities and the coordination of state organs, social organizations, enterprises, and 'autonomous mass organizations'.

Contemporary criminal justice strategy reflects Chinese cultural preferences as well as deliberate adaptation to international norms. 'Localization' and 'internationalization' are both at work, and it is not always that reform surrenders to tradition. The traditional focus on collective criminal responsibility, for example, has been challenged. Even in the sensational case of 'organized crime' where there is new legal emphasis on the criminal nature of membership in particular collective organizations, the emphasis is on the individual's conscious decision to join an association that participates in criminal activity. In today's China, there is no automatic criminal association of family members with the individual criminal.[16]

In the reform era, the Chinese state has slowly but surely become more involved with legal countermeasures to insure the integrity of the modern family under stress. At the outset of reform, the CL79 Article 169 meted out punishment in relation to the 'social harm' done to women forced into prostitution. Article 182 referred to the 'abuse of family members'. Prevailing legal theory lumped together the 'rights and interests' (*quanyi*) of women, children, and the elderly as a 'special grouping' (*teshu qunti*) that required the law's protection as against the harsh competitive vicissitudes of a fast-paced and bewildering economic reform that tended to marginalize the weakest members of society.[17] Article 182, in practice, referred mainly to children and the elderly. The force of this article was not seen as particularly relevant to working adults.

CL79 Article 160 made interesting reference to the 'humiliation of women' when it enumerated a basket of unrelated crimes under the catchall category of 'the crimes of hooliganism' (*liumangzui*).[18] This particular basket could be 'flexibly' used to extend morality into law and the justice system so as to cover unstipulated, but socially reprehensible 'crime' relating, for example, to homosexuality, orgies, and distributing pornography.

While drawing on aspects of earlier Soviet law and focusing on such crime as an offence against public order, the Chinese construction of 'hooliganism' focused on the public harassment of females by males.[19] Harold M. Tanner provides an interesting case of hooliganism whereby a young worker just 'for a lark' threw a white cabbage at a woman pedestrian. Unfortunately, the woman died on the spot of a heart condition. As the worker was unaware of her condition, there was no intent to commit homicide, nor was 'causing death by negligence' an option as one would not normally expect that a blow caused by a cabbage would result in death. However, as the worker had a history of harassing and striking women with cabbages, he was, therefore, charged with the crime of 'hooliganism'.[20]

The 1990s witnessed a whole new range of human rights legislation, of which, 'Law on the Protection of Women's Rights and Interests' (April 1992) was among the most important. This law explicitly addressed the gender inequality associated with property ownership in the heated context of the transition to the market, but it did not specifically address 'domestic violence'. The latter was only vaguely anticipated in Article 33's insistence that women enjoy the same 'personal rights' as men. Article 40 added that women are to enjoy 'the same rights of family and marriage with men'.[21]

The first official reference to domestic violence came in the August 1995 National Program for Women's Development. This statement of government policy called for strict punishment against such activities as kidnapping, abandoning, maltreating, persecuting, and insulting women. The program also called for the resolute 'curbing of family violence'.[22]

1996–7 criminal justice reform responded to the new economic dimensions of crime and to the new self-conscious 'balance of values' that presumed the protection of the personal rights of women. The CL97 incorporated several articles relating to criminal prosecution of acts of force such as in Article 232, the crime of intentional murder; Article 234, the crime of intentional injury; Article 236, the crime of rape; Article 237 the crime of 'indecency'; and Article 260, the crime of 'abuse'. The crimes of injury and abuse more commonly relate to what is now called 'domestic violence'.

In particular the 'crime of abuse' concerns family members as special subjects; however, it involves an extraordinary high criterion for conviction. The Centre for Intervention and Research Against Domestic Violence has recently reported on the case of Li versus Zhang. Even though the husband had committed battery against his wife thirteen times over twenty years, the SPC upheld previous court decisions that, in light of the victim's remarriage to her husband, the beatings were not sufficiently regular, continuous, and consistent so as to constitute the 'crime of abuse'.[23] Apparently, the evil circumstances that are needed to establish criminal liability are ill-defined, and law in contemporary China often has a problem in objectively responding to shifting value structures in society.

As for the 'crime of intentional injury' this too very much depends on the proactive approach of well informed and favourably disposed public security officials. The law requires the forensic authentication of at least a 'flesh wound', and the victim is dependent upon public security to endorse the formal request for such authentication. Public security may, however, decide not to process such a request if it is overly concerned with the interests of the whole family as traditionally distinguished from the interests of particular family members.

Culture can still trump legal professionalism. One might argue that the latter has been articulated as a desired goal, and that there is some evidence that it is beginning to take hold, but external observers are likely to draw the following conclusion: 'A policing style as based on a culture of police professionalism cannot be developed in a short time in China because, in China today, psychological and emotional ties to the family, the work group and society remain strong; and the Chinese police executives have hardly changed their traditional philosophy of policing.'[24]

Victims who have suffered serious injury may decline to press criminal charges, but may consider that the competent public security authority alternatively enforce Article 22 of 'The Regulations on Punishment in respect of the Management of Public Security'. Under this article an abusive husband could be detained administratively for violence that was presumably not considered as 'continuous and consistent' as under the Criminal Law's provisions. However, even this lesser form of punishment for the infringing of the 'personal rights' of an individual is sometimes neglected by vacillating public security officials, who are reluctant to apply the appropriate administrative regulations ostensibly for the sake of preserving the family.[25]

Public morality is especially meaningful in its incorporation into the new CL97 Article 237. The latter updated the earlier language of CL79 Article 160 concerning 'hooliganism' and assembly to create brawls and humiliate women, by adding the following provision: 'Whoever acts indecently against or insults a woman by violence, coercion or any other forcible means shall be sentenced to fixed-term imprisonment of not more than five years or criminal detention.'[26] This notion of a 'coercive indecent act' relates specifically to adult women as victims. The Peking University's Centre for Women's Law Studies and Legal Services provides the following informative gloss on the subjective aspect of this crime as follows: 'The subjective aspect of crime is intentional crime, whose main motive is mainly on account of spiritual emptiness and to seek abnormal sexual satisfaction and obscene shameless spiritual excitement.'

Apparently, the issue here is not the act of fornication, itself, but the accompanying degradation that accompanies the coercive obscene shaming of a woman. The Centre enumerates the following acts as examples:

> For example, forcing a woman to masturbate him and suck his genital, etc. [sic] Insulting a women refers to the act that the actor takes [such a] mean and obscene action against a woman to induce [in] her a sense of shame, for example, philandering in public places with mean and obscene language, cutting a women's underwear stealthily, making a woman disgraced, stripping a woman naked and showing a woman his genital, etc. [sic][27]

Article 237 on indecent sexual acts and Article 236, as they pertain to the 'raping of a number of women' and 'indecency' were recently applied separately in the case of Dai Xinglie of Ningbo, Zhejiang. This gynaecologist was accused of indecent sexual contact and of sodomizing 16 of his patients over a period of 4 years. These criminal acts resulted in the assignment of the death penalty by the local intermediate court.[28]

With the new formal trend towards the stipulation of crime relating to violence against individual family members, the state was expected to grab hold of the law and to become more directly involved in upholding the human rights of individual family members. International standards and norms are more freely circulating within Chinese society, and the stability of the family is readily associated with society's stability in the context of accelerated economic growth. Chinese jurists and lawmakers are sensitive to argument concerning the need to develop a 'rule of law' that has 'Chinese characteristics', but, at the same time, they have a lower threshold of tolerance for violence in familial and social relationships.

Contemporary social science research has established that violence against women such as assault, rape, and robbery is more likely to occur inside, rather than outside, family relations.[29] For both purposes of public order and human rights protection, the state is now expected to become an 'honest official' who will directly intervene against family violence. There are continuing problems with regard to the lack of enforcement of related law, but the notion that violence against individual family members ought to be dismissed as 'family conflict' is under increasing political and legal challenge.

The limits of criminalization and the mixed blessings of 'virtue'

As noted earlier, the Party's response to the Falungong and 'wholesale Westernization' focused political attention on the need for a combined rule of law and rule of virtue in order to deal with the stability of the family and society. There is a very interesting debate on the wisdom of this combined approach. Some have argued that such a combination is essentially innocuous. They think that after all is said and done, the law will succeed only if it appropriately reflects society. In fact, it is a specifically Chinese approach that will insure the law's effective balancing of rights protection and public order. Some reformers, however, worry lest the comprehensive and explicit correlation of law with politically determined virtue resurrects the 'rule of man' and adversely affects the struggle for the 'rule of law'. They ask whether at a contemporary critical point in the struggle for the 'rule of law' the pre-eminent concern for virtue will trump the supremacy of law and whether the law's august authority will be weighed down with the conservative politics of morality.

They suggest that talk of virtue, in an abstract, or woolly sense, can generate legal confusion. Reformers fear that 'rule by virtue' might facilitate a return to the 'rule of man'. The latter of course not only contradicted the mass-line assumptions of the CCP, but it stood in the way of the principle of equality before the law in that the 'spirit of the leader', as it was predicated in 'personality cult', assumed that some people in positions of power might be more virtuous than others.[30] Moreover, one might assert that the new emphasis on a 'rule of virtue' could easily deflect the thrust of legal reform, based upon the principle of legality, namely, 'no crime and no punishment without law'. Furthermore, in dealing with the urgency of ideological decline and value change, political leaders may be under great political pressure to skip over the normal law-making process so as to rely on administrative sanctions, which are applied outside of the criminal and criminal procedural law context.

Indeed, there are obvious difficulties in the comprehensive stipulation of law in a fast-changing society that is undergoing profound value change. In its struggle to insure social control and public order the Party is politically sensitive to spreading anomie and stress. However, with the deepening of social change, Chinese law-making has sometimes had to make politically uncomfortable moral choices. The related revision of the Marriage Law not surprisingly attracted enormous public interest and revealed significant differences of generational opinion on the legal and ethical dimensions of married life.

While the younger generation may have become more liberal, in its views of marriage, family, and sex, Party authorities were vitally concerned about the rising divorce rate, the integrity of family life, and relation of monogamy to social stability. In 2000, there was a 10.8 per cent drop in marriage rate and a 51.25 per cent increase in the divorce rate over 1990.[31] The Marriage Law amendments, therefore, attracted an unusual degree of animated public discussion about the direction of related law, and this resulted in intense political bargaining within the NPC's legislative process.

The issue as to which of the newly identified social behaviours were to be criminalized was a matter of hot controversy, and apparently, there were a great many outstanding proposals for revised wordings. The first draft of the revised Marriage Law, prepared by senior legal scholars, included 266 articles. The scholars were advised to whittle these down to 154 articles and then these were subsequently reduced in the political process of legislative committee consideration to a total of 51 articles, which made it into the amended Marriage Law of April 2001.[32] Thirty-three major alterations were made to the former 37-article law, and at the time of promulgation it was widely anticipated that the SPC would quickly issue formal interpretations to 'curb acts that lead to serious consequences to family relations'.[33]

The controversy over the amendments was predictably hailed as an instance of a new process of democratization highlighting public participation in law-making. From the point of view of Party conservatives, however, more than just flies were coming through China's 'open door'. The Party addressed the fundamental issue of society's ideological purity. Morally bankrupt Western culture was undermining the Chinese family as it struggled with the bewildering and socially distressing consequences of economic reform. Pornography and casual sex, for example, had become all too common. Families were being ripped apart over property rights. And economic reform had even generated conditions favourable to the resurrection of the traditional vices of concubinage and bigamy.

In Guangdong, for example, 95 per cent of all criminals who were accused of economic crime were identified as having at least one concubine.[34]

There was a growing political concern that the institution of marriage was under attack. Chapter 2 in both the 1950 and 1980 Marriage Laws, as a matter of general principle, had referred to how 'third parties' (*disanzhe*) would not be allowed to interfere with the marriage contract. In light of the contemporary challenges to family life brought on under accelerated economic reform, conservative moral opinion wanted to go beyond the earlier rhetorical admonition in the law to criminalize 'third parties' for their role in precipitating divorce.

Indeed, the issue of adultery has had a very long legal history. The imperial tradition had formally criminalized the commission of adultery, but such law was not always applied with rigour. Qing law specifically granted immunity to a husband who in a fit of 'righteous' rage killed his wife and her lover in delectio flagrante.[35] Although later Kuomindang (or Guomindang) criminal law sought to bring rights into the law, based upon a new notion of gender equality, the 1935 criminal code provided for the punishment of not more than one year's punishment for either the husband or the wife who committed adultery with a third party.[36] During the Mao era and through to the early reform period, while adultery had not been criminalized, adulterers were occasionally arrested for the crimes of 'rape' or 'hooliganism' and then subjected to administrative detention without trial.[37]

In 2001, the NPC's Law Committee ran into difficulty in its attempts to enumerate acts in violation of the 'statutory principle of monogamy'. At the end of the day, the conservatives were unable to muster sufficient NPC votes to criminalize adultery. This was the case even in the face of strong public opinion. The national debate over extra-marital affairs, concubinage, and domestic violence had been prefaced by an ACWF survey. Ninety-five per cent of the 4,000 people surveyed from ten provinces and cities including Beijing, Guandong, and Sichuan wanted to criminalize extra-marital affairs for the harm done to marriage relations. According to the same survey, 8.2 per cent of respondents acknowledged that they had had 'illicit sex' and 2.4 per cent claimed to have concubines.[38]

Despite the hand-wringing of the conservatives and the trend of public opinion, the NPC delegates consigned adultery to the non-legal, and arguably less compelling realm of ethics. Criminalization would have tied up tremendous institutional resources, and, in this important instance, the NPC chose to ignore the connection between the 'rule of law' and the 'rule of virtue'.

The NPC Law Committee steered clear of conservative attempts to police changing sexual relationships, except in the politically sensitive area relating to military personnel. NPC delegates were well aware of the Party's very low tolerance for any family trouble that might de-stabilize the army. On the issue of divorce affecting military personnel, Article 33 of the new law retained the past wording: 'The spouse of a service member requesting divorce shall get concurrence from that service member.' The full impact of this was softened in the drafting process. The final version of this article included new reference that gave a suffering spouse some hope when it added the rather fuzzy qualification, 'except in the case that the service member has a serious fault'.[39]

Past criminalization of 'third party' interference with the sanctity of the marriage of military personnel was duly carried forward into the 2001 revised text of the Marriage Law. This criminalization was treated as a legitimate example of 'localization', but the most important point is that the NPC did not criminalize civilian adultery.[40] Indeed, the criminalization of adultery would possibly have enflamed already significant generational tensions, and it might have also placed an impossible logistical burden on the law's operation in society at the expense of its own authority and dignity. The new law did, however, place new criminal emphasis on 'cohabitation with married persons'.[41] Living together over time was treated as more insulting to society than adulterous casual sex.

The issue of virtue, as it related to the 1992 socio-legal approach to the protection of women's 'rights and interests' (*quanyi*) informed related changes to jurisprudence and legislation. In turn this affected the understanding of the socio-legal approach embedded in the 1992 women's law. The amended Marriage Law formed part of an existing comprehensive strategy to deal with apparently undesirable social change, hence the Xinhua News Agency editorialized:

> The vast numbers of the masses should study the law, understand the law, and regard the revised Marriage Law as the code of conduct in their marriage and family lives. The propaganda of the legal system in this aspect should be effectively integrated with the education of the socialist marriage and family morality.[42]

'Domestic violence' in the politics of law and virtue

The correlation of law and virtue was again tested in political and legislative debates over 'domestic violence' (*jiating baoli*) and revision to the Marriage Law. The ACWF's 2000 survey had shown 46.2 per cent support for the new assignment of criminal penalities to those convicted of 'domestic violence'. Another 26.8 per cent of respondents indicated their alternative preference for related 'education'.[43] Reformers contended that 'maltreatment', as it had been developed within past criminal law, had failed to keep up with new phenomena relating to 'domestic violence'.

Under 'maltreatment' the criminal law had dealt with 'causing death by negligence' (*guoshi sharen*). The general category of 'maltreatment' (*nuedai*) had, however, failed to cover the increasing incidence of husbands beating their wives to death in unpremeditated rage.[44] Such violence turned gender equality into a life or death issue. An implicit cross reference to 'domestic violence' in the Marriage Law was seen as a way of strengthening the law's multidimensional response to the changing circumstances of 'causing death by negligence' in contemporary society.

Prior to the 2001 revision to the Marriage Law, there was no definition in law of 'domestic violence'. This reflected a lack of political consensus and priority with respect to entwined domestic and international social change. In the past, 'domestic violence' was not considered sufficiently serious as to warrant punishment under the criminal law.[45] However, the 4th World Conference on Women in Beijing provided reformers with new political opportunity to highlight the issue in domestic politics. Reformers highlighted the UN Declaration on the Elimination of Violence against Women where it indicated: 'violence against women indicates any rough behaviour based on social sexes which has caused or will probably cause women injury of pain in mind, body, and sex, including threatening to use such violence, forcing to deprive freedom, or depriving freedom at will, no matter where it happens, in public or in private life.'[46]

The UN declaration provided an open-ended understanding of 'violence against women' that included physical, sexual, and psychological violence that occurs 'privately' within the family such as wife-battering, the sexual abuse of female children in the household, dowry-related violence, marital rape, female genital mutilation, and violence against exploitation. These areas of violence also included the more 'public' dimensions of abuse relating, again only by way of example, to non-spousal rape, sexual abuse, harassment and intimidation in the work place, forced prostitution, and the trafficking in women.[47] The 'Action Guiding Principles' that were passed in Beijing included 'domestic violence' in its listing of twelve key issues.

Article 237 of the CL97 subsequently included the following expanded reference to 'violence' against women: 'Whoever acts indecently against or insults a women by violence, coercion, or any other forcible means shall be sentenced to a fixed-term imprisonment of not more than five years, or criminal detention.'[48] This article added to existing law regarding the 'humiliation' of women under the catch-all categories of 'hooliganism', but it was still something of a blunt instrument that was not really designed to remedy the wild spread of familial abuse in economic reform.

In February 2000, Liaoning Provincial Court, Public Security Office, the Office of the Committee for the Comprehensive Management of Public Order and provincial branch of the ACWF approved a set of regulations (*guiding*). The latter's definition of 'domestic violence' anticipated the December 2001 SPC definition, and the regulations approximated the socio-legal strategy that had informed the 'Law on the Protection of Women's Rights and Interests'. The regulations assumed a close working relation between government departments, mass associations, and popular organizations in taking coordinated remedial action to prevent domestic violence.[49]

For the first time in Chinese legal history, 'domestic violence' was stipulated as a crime in the 2001 revision of the Marriage Law. A great variety of associations and government departments, not to mention interested jurists, lobbied and made submissions with regard to the question as to the criminal scope of domestic violence. There was a strong opinion to the effect that any revision to the Marriage Law should be expansive in nature so that this law not only dealt with the issues concerning marriage, itself, but also the revision would deal with the cognate issues of marriage concerning, for example, the handling of new property issues as well as the development of a strategy to combat 'domestic violence'.[50]

The NPC drafters recognized domestic violence as a growing problem in a traumatized society, the stability of which required new forms of state activated legal redress. The ACWF survey had helped convince them that domestic violence was estimated to occur in 30 per cent of Chinese families. The drafters, however, were concerned about institutional costs and how the issue and related remedial legislation would play out in Chinese society. They were well aware of socio-cultural preference that alternatively focused on extra-legal, 'private' remedy to domestic violence from within the inner precincts of the family, itself. The legislators, therefore, sought a middle ground, which would criminalize domestic violence, but which would also limit its legal scope in accordance with their own specifically nuanced sense of contemporary social preferences and related value change.

Even with the new political prioritization of the issue, reformers were unable to secure a stand-alone article on 'domestic violence'. The symbolic significance of the latter was diminished in so far as it was lumped together in the omnibus stipulations of Article 3, which also dealt with a range of other, if nonetheless important, categories relating to 'bride-trafficking', 'mercenary marriage', bigamy, and concubinage.[51] To be sure 'domestic violence' received new priority in that, for the first time, it was designated as a 'crime'. However, the clarification of the content of this newly stipulated crime suffered as the result of the politics of legislative bargaining. Although the legislators did agree on the importance of insuring greater organizational responsibility for dealing with 'domestic violence', they did not address the difference between 'domestic violence' and 'maltreatment' in law. Nor did they attempt to detail the categories of 'domestic violence' in the revised Marriage Law.

Moreover internal debates over whether 'domestic violence' ought to move beyond physical assault to include sexual and psychological abuse were largely left without criminal law resolution. Also, the newly revised Marriage Law was the product of political compromise between legal scholars, judicial practitioners, and legislators. Some reform scholars wanted to parallel new international legal norms incorporating all three categories of domestic violence, including sexual abuse, psychological abuse, and physical violence. The legislators were more inclined to consider only the last category. Moreover they focused on the relation between husband and wife and did not attempt to deal with common law spouses, ex-spouses, or boy- and girl friends.

The jurists, themselves, have not gotten very far with debates concerning 'rape in marriage' (*hunnei qiangjian*). A women's right of refusal continues to apply only to non-spousal relationships.[52] Some jurists have maintained that China's tradition is still very much alive in contemporary society and that related legislation cannot move too far ahead of society. Legislation must, therefore, await the development of appropriately supportive public opinion. In the meantime the authorities were encouraged to focus on saving the victims, first, and then later worrying about whether rapists inside the marriage ought to be punished.[53]

Not surprisingly, NPC legislators have also tended to steer clear of the developing reform focus on the public dimension of workplace sexual harassment.[54] On the other hand, while some conservative Party authorities may have wanted the law to provide a strong moral guidance to society, the NPC was reluctant to legislate against all the categories of behaviour that were deemed immoral.

The prevailing political line on converging the rule of law and rule of virtue did not directly challenge the 1990s strategy whereby social stability and rights protection are to be achieved on the basis of a comprehensive socio-legal strategy encompassing society and the state. The 2001 Marriage Law re-affirmed the unified state–society strategy embedded in the 1992 women's law. And indeed over the next several years jurists and legislators are expecting to consolidate this strategy in a host of new local regulations and organizational initiatives.

However, soon after the revised Marriage Law was signed into law, reform jurists complained about the Law's shortcomings in terms of its weak definition of standards regarding the measure of family violence causing severe injury.[55] Currently, the Centre for Intervention and Research Against Domestic Violence is lobbying NPC delegates to adopt the Centre's extensive proposals regarding the drafting of new national legislation that exclusively focuses on the definition of the crimes of domestic violence and a related socio-legal organizational strategy.

Chapter 5 of the 1980 Marriage Law was simply entitled 'Fu Ze', or supplementary rules, but it was greatly extended so as to address issues of remedy under a new title, 'Countermeasures and Legal Liability' (*jiuzhu cuoshi*). In 2001, new articles 43 through 47 were added. Chapter 5 essentially reiterated the 1992 socio-legal strategy. Remedial action in this chapter was calibrated in relation to the severity of the violence so that an aggrieved party might initially request the assistance of the neighbourhood committee to mediate. The next level of severity and response involved a request to Public Security to impose penalties under public security administration. Article 45, as indicated in the following wording, newly envisaged either public or private prosecution of related crimes:

> The person who commits bigamy, family violence, maltreatment or abandonment of a family member, if it constitutes a crime, shall be investigated for criminal responsibility in accordance with law. The victim may, in accordance with the relevant provisions of the Criminal Procedure Law, lodge a private prosecution with the People's Court; the public security organ shall investigate the case in accordance with the law, and the People's Procuratorate shall institute public prosecution in accordance with the law.[56]

Conceivably, for those with resources and inclination, private prosecution offered a new way round any potential cultural resistance, or default within the standard judicial process. On the other hand, a greater reliance on private resources and initiative might possibly highlight the public system's failure to provide an even application of rights protection under the law.

The relation of 'domestic violence' to 'maltreatment of family members' needed clarification in law. Article 43, for example, refers ambiguously to 'the aggrieved party in domestic violence or the maltreatment of family members'. However, the 2001 Marriage Law calibrated the degrees of severity of the domestic violence and correlated these degrees with particular socio-legal strategies. Related intervention and countermeasures varied from informal community response through criminal court proceedings, including a new emphasis on private criminal law prosecution. The revised law endorsed the resort to neighbourhood mediation so as to educate violence offenders in the community. In more severe cases the offender could be taken to court and criminal punishment could then be meted out.[57]

A NPC Standing Committee member close to the revision process, Nei Li, argued that the new law had to encourage both police and community organizations to be proactive in the protection of family members against domestic violence. Their respective official responsibilities had not been emphasized in either the 1950 or the 1980 laws. The final draft of the 2001 new Article 43 included a sentence that squarely addressed the persisting lackadaisical performance on the part of responsible officials: 'When the victim advances a request, the public security organ shall, in accordance with the legal provisions on administrative penalties for public security, impose an administrative penalty on the person who commits family violence or maltreatment of a family member.'[58] The newly created Article 45 of the 2001 Marriage Law, also made specific reference to neighbourhood committees and public security:

> Those who commit the crimes of bigamy, domestic violence of family maltreatment and abandonment of family members shall be prosecuted for their criminal liabilities. The victim can initiate a private

prosecution according to relevant stipulations of the Criminal Procedure Law, while public security organs shall conduct investigations according to the law and the People's Procuratorate shall proceed with public prosecution according to law.[59]

Moreover, in the earlier drafts of the 2001 revised law, chapter 5 was simply entitled 'Legal Responsibilities'. The final approved version gave more emphasis to remedial institutional and neighbourhood support in the inclusion of its title of support, or countermeasures, or salvaging measures (*cuoshi*).

Consistent with recent reform emphasis on the protection of individual rights, chapter 5 several times highlighted new language relating to the victim's 'right to request' (*you quan tichu qingqiu*) community and public security interventions.[60] The NPCSC delegate, Shu Huaide, gave part of the reasoning for emphasizing state involvement even in the absence of a request for help:

> it is possible that the victims are not able to ask for help because of threats and surveillance by the family member who is violent or the victim is unable to ask for help because they are too young or too old.[61]

Also, the victim may simply demur and not seek legal aid when confronted with tradition and related stigmatization, and this can give the public security authorities the opportunity not to file even in cases of sexual violence. Reformers described such phenomenon as 'the vanishing case' (*xiaoshide anjian*).[62]

Article 98 under 'Other Provisions' of the CL97 started to address this kind of cultural dilemma in its consideration of the terminology, 'to be handled only upon complaint':

> 'To be handled only upon complaint' as mentioned in this Law means that a case shall only be handled if the victim brings a complaint. However, if the victim is unable to bring a complaint because of coercion or intimidation, a People's Procurator or a close relative of the victim may bring a complaint.[63]

More specifically, however, the CL97 had failed to anticipate coercion by a family member to prevent the victim from filing a complaint.

The legal issues with regard to 'domestic violence' are now only emerging. Currently, the Centre for Intervention and Research Against Domestic Violence is lobbying NPC delegates to adopt the Centre's proposed draft law on domestic violence. Reformers at the Centre have pinpointed certain areas for related debate and legislation. First of all, 'domestic violence' as it is incorporated into the revised Marriage Law and as it anticipates the application of Criminal Law punishment in the most serious cases has focused too exclusively on violence to the body. These reformers are urging NPC delegates to consider investigating new criminal liability for 'the violence to the mind of females, and for the threat of life, health, personal freedom, reputation or property of the victims or their relatives and friends when causing serious consequence.'[64]

Furthermore, although the 24 December 2001 SPC 'Interpretation on Several Questions concerning the Revised Marriage Law' has interpreted the reference in Article 46 of the 2001 Marriage Law to 'compensation for injury' (*sunhai peichang*) to include harm relating to the mind as well as the body,[65] the Centre's reformers remain concerned that the holding of 'joint property' in marriage continues to prevent an abused wife from gaining civil compensation for both physical and spiritual harm. To fix this, reformers are urging that the Civil Law be revised so as to expedite such compensation by 'the suspension of joint property'.[66]

Centre reformers have also highlighted the haphazard nature of punishment for 'domestic violence' and the need for more consistently dependable protection for battered women. They are now vetting the American legal notion of the protection order as a means of filling this gap in existing countermeasures.[67] While the revised Marriage Law attempted to deal with outstanding matters relating to official non-performance regarding the punishment of 'domestic violence', these reformers have also argued that the time has come for new national legislation on domestic violence that will draw on the growing body of local regulations that are presently used to insist upon the intervention of the legally responsible agencies to deal forthrightly with the crime of 'domestic violence'. These reformers have also sought to develop further 'pluralized mechanisms' that will address the socio-legal protection of women, and hence they support the creation of a new generation of special family tribunals to deal with cases 'specially in consideration of the privacy and reiteration of domestic violence, to emphasize active intervention in the investigation of evidence, to promote the training of the judges of the family court, and to eliminate the subjective understanding of domestic violence in order to handle the cases of domestic violence timely and fairly (*sic*).'[68]

The reform response to the trafficking of women and children

When one considers the law's response to the affects of violence on the contemporary Chinese family as it struggles to cope with the social consequences of economic reform, 'domestic violence' is not the only front on which reformers are battling for the recognition and legal protection of human rights. Article 6 of the UN Convention on the Elimination of All Forms of Discrimination against Women specifically called upon states to legislate against the trafficking and prostitution of women. The leaders of the CCP have become deeply concerned about the abduction and sale of women and children. This phenomenon had plagued traditional Chinese society. In the early 1950s, the vigorous new 'people's' regime quickly and resolutely suppressed all such trafficking. The resurgence of such ugly phenomena affects the Party's own legitimacy in the reform period, as it is a distressingly painful and embarrassing reminder of the depth of moral decline in contemporary society.

The development of such crime has been through a number of stages. By 1990 it statistically peaked in its spread and occurrence, but in the 1990s the basis for this crime demonstrated increasing organizational sophistication especially in areas of Sichuan, Henan, and Shanxi. In 1996, in Fuyang County, Anhui, specific villages that had become especially adept in the abduction and sale of women and children were labelled as 'specialized villages'. In Mananzhao village, for example, 60 per cent of the village population of 500 were estimated to have participated in related activities.[69]

Zhu Yantao, an official with the Crime Investigation Division of the Public Security Ministry, indicated that there were 20,000 cases of trafficking women and children in 1992. After 1992, there was a decrease such that by 1997 there were only 6,000 cases.[70] The numbers have started to climb once more. In 2000, the authorities initiated a national wide campaign entitled '*daji renfanzi, jiejiu beiguaimai funu ertong*' (attacking human traffickers and rescuing abducted and sold women and children) under the auspices of a new special office, established within the Ministry of Justice.[71] Professors Ye Gaofeng and Liu Defa reported that in the province of Henan alone, 2,100 human traffickers had been arrested and 5,700 abducted women and 1,000 abducted children were rescued from the criminal traffickers.[72] This crime was especially prevalent in the rural areas where organized criminal groups formed along kinship lines. Within the organized group there were branches that specialized in abduction, transport, and the sale of women and children. More than 60 per cent of the women abducted were 18 years of age, and these women, many of whom originated from the remote and poorer areas of China's hinterland, were often lured into trafficking with false promises of finding a husband or a business partner.[73]

Such criminal practice was driven by interactive socio-demographic pressures and crude economics. The rural imbalance in the ratio of males to females is particularly acute. While rural women preferred to marry men in the urban and more developed rural areas, men in the rural areas, who were looking to maintain the family line, found that the purchase of a bride was a cheap alternative to the cost of a legitimate wedding involving household expenditure on new furniture, appliances, and electronics.

The proliferation of such crime in remote areas is also conditioned by a lack of awareness of related human rights law.[74] Moreover, rural village officials often covered up for those purchasing wives in the belief that this was the only practical way for them to start up their families. In fact, there are even examples of village officials and Party cadres organizing the villagers to forcefully obstruct the public security authority in its attempts to rescue the victims of abduction.[75] Also, in some areas there was a 'local protectionism' whereby local government organization focused on the saving of abducted women, but did not prosecute those who had purchased the women victims.[76] Those organizing criminal abduction are increasingly targeting younger women who are often forced into prostitution. Also, there is a pattern of sale of male babies sometimes for purposes of extortion and often as the means of remedying the infertility of rural couples anxious to maintain the family line.[77]

Luo Gan, a Politbureau member and Secretary of the CCP Central Committee's Politics and Law Committee, placed the 2000 crackdown campaign on human traffickers within the wider policy frame concerning the comprehensive management of China's huge floating population. Abduction created more related problems as women had become targets of opportunity at the railway stations, bus stops, and wharves in the big and medium-sized cities, and in Luo's view the relevant special work within the justice system had to be combined within a comprehensive strategy that would make the most of mass-line initiatives at the key points of trafficking.[78]

In a June 2000 'Notice' of the Ministry of Public Security, police units across the country were ordered to help resettle women and children who were the victims of abduction and trafficking. Public Security was asked to reinstate these victims' registration as the latter had often been routinely cancelled after their disappearance. Perhaps in an interesting twist on human rights protection, the same 'Notice' required Public Security to respect the wishes of newly freed women who opted to stay married with 'husbands' who had purchased them from the traffickers.[79]

The changing law on abduction and trafficking

At the time of the approval of the CL79 and CPL79 the ugly criminal issue of abduction and trafficking had just begun to become manifest, especially in the wake of the social turmoil and destruction of normal family relations that had been wildly fostered in the Cultural Revolution. CL79 Article 141 stipulated that, in particularly serious cases, the abduction and sale (*guaimai*) of human beings might attract no less than 5 years and not more than 15 years of imprisonment. Although the 'object' of such crime was human beings in general, women and children were almost exclusively the victims of such crime.

The rising crime rate for abduction and trafficking in the early 1980s prompted wholesale resort to more severe penalties. In a controversial 1983 decision, that later attracted significant reformer criticism, the NPC increased the maximum punishment for the leaders of the crime from fifteen year imprisonment to the death penalty. This 'Decision Regarding the Severe Punishment of Criminal Elements who Seriously Endanger Public Security' relied heavily on criminal law deterrence, and it was intended to provide a quick fix to a social problem that was spiralling out of control, but the 'Decision' provided very little basis in law for dealing with the practical detail that increasingly characterized the sophisticated organization of human abduction and trafficking.

Moreover reformers attacked the 'Decision' for its failure to arrest such phenomenon. The wider application of capital punishment, in their unconventional, if not daring view, had proved to be an ineffective deterrent. The Chinese authorities were increasingly sensitive to reformer criticism in light of growing social instability and public opinion concerning violent crime. And at the same time the death penalty had attracted criticism that disparaged China's international image.[80]

In order to deal with the lack of clear stipulation concerning crimes of abduction and trafficking, the NPCSC, in 1991, issued a new decision, 'Decision Regarding the Punishment of Abducting, Kidnapping and Selling of Women and Children.' The 'Decision' provided closer detail concerning the punishment of related crime. It, for example, separated the new crime concerning the abduction of women and children from 'human trafficking'. This new crime required a minimum of five years in prison.[81] This 'Decision' was, nevertheless, subject to another round of reform criticism. Reformers attacked the 'Decision', as it was not well organized, and it lacked definition of key terms governing the law's implementation. While there was great concern over the lack of definition in the law, there was a problem in achieving an appropriately rational form of 'flexibility' in light of the lack of clear and comprehensive stipulation in law.

To deal with outstanding issues of implementation, the SPC and SPP jointly issued in 1992 'Answers to Several Questions concerning the "Decision Regarding Punishment of Abducting, Kidnapping and Selling Women and Children."' The 'Answers' highlighted the 'Decision's' stipulation of several different crimes concerning women and children, including the crime of abducting and selling women and children, the crime of kidnapping women and children, the crime of kidnapping women and children for the purpose of extortion, crime relating to the organizing of populace to obstruct the rescue of women and children, and the crime concerning official failure to respond to obstructed rescue of women and children victims.[82]

The 'Answers' also clarified the crime of stealing babies. In the 1980s, there was some confusion in judicial practice as to which CL79 article might be used to punish this particular crime. The 1991 'Decision' had provided that such conduct should be punished as the 'crime of abducting and selling women and children'. The 'Answers' further clarified the crime's 'object', making formal distinctions between (a) 'babies', or 'infants' (*yinger*) that were less than 1 year old, (b) 'young children' (*youer*) that were between 1 and 6 years old, and (c) 'children' (*ertong*) that ranged from 6 to 14 years old.

The minimum penalty for committing abducting, kidnapping, and selling and buying women and children was established as not less than five years' imprisonment. The 'Answers' broadly extended the death penalty to those, who acted as the leaders of a related organized crime group, for the abduction, sale or purchase of more than three women or children, for those who raped abducted women, for those who forced abducted women into the sex trade, or who sold abducted women to others who would then force these women into prostitution, for action resulting in the injury or the death of abducted women, children, or their family members, and for the abduction and sale of women and children abroad. The 'Answers' also made new provision for the introduction of fines and the confiscation of an offender's property, thus denying to offenders the financial ability to pursue related crime in the future after having served their sentences.

When compared to the 1983 'Decision', the 1991 'Decision' provided much more detail concerning related criminal punishment. For the first time, buyers of abducted women and children and those who were guilty of using violence to prevent the police from rescuing the victims were to receive severe punishment. Moreover, the 'Decision' started to address outstanding problems relating to the circumvention of the law and non-compliance. It may seem rather extraordinary that the 'Decision' had to prohibit buyers from seeking financial compensation from the victims' families after the buyers were ordered to return the women and children to their families.

Chinese legal scholars have often affirmed that the 1991 'Decision' constituted an important improvement over both the CL79 and the 1983 'Decision'. Indeed the 1991 'Decision' helped provide for a new legal basis in the revised CL97. The latter necessarily drew on past stipulations concerning the trafficking of women and children. CL97 Articles 240, 241, and 242 consolidated and simplified the aforementioned 6 crimes into 3 crimes, namely, the crime of abducting and selling women and children, the crime of purchasing women and children, and the crime of obstructing the process of rescuing abducted women and children. The previous categories of crime concerning the kidnapping of women and children, the kidnapping of women and children for the purpose of extortion, and the stealing of babies were newly treated as 'special circumstances' relating to the root three crimes. The various punishments stipulated in the 1991 'Decision' were carried over into the CL97.[83]

Not surprisingly, reformers have critically reviewed the related provisions of the CL97 calling for further revision of the criminal law. These critics, for example, have complained that the law has not articulated clear distinctions between the different types of actors involved in abduction and trafficking. In particular, the CL97 made insufficient provision for the punishment of those who have non-violently interfered with state officials in their attempts to rescue the victims of abduction and trafficking.

In addition to this proposed extension of the terms of 'criminal liability', some have also argued for heavier penalties in cases where 'criminals' obstruct the rescue of victims; they would, for example, increase the penalty for the latter 'crime' from 5 to 7 years of imprisonment.[84]

Perhaps too often politics has willy-nilly directed the law to promote 'heavy penalty-ism' in order to promote the state's immediate objectives of social stability and public order. Certainly, in the response to the abduction and trafficking of women and children, one can see some of the problems that have complicated the struggle to achieve a new strategy for criminal justice reform. The law, in fact, has never been sufficiently comprehensive as to obviate the practical need for the more rational forms of 'flexibility' to fill in the perennial gaps left by formal legislation.

Conclusion

The above analysis suggests that the score-card for legal reform, based upon the newly proposed balancing of human rights and social protection, has a rather complex format, and that many of the related legal battles are developing simultaneously in a haphazard manner. Jurists and legislators are helping to promote meaningful political and legal discussion of how the modern Chinese family copes with the unprecedented stress and anomie of reform even while the Party's leadership is seeking some new synthesis combining the 'rule of law' with the 'rule of virtue'.

How should one evaluate the importance of this new Party focus? To what extent should one assume that it represents a serious neo-traditional tendency that contests the superiority of the 'rule of law'? What is the difference between legitimate 'localization' and 'cultural relativism'?

For a very long time the penal code of imperial China deliberately and directly reflected the moral requirements of propriety or decorum (*li*). However, if today's 'rule of virtue' professes a strong interest in 'Chinese characteristics', there is no doubt that family and society are undergoing multidimensional and episodic change and that moral understandings as to the purposes of the law in society have become more complex. In the contemporary context which attempts to synthesize *baohu* and *baozhang*, there is new emphasis on the rights of individual family members, gender equality in law, and the protection of human rights. There is also related emphasis on the activist state taking countermeasures to insure such rights.

The debate over 'third-party' affects on monogamy and the divorce rate and the debate over the scope of domestic violence both took place within the political context of the Party's new found interest in Chinese morality. While reformers have called on the state to play a new proactive role in supporting rights, conservative viewpoint that focuses almost exclusively on the problems of public order argues that the combined rules of law and virtue are needed so that the state can actively criminalize and police immorality in society.

However, even in this muddied context of reform, conservative viewpoint failed to widen the scope of the CL97 in order to achieve a rule of virtue based upon a closed ideological notion of the state serving as the custodian of morality in society. Not only have civilian 'third parties' escaped criminal penalty for actions against familial harmony, but the state has also been given a new role to play in establishing countermeasures to arrest the growing pattern of abuse within the modern Chinese family as individual family members contend with the difficulties of China's 'social environment'.

Despite great controversy, China's jurists and law makers have, since the 1996–7 revisions, managed to move forward, albeit, one step at a time, to emphasize the state's adoption and implementation of countermeasures dealing with the spread of domestic violence among individual family members. Reformers are continuing to develop the 1992 socio-legal approach as the means by which to achieve the newly declared balance of rights and social protection. The right of women, children, and elderly to protection against violence and abuse has received greater if somewhat qualified legal attention in a cautious synthesis of the requirements of *baohu* and *baozhang*.

Even with political change asserting the importance of public order and social stability in light of the Falungong, terrorism, and 'splittist' threats to national unity, the conservatives were unable to force legal reform and the NPC along the path of a rigid rule of virtue that sacrifices rights to the gods of public order and familial harmony. The jurists and their NPC allies successfully criminalized 'domestic violence'. On the other hand, they could not get a stand-alone provision on such violence and the issue of 'rape within marriage' was postponed.

Meanwhile, in terms of the organization of practical remedies, reformers have worked from both the bottom up, and the top down. They have found the conventional emphasis on the top-to-bottom strategy for the 'comprehensive management of public order' needs important qualification. They are becoming adept at coordination of the organizational efforts of 'plural mechanisms' that include NPC and State Council agencies, the ACWF, and over 5,800 non-governmental women's organizations.[85]

From the top bottom, there is growing emphasis on the activist state intervening in society to protect human rights. There has been important if qualified progress in the area of 'domestic violence'. This issue has been joined in a self-conscious political manner, but of course practice is another matter. Even the victims in society are, themselves, still predisposed in looking for a behind-the-scenes remedy for 'domestic violence'. With the complicity of officials within the judicial system cases still have a tendency to 'vanish'. At an abstract level, one might approve of 'localization' and the practical need to adapt the 'rule of law' to 'Chinese characteristics'. However, the meaning of these characteristics is in flux. Reformers want the state to be proactive in the protection of rights, but they have to deal with an inherent Chinese disposition towards mediation rather than open court proceedings.[86]

If reformers have encouraged the activist state to intervene with the law in family relations to protect human rights, they have also moved beyond the conventional limitations of Party-led mass organization to encourage the development of new social organization that is focusing on the coordination of state and community organization in the socio-legal protection of rights. As distinguished from Party-controlled mass association that takes exclusive responsibility for all organizational activity within a single sphere such as women's work, there is currently a more complex emphasis on expanding the Party's traditional organizational terms of reference so as to include new bottom-up and horizontal initiatives that deploy semi-autonomous 'community intervention' in remedying the problem of domestic violence.[87] Even while they have availed themselves of international resources and norms, reformers have often justified such an updated organizational strategy as appropriate to China's culture and particular 'national conditions'.

Also, this networking is compatible with the emphasis in the economy on 'small government and big society'. It reflects the organizational decline of the work unit and the development of a new generation of popular organization at the community level. One of the most successful examples of this is the Centre for Research and Intervention against Domestic Violence. The latter was deeply involved in the 2001 revision of the Marriage Law and is now pushing its own draft proposal for national legislation on 'domestic violence'. An example, at the local level, would certainly include the formation of new Anti-Domestic Violence Teams such as the 'Community Intervention in Family Problems' team in Tianjin.

Both examples reflect the impact of 'globalization' in terms of the international inflow of new resources and the deliberate adaptation to international legal norms and experience. The Centre has been generously funded by several international human rights centres and the latter has been supported by Germany's Heinrich Boell Foundation, the Ford Foundation, and the Tianjin local government.

Dagmar Woehlert of the Heinrich Boell China project has advocated the integration of various organizational and institutional initiatives to combat domestic violence, and in a related report, the Xinhua News Agency commented:

> In the past, the lives of Chinese citizens were largely centered on institutions or enterprises, which were responsible for handling the various problems of their employees, including marital problems. However, with the establishment of a market-oriented economy in China, various community and professional organizations started to take the initiative in handling such problems as domestic violence.[88]

Reformers have often approached the Party rationalizing new organizational initiatives as the progressive updating of the Party's own mass line. Also, they have sought to generate new and improved legal standards through a newly upgraded form of praxis at the local level. Local experiential learning and adaptation is often researched and incorporated into proposals for new national legislation. Reformers have also made effective and self-conscious use of international human right standards to build the case for new national legislation on 'domestic violence'. In this progress, they have played on leadership concern over China's 'good image', and they have been able to secure NPC support for moving beyond the limitations of extant criminal law.

A review of the last twenty years of related legislative development during 'reform and the open door' reveals a progressive if at times some qualified and even opportunistic attempt to address the 'balance of values'. To be sure, severe punishment and the death penalty were initially deployed in a conservative attempt to maintain public order and social control; however, jurists have since rallied against the early 1980s' extension of the death penalty. The 1983 Decision was denounced as in spurious opposition to the CL97 emphasis on 'the punishment must fit the crime'. Even as one considers the problems of tradition as an ongoing concern within society, one might still argue that particularly in the area of women's and children's rights one is witnessing the beginnings of a paradigm shift in the conceptual understanding of the state's use of law to insure the protection of individual family members' rights. Increasingly, the state is expected to act as 'the honest official' who will interfere in family affairs to protect these rights.

In the first place, one might argue that, especially in comparison with the period prior to the contemporary reform period, the law, as a matter of domestic political preference, has become increasingly detailed. Second, the international influence on Chinese legal thinking and practice is much easier to discern. The change in family law, as it relates to crime and rights protection is especially noteworthy given the resilience of tradition in contemporary society. However, there are a lot of loose ends. Reformers, at this time of writing, are still lacking national legislation on domestic violence, and in many other areas of the law's development, it would appear that it is easier to declare a comprehensive stipulation of the law than it is to actually accomplish such comprehensiveness. Most importantly, the available forms of compensating 'flexibility' need to be carefully defined and assessed in the absence of planned comprehensive stipulation of the law.

Legal reform, in the area of familial violence, has provided some grounds for qualified optimism. However, reform has, even in this area, encountered significant resistance. Furthermore, the entirety of the post-1996–7 experience suggests just how difficult it is to anticipate correctly the fast-changing nature of crime and casts some doubt on the ability of the judicial and legislative systems to stay ahead of the curve of societal and political change. The post-1996–7 strategy for criminal justice reform is trying to expedite a continually updated comprehensive stipulation of the law even as it contends with the politically uncertain implications of the 'globalization' of criminal law norms and the 'pluralization' of China's domestic value system.

4   'Organized crime', politics, and the law

The Western scholarly literature on transnational crime is robust particularly as it deals with transnational crime committed by ethnic Chinese and their criminal organizations outside China, such as in the various Chinatowns in the United States.[1] However, when it comes to analysis of the domestic PRC understandings of 'organized crime', the Western literature is very modest indeed.[2] There is good reason, therefore, to introduce and study the basics in terms of how Chinese jurisprudence has defined 'organized crime' and how this definition is reflected in related national legislative stipulation and judicial and administrative interpretation.

The following analysis may seem tedious and arcane but it is important to assess how the underlying politics of the law have substantively influenced the conceptual and legislative understanding of 'organized crime' in the PRC. Chinese legal reformers and their Party patrons have experienced tremendous difficulty in establishing a commonly accepted definition of 'organized crime' as new crime since 1996–7. Of particular importance is the analysis that helps to explain (a) why and how the basic concepts relating to 'organized crime' have had to be continuously revised by legislators, responding to public demands for public order and social stability and (b) how related controversy has affected the 1996–7 criminal justice strategic balancing of public order with human rights protection.

Since the early 1980s, 'organized crime' (*zuzhi fanzui*) has spread like wildfire, and this has served as a poignant reminder of the fallibility of the CCP. The return of organized crime calls into question the survival of the revolution as well as the Party's own credibility in dealing with morally degenerate 'Westernization' and the corruption of old society. 'Organized crime' also seriously threatens the social stability that is critical to the Party's strategy to make the Chinese people 'well off'.

Even in the Western established 'rule of law' context, politics requires law to respond to prevailing public values, particularly as the latter concern public order and safety in the post-9/11 world. Perhaps, it is a matter of degree, but given the persistence of the *zhengfa* system and traditional assumptions about deterrence and heavy penalties, the public order issue in China is hugely important. The countervailing emphasis on the protection of human rights appears only intermittently in the new law concerning 'organized crime', and the post-1996–7 strategy for criminal justice has become mired in very confusing jurisprudential controversy, conflicting judicial, administrative and legislative interpretation, unclear legislation, and the highly politicized stipulation of crime.

The political pressure on criminal justice to serve as a 'weapon' is intense, and the politics of 'crime' treats procedural justice as if it were a frivolous drag on the state's life-and-death struggle to insure public order. The latter is widely recognized as critical to the continuance of China's economic miracle. In such a context, the importance of punishment outweighs reform subscription to new due process. A high premium is placed on developing the formats of 'flexibility' within the *zhengfa* system. The jurists are struggling to deal with this adverse situation. Much of their related criticism focuses on the law's failure to provide clear definitions and concepts. However, they, themselves, have made many and often conflicting recommendations to improve the law and its implementation.

The controversies in China started with division over how to define the most basic term of reference, namely, 'organized crime'. Apart from related political factors concerning 'organized crime' and the legitimacy of the Party-State, the lack of appropriate definition reflects the accelerated metamorphosis of new crime within China's new market economy. Within the dual context of heady transition to the marketplace and the impact of economic globalization on China, 'organized crime' has cut across a wide spectrum of newly defined criminal liabilities concerning terrorism, membership in 'criminal organization with a triad nature', the selling and buying of women and children, drug trafficking, prostitution, gambling, the smuggling of emigrants, armed robbery, automobile theft, and the manufacturing and selling of pornography and adulterated products.

The spread of 'organized crime' in social context

Organized criminal organization has a long history in China. By the midway point of the Qing dynasty, these secret societies had already become powerful political forces. Their enduring resilient coherence derived from their secretive nature and their ability to control their members' activities with various rigid but highly effective codes of conduct and discipline. In the beginning of the twentieth century, the secret societies played an important role in the Boxer rebellion and the movement 'to overthrow the Qing and to restore the Ming'. They were also involved in early attempts to precipitate revolution and helped to establish the Republic of China in 1911. The father of the Republic, Sun Yatsen, himself, was once a triad member.[3]

After 1911, the values of Confucian society came under increasing challenge, and the secret societies and triads no longer had a dynastic government to rebel against. They often developed into malevolent criminal organization that specialized in drug trafficking, gambling, prostitution, and occasionally, spectacular political assassinations. In April 1927, the so-called 'Green Gang' helped Chiang Kai-shek to massacre the Communists in Shanghai. In 1949 the 'Green Gang' joined Chiang's exodus to the island of Taiwan to escape the PLA's advancing juggernaut.

In the early 1950s, the revolution caught up with all of the remaining secret societies. The CCP launched a series of political campaigns, including 'The Suppression of Counterrevolutionaries Campaign' and 'The Rooting Out of the Secret Societies Campaign'. These movements practically wiped out the triads. A large number of triad members were imprisoned, or executed, and many of those who managed to escape relocated to Hong Kong where they took 'root'. For thirty years in the PRC there was hardly any sign of the once powerful secret societies and triads and the CCP could rest easy, taking pride in the social accomplishments of the revolution.

However, organized crime re-appeared and rapidly spread in the early 1980s context of reform. In order to control the related 'crime waves', the regime once again turned to its mass-line strategy, launching a series of 'strike hard' campaigns in 1982–5. At first, these campaigns, especially, the one in 1985, significantly reduced organized crime. Public order was considerably improved. However, not long after 1985, organized criminal activities regained their momentum. Police statistics in Table 1 indicate that the number of criminal organizations prosecuted has increased annually since 1986, and up until 1994, when the numbers started to fall. During this period, organized crime constituted about 75 per cent of the most serious crime known to the police. Table 1 indicates the extensiveness of organized criminal activities in China in the first part of the 1990s.[4]

In order to eliminate the rising pattern of organized criminal activity, the jurists needed to understand the underlying causes of the new categories of 'organized crime'. In the past, Chinese criminological research explicitly drew upon a Marxist approach, tracing the roots of crime to the inherent pathological tendencies of the capitalist social system. In the New China, there was not enough capitalism to explain the social foundations of post-revolutionary organized crime, and criminology concluded that the origins of modern organized crime lie in the persistence of a 'semi-feudal' society within modern China.[5]

Contemporary criminology, on the other hand, has sought an alternative explanation of organized crime within new social scientific research. The research of Professors Ye Gaofeng and Liu Defa, for example, correlated rising organized crime with the social, economic, and demographic factors of the reform period.[6] Chinese scholars have generally highlighted the effects of increasing population mobility, official corruption, and judicial corruption. Their studies show that the members of criminal

Table 1 Criminal organizations and the number of arrests of members of organized crime in the period 1986–98

Year	The number of criminal organizations known to the police	The number of members of criminal organizations arrested
1983	100,000	n.a.
1984	31,000	130,000
1985	197,000	876,000
1986	30,476	114,452
1987	36,000	138,000
1988	57,229	213,554
1989	97,807	353,218
1990	100,527	368,885
1991	134,000	507,000
1992	120,000	460,000
1993	150,000	575,000
1994	150,000	570,000
1995	140,000	500,000
1996	136,225	495,878
1997	n.a.	n.a.
1998	102,314	361,927

Source: This table is based on the statistics provided in Yu Zhigang, *Redian fanzui falu yinan wenti jiexi* (Analysis and Explanations of Difficult Legal Issues Concerning Hotly Debated Crimes), vol. 1, Beijing: Zhongguo renmin daxue chubanshe, 2001, pp. 175–76.

organization consisted largely of '*mangliu*' (mobile population that has no specific destination). The '*mangliu*' were largely surplus rural labourers, who in their desperate search for work, migrated to the cities. While this 'floating population' steadily increased in numbers, urban employment opportunities declined, particularly in light of state-enterprise reconstruction and lay-offs. Faced with this grim reality, rural migrant labour increasingly turned to crime.

In Beijing, in recent years, for example, migrants have been responsible for about 50 per cent of the total crime. Many Beijing residents denigrated these migrants, describing them as '*wusuo buwei, wuluan buzuo*' (people doing all kinds of work and committing all kinds of crime).[7] In addition, among the rural emigrant population there were '*sanwu renyuan*' (individuals without identifications, jobs, and permanent residence). This part of the migrant population was considered the most dangerous and the most likely to join organized crime. Many of them were either ex-convicts, or they were on the police wanted lists. Re-education through labour has been extensively used to control this '*sanwu*' population.

At the same time, the rise in official corruption helped spawn the development of organized crime. Many criminal organizations became adept in bribing government and judicial officials. Some of the latter directly participated in smuggling and drug trafficking operations and many others either bent the law out of shape or violated it so as to protect their criminal patrons.[8] Responding to this deteriorating situation, the government issued successive regulations to control the transient population and judicial corruption, and the NPC attempted to create a new generation of legislation in order to fight 'organized crime'.

The definition of 'organized crime' in political context

The criminal law is the first line of defence against organized crime; however, the provisions on organized crime and criminal organization were only codified, for the first time, in the CL97. Cognate terms, such as 'to organize' (*zuzhi*) and 'to organize the populace' (*juzhong*) had first appeared in the 1951 'Provisions for Punishing Counterrevolutionaries'. In 1979, organized crime was not even on the NPC's radar screen. The CL79 did not refer to 'organized crime'. The CL79 did, however, address the related issue of 'joint crime' (*gongtong fanzui*). The CL79 punishments for joint crime were nowhere near as severe as those stipulated in later legislation.

CL79 Article 22 defined 'joint crime' as 'an intentional crime committed by two or more persons jointly', and joint crime has to be committed by criminal organization.[9] The CL79 established four categories of 'subject' relating to 'joint crime', namely, *zufan* (principal offenders), *congfan* (criminal accessories or accomplices), *jiaosuofan* (criminal instigators), and *xiecongfan* (offenders who are coerced or induced to participate in a joint crime).[10] The most senior authority on the CL79, Professor Gao Mingxuan, traced the thinking underlying this classification to the Continental and former Soviet Union Criminal Law Traditions. These traditions focused primarily on the criminal offenders rather than the commission of crime, *per se*.

Technically, the CL79 stipulations on joint crime could be used to fight against organized crime and related criminal organization, but many jurists expressed doubt whether the CL79 provisions were sufficiently forceful to provide effective deterrence. Professor Yu Zhigang of the Chinese People's University (Renda), for example, was concerned that these provisions could not be effectively used to punish offenders, who either actively participated in or led and actively organized a criminal organization, but who could not be proven to have carried out specific criminal acts.[11] Yu, as well as the public, demanded heavier punishment as well as a bigger net for catching criminals.

Beginning in 1982, the NPCSC made several attempts to revise the CL79 stipulations through a number of its own decisions. The first two NPCSC Decisions came in 1982 and 1983. The 1982 NPCSC 'Decision on the Severe Punishment of Criminals Who Seriously Undermine the Economy', and the 1983 'Decision Regarding the Severe Punishment of Criminal Elements Who Seriously Endanger Public Security' responded to an early 1980s rise in criminal activities that concerned 'organized hooligan activities' (*liumang fanzui*), and the 'organized abduction and sale of human beings' (*guaimai renkou*), smuggling, and drug trafficking. These particular activities seriously undermined public order, causing growing public outrage. Also, the rise in such crime was particularly noticeable given the extraordinary levels of security that the public had enjoyed in the immediate past.

Drawing on its mass-line experience, the Party-State acted swiftly, launching a series of 'strike-hard' campaigns (*yanda*). The legal basis for these campaigns was located in the two NPCSC 'Decisions'. The latter referred to 'organized crime' (*zuzhi fanzui jituan*), especially as it relates to 'hooligan criminal organization' (*liumang fanzui jituan*), and 'criminal organization for the purposes of abducting and selling human beings' (*guaimai renkou jituan*). The 'Decisions' clamped down on such crime with more severe punishment that included the death penalty.

Subsequently, China's jurists vociferously criticized the NPCSC decisions on a number of counts. In the first place, the 'Decisions' had been drafted in unconscionable haste so as to meet immediately the demands of the public and the Party leaders for public order. Second, the 'Decisions' were faulted for their failure to provide detailed descriptions of related criminal activities, and they had failed to define the key terms that were used for the first time in Chinese criminal legislation, such as 'hooligan criminal organization'. Third, the jurists criticized the 'Decisions' for an unacceptably wide range of punishment that included 6 months to 15 years of imprisonment, life imprisonment, and the death penalty.[12] Also, the 'Decisions' purportedly endowed the judiciary with too much 'flexibility', thus opening the door to the abuse and misuse of judicial power at the expense of human rights protection. Also, the 'Decisions' contributed to inconsistent law enforcement. This was withering criticism indeed! The persistent and widespread reaction to the 'Decisions' helps explain the later 1996–7 emphasis on the comprehensive legislation of criminal law.

The 1983 stipulation on 'hooligan criminal organization' is a case in point. Although the 'Decision' focused on the punishment of 'hooligan criminal organization' (*liumang fanzui jituan*), the question as to what is hooligan organization was not discussed. To make matters worse, the CCP Central Committee issued in late 1983 its own internal notice, known as Document #31. This 'Notice' called for the severe punishment of hooligan activities. But it used the term 'hooligan gangs' (*liumang tuanhuo*), instead of 'hooligan criminal organization'. The inconsistent use of key terms caused further confusion and controversy, and the legal circles were embroiled in heated debate over the relative superiority of these terms.[13]

What were the differences between a 'criminal gang' (*fanzui tuanhuo*) and a 'criminal organization' (*fanzui jitua*)? Some scholars believed there was no real difference. Others disagreed, arguing that 'criminal organization' was better organized than a criminal gang. Professor Ye Gaofeng claimed that the whole matter was moot because 'criminal gang' was not a stipulated terminology and that the terminology's only sanction was in its use by public security personnel to describe a criminal group consisting of no-less-than three members who commit a joint crime.[14]

In the hope of putting a stop to all the confusion, the SPC, the SPP, and the Ministry of Public Security jointly issued, in May 1984, 'An Opinion on How to Identify and Adjudicate Hooligan Criminal Organization'.[15] The 'Opinion' distinguished between hooligan gangs and hooligan organization. The 'Opinion' defined the legally more important term 'hooligan organization' as an organization that consisted of at least three members, including some long-term members and obvious leaders. The members of such organization were presumed to have been frequently involved in criminal conspiracies and to have carried out criminal activities in a well-organized and planned manner.

The 'Opinion' listed the following activities as 'organized hooligan activity': organizing serious brawls and fighting with weapons in public places; verbally insulting and physically assaulting innocent citizens; racketeering in market places; disturbing public order and routine economic activities; robbing, sexually assaulting, and verbally insulting women, and participating in sexual orgies. This listing threw together different types of activity that were receiving contemporaneous political attention. The listing did provide one element of clarity when it stated such organized hooligan crime did not apply to youth with bad living habits such as drinking, wandering around, and occasionally committing joint minor offences. Indeed, CCP policy and related law has been predicated in a policy focus on the rehabilitation rather than the punishment of youth.

The 'Opinion' cleared up the confusion surrounding 'hooligan criminal organization' and 'hooligan gangs', but it too failed to define 'organized crime'(zuzhi fanzui). And it was this last key concept that was most urgently needed. In June 1984, the SPC, the SPP, and the Ministry of Public Security jointly issued 'The Answers to Questions Regarding the Application of Law in Dealing with Cases Involving Criminal Organization'. The 'Answers' focused exclusively on the definition of 'organized crime'. To qualify as 'organized crime', under Article 2 of the 'Answers', prospective 'organization' had to exhibit all of the following attributes: the organization had to have at least three members, including some long-term key members and obvious leaders, or organizers, and these members had to have committed one or more serious crimes in a well-planned and organized manner. This definition obviously approximated the 1983 'Opinion' definition of 'hooligan criminal organization'. The 'Answers' perpetuated an existing wisdom, but they tried to indicate how the definition might inform judicial practice. The 'Opinion' and the 'Answers' both served effectively as judicial interpretation that was later incorporated into the CL97.

'Organized crime' in the CL97

Judicial interpretation assisted the CL97 with a definition of 'organized crime'. Building on this definition, the CL97 established three related categories of organization, namely, 'ordinary criminal organization', 'criminal organization with a triad nature' (*heishehui xingzhi zuzhi*) (COWTN), and terrorist organization. Stipulation regarding 'ordinary criminal organization' was placed in the General Provisions of the law, which served as a guide in implementing the Special Provisions of the law. The other two categories were located in the secondary Special Provisions. This classification confirmed that, in accordance with Chinese criminal theory, the determination of 'organized crime' very much depends upon the determination of the nature of the organization with which offenders are associated.

In order to identify accurately organized crime, both Chinese lawmakers and jurists are very much interested in the nature and constitution of a criminal organization. 'Criminal organization', *per se*, is defined by CL97 Article 26 as 'a long-term and relatively stable organization that consists of at least three persons and that is formed for the purpose of jointly committing crime'. This provision identifies both the leaders and organizers of a criminal organization as principal offenders and stipulates the same penalty for both. In effect, both categories of offenders were to assume entire criminal responsibility for a crime committed by an entire criminal organization. However, this complicates the established differentiation in criminal law between the leaders of an organization and the secondary offenders who play a minor role in the organization and its criminal activities. Obviously, the underlying intention of Article 26 was to punish severely all of the individuals involved in criminal organizations. This organizational approach to organized crime is rather unique to Chinese criminal law and its preference for heavy penalties across a wide range of criminal liability.

In the West, the definition of 'organized crime' was also the subject of considerable controversy. Michael Maltz provided ten different definitions of organized crime. These incorporated constitutive elements emphasizing developed organizational structure, hard-core organized criminal activity, specific language and rules, the presence of a 'top man', and the criminal conspiracy of a criminal syndicate.[16] Based on these definitions, Maltz defined organized crime as 'a crime committed by two or more offenders who are, or intend to remain associated for the purpose of committing crimes'.[17] He further elaborated the definition/typology of organized crime using a 5 by 6 matrix. Maltz sought to incorporate the elements of organized crime, listed in his ten definitions, with an emphasis on the means and objectives of the crime that does not entirely depend upon organizational structure.[18] Essentially, organized crime in the West presumes 'crime' committed by criminal syndicates, the purpose of which relates to their own financial interest.

Comparatively, 'organized crime', in Chinese criminal legislation, stipulates three different types of organization that have different purposes. This suggests that the concept of organized crime in Chinese criminal law is more loosely and broadly construed when compared with its Western counterpart. Many ordinary crimes committed by more than two offenders, which are not considered criminal in the Western context, are regarded in China as organized crime, and such crime has often attracted severe punishment under the CL97. Again, this confirms the Chinese intention to punish severely any crime committed jointly by more than two persons in order to protect society.

The conceptual differences in criminal organizations and consequently, organized crimes, between China and the West have been researched by Professor Yu Zhigang at one of the leading centres of criminal law research, the Chinese People's University. Yu concluded that, in China, organized crime is simply equated with the criminal activities of offenders who belong to any of the three types of criminal organization. The Chinese system operates with a broader concept of organized crime. This approach enhances the severe punishment of organized criminals while it minimizes the very notion of organized crime in Chinese criminal legislation. Yu argues that 'organized crime' is linked only to two specific types of criminal organization: criminal syndicates or underworld societies (*heishehui zuzhi*) and COWTN.[19]

In light of the severe consequences that come with the identification of those who participate in organized crime, Chinese jurists have insisted on a very careful application of Article 26 so that 'organized crime' is not confused with other crime that might share 1 or 2 characteristics with organized crime. The Chinese criminal law literature contains extensive elaboration of the differences between 'organized crime', on the one hand, and 'organizing populace for criminal purposes' (*juzhong fazui*) and 'crime committed by a work unit' (*danwe fanzui*), on the other.

For instance, 'organized crime' is substantively different from 'crime committed by organized populace' (*juzhong fazui*). Although 'organizing populace' (*juzhong*) was mentioned in both the CL79 and CL97, it was not defined. An organized crime and a crime committed by organized populace have some common characteristics, including references to 'no less than three offenders', organization by leaders, and participation in many different kinds of criminal activities. Nevertheless, they are essentially two different kinds of crime.

An organized crime can only be committed by a criminal organization in a well-planned and organized way. The time-line of organizational maturation is critical. In contrast, the organizational structure associated with organizing a populace for conducting criminal activities is a temporary one; it is formed spontaneously to engage in particular criminal activity. Its organizers or leaders are the only persons who are presumed to have criminal intent, and they are accordingly liable to severe punishment.

Other participants who were duped into committing crimes and who lacked criminal motivation were to receive less punishment.[20]

Similarly, 'crime committed by a work unit' (*danwei fanzui*) has some characteristics in common with organized crime. The former is similar to a crime committed by a 'legal person' or entity in the Western criminal legislation. Compared to a legal person or entity defined in civil law, however, 'work unit' is a loosely construed concept so that it includes a wide range of social organizations, which are not automatically legal entities under civil law, such as research and education institutions, government organizations, and mass associations.

Two eminent criminal law professors, Zhao Bingzhi and He Xingwang, have explained that the use of the term, 'work unit', in the CL97 Article 30, was in deliberate reference to 'legal person'. The latter is more compatible with Chinese reality where many organizations have yet to become civil-law entities, even after so many years of economic reform.[21]

'Crime committed by a work unit' is usually for the financial interests of an entire work unit. Nevertheless, a work unit and the individuals in charge of the unit plan can carry out 'criminal activities'. Therefore, according to CL97 Article 30, a work unit and the person in charge shall bear 'criminal liability' and face punishment. A work unit, however, could be punished only with a fine, while the individuals in charge could be punished with both fines and other types of penalties, including imprisonment.

'Crime committed by a work unit' and 'organized crime' share the fact that both are committed by an organization; however, they are different in nature. A crime committed by a work unit is committed by a social organization that is legally established according to law and regulation, while an organized crime is committed by a criminal organization that has no such legal status.[22]

Within this shifting continuum of different criminal organization forms, triad organizations (*heishehui fanzui zuzhi*) or criminal syndicates are regarded as the most dangerous and insidious types of organized criminal group. They are similar to the Italian Mafia, Chinese tongs, Japanese yakuza and boryokudan, the Wo Group, the 14K in Hong Kong, and the Brother Gang and the United Bamboo Gang in Taiwan. These organizations are well organized and are very sophisticated in their changing tactical responses to law enforcement.[23]

In the process of revising the CL97, there were two conflicting viewpoints as to whether 'triads' actually exist within China's borders and what type of criminal legislation is necessary to suppress the development of criminal organization. In the *People's Daily*, Gao Jinghong, affirmed the existence of such organization within China's borders:

> In recent years, with the increase in China's ties with foreign countries, criminal syndicates have crossed borders to infiltrate the hinterland and to engage in criminal activities that have grown increasingly

conspicuous. Consequently, the triad forces have grown and spread in some localities in China. Statistics show that of the 523 cabarets operated by persons from outside our borders, 22 were run by triads. In recent years, approximately 100 lawbreakers with triad connections were uncovered in Fujian. Most were involved with triads beyond our borders, such as 'the 14K' and 'Wo Shing Tong' from Hong Kong and Macau, and 'Chuk Luen Bong' from Taiwan. Triads are also active in Yunnan's Dehong, Baoshan, Dali, and Kunming Cities. Triads from Hong Kong's 'Wo Shing Tong' and 'Sun Yee On' have on several occasions engaged in drug-trafficking via Yunnan.[24]

Had not the triads been expelled from China? Did their development not stop at the border? These are serious political questions. Not surprisingly, some Chinese criminal law experts flatly disagreed with Gao Jinghong. They contended that there is no evidence to support the material existence of triad organizations in 'socialist' China. China, in other words, does not have the social foundations upon which these organizations can fully mature. Such criminal organizations can only flourish in Western capitalist society.[25]

In his rebuttal, Yuan Fanmin of Hongzhou University pointed to the alarming proliferation and metamorphosis of criminal organizations in China. In his view many ordinary criminal organizations, including hooligan criminal organizations, were actually in the process of transforming themselves into genuine triad criminal organizations at some cost to China's socio-economic order and stability.[26]

This judgment was originally reflected in the early consideration of the revisions to the CL79. In that context, Professors Chan Minghua and Guo Xiaoming of the Chinese Northwest University of Politics and Law first used the term, 'criminal organization with a triad nature' (heishehui xingzhi fanzui zuzhi) to describe the metamorphosis of an ordinary criminal organization into triad organization.[27] The term 'criminal organization with a triad nature' (COWTN) was embedded in the final draft of the CL97. Wang Hanbin, Vice-Chairman of the NPCSC, in his related report to the NPC endorsed the use of this term when he stated: '...there are no typical triads in China. However, there is a rapid increase in criminal organization with a triad nature.'[28]

The CL97 declined to acknowledge the existence of full-blown triads in China. It focused instead on the punishment and on COWTN members and organization. CL97 Article 294, for the first time, stipulated the crimes of organizing, leading, and actively participating in a COWTN, the crime of COWTN membership, the crime of crossing state borders to recruit members, and the crime of state functionary protection of and involvement with the COWTN. Offenders were to be punished with 3–10 years of imprisonment, except for the state functionaries and 'other participants', who, under 'ordinary circumstances', would receive no more than 3 years' imprisonment.

The stipulation of 'COWTN' was built upon roughly calibrated degrees of organizational development. Those jurists who succeeded in getting the NPCSC's recognition of the new term, COWTN, were concerned that many prospective criminal organizations, in terms of their organizational and operational sophistication, lie somewhere in the middle of the continuum between 'ordinary criminal organization' and the full-blown triads.

At stake was 'public feeling' and the political question of the law's scope for conviction and punishment. Without legislation on the triads, many criminal organizations would have to be identified as 'ordinary criminal organization' and their members might possibly escape 'righteous' prosecution and punishment.[29] On the other hand, if criminal legislation had focused on the triads, fewer organized criminal elements would face punishment. At first blush, the 'COWTN' concept seemed to offer a way out of this predicament. The COWTN offered some advantage in the protection of society from serious crime. It equipped the judiciary with a format that allowed for the immediate punishment of the members of triad organizations as well as for the punishment of members who belonged to quasi or semi-developed triads. However, this format may have been just a bit too clever as it invited subsequent rounds of controversy.

Controversies in defining 'COWTN'

The CL97's failure to define 'COWTN' set the stage for more controversy. The jurists became quite creative in their preferred definitions of this key term. Some definitions highlighted that COWTN organizational stability is based on the disciplinary codes used in triad organization. Others emphasized that the COWTN has to have an organizational complexity and financial interests similar to that of a triad society.[30] Gao Jinghong offered up what might be considered as 'the mother of all definitions':

> [The COWTN] refers to a kind of complete, multi-tiered criminal organization formed by lawless elements from various social professions in an orderly way, that are generally branches of criminal syndicates beyond the border but set up in the hinterland, or major criminal gangs under the control of criminal syndicates beyond the border, which act on their orders to engage in organizational development and criminal activities.[31]

There was jurist division on the question of how to determine the criminal nature of the COWTN. Mindful of the importance of the law's own rationality, Professor Yuan Fanmin, at Hangzhou University, contended that an organization could not be deemed to be 'criminal' unless its members actually commit illegal acts.[32] Zhu Erjun, a researcher at the SPC, focused on controlling the spread of new crime and countered that leading, organizing, and participating in a COWTN were criminal, *per se*, and that, if members committed other criminal activities, such as robbery or assault, they should receive additional punishment based on the criminal law principle of combined punishment for committing more than one crime.[33]

The SPC, on 4 December 2000, attempted to put an end to jurist dissonance with a timely judicial interpretation. The 2000 SPC 'Explanations for the Application of Laws Concerning the Adjudication of Cases Involving Criminal Organization With a Triad Nature' offered seven articles, providing detailed descriptions relating to the stipulated content of CL97 Article 294.[34] Article 1 of the 'Explanations' detailed four constitutive elements that were necessary to the recognition of the COWTN in law. These distinctions were already quite familiar. In the first place, the organization in question has to have a tightly developed organizational structure that comes with internal rules of conduct and discipline, a significant membership, the presence of leaders, and long-serving members.

Second, the prospective COWTN has to be financially independent and the purpose of its criminal activity is financial gain. Third, a genuine COWTN is expected to bribe, threat, induce, or force state functionaries to participate in the organization's illegal activity and to provide illegal protection. (It was this third element that was to generate the most controversy.) Fourth, a criminal syndicate is characterized by the use of violence, or the threat of violence, and disruption as it engages in racketeering and the monopolizing of commercial establishments, organizing violent brawls, trouble-making, the physical assault of innocents, and other criminal activities that seriously undermine social and economic order. To insure that the law's net is cast as wide as possible, this last constitutive element made use of analogy (namely, 'and other criminal activities') thus ignoring the prerequisites of the 1996–7 criminal justice reform.

The 2000 'Explanations' also declared that those ordinary members of the COWTN, who only took part in the criminal organization due to 'threats or deception' and who had not committed any crime would not be deemed guilty of the crime of participating in a COWTN.[35] Second, in Chinese legal theory, state functionaries are often exposed to more harsh punishment because their failed example is considered more 'harmful' than that of the average citizen. The 'Explanations' asserted that state functionaries who lead, organize, or participate in a COWTN would be more severely punished than an ordinary citizen who commits the same crime.[36]

In judicial practice, it became extremely important to differentiate a COWTN from an ordinary organized criminal group. The CL97 treats them differently in terms of punishment. The law does not punish activities of leading, organizing, and actively participating in 'ordinary criminal organization'. The members of an ordinary criminal organization can only be punished based on actual discrete criminal activities, such as robbery, breaking and entry, etc., but not on the basis of membership in such organization. In contrast, being a member of a COWTN is a 'crime' in and of itself.

Chinese jurists focused on defining the differences between a purportedly full-blown triad organization and a COWTN. A COWTN is purportedly less complex in its organization and less sophisticated in its operation. Zhu Erjun, in a SPC official publication, dropped down into pedantry when he stated that if a triad organization was located outside of China, it should be named as a triad organization, while if a pseudo-triad organization was found operating within China, it should be called a COWTN.[37] It has been clear thus far that Chinese academic discussions on these critical differences in organizational development were rooted in competing understandings of political realities.

Compared to 'ordinary criminal organization', as defined in CL97 Article 26, the most unique and important feature of a COWTN is that it involves state functionaries in its activities. Song Xiaoming explained that bribery is the way for COWTN organizers to pull state functionaries into their organizations. Song focused attention on how state functionaries use their positions in government and judicial institutions to protect or harbour the organized criminals from criminal prosecution and to conveniently launder their illegal profits.[38] Consistent with these discussions, the 2000 SPC 'Explanations' clearly indicated that having a state functionary as an organizational member was a necessary element of the COWTN. This stipulation in the 'Explanations' incurred the ire of some members of the judiciary, not to mention the outrage of the Ministry of Public Security.

Hu Kangsheng, Deputy Director of the NPCSC's Legal Affairs Committee, tried to assuage this inflamed opposition, patiently explaining that the COWTN cannot exist without the illegal protection of state functionaries. He was even ready to concede that there were some examples of criminal organization that enjoyed such protection without the benefit of state functionary membership. Hu also addressed the question whether the state functionary requirement in the 2000 SPC 'Explanations' might restrict the scope of prosecution, allowing some COWTN members to escape punishment.

In some cases the judicial authorities had regrettably been unable to establish the involvement of state functionaries in COWTN. This had resulted in an unfortunate misclassification of the COWTN as 'ordinary criminal organization'. Some members of judiciary had complained that the use of the state functionary element had 'tied [the] hands of judicial personnel' in punishing and eliminating the most dangerous criminal organizations and their leaders.[39]

For two years the SPC and SPP battled over the inclusion of the state functionary element in the law. According to the State Constitution, legislative interpretation trumps judicial interpretation.[40] On 28 April 2002, the NPCSC sided with the critics of the SPC 2000 'Explanations', and it issued a legislative interpretation deleting the state functionary element from the law. This was, indeed, a rare move that ignored the thrust of reform research and discussion on questions of interpretation.

In the past, the NPCSC had focused on revising substantive criminal legislation. It was not in the habit of issuing legislative interpretation so as to clarify unclear legal terms. The NPCSC usually deferred to the SPC, SPP, and sometimes the Ministry of Justice to provide reinforcing judicial interpretation. Its involvement in this case confirms the critical political importance attached to public order and the war on 'organized crime'; it also suggests the seriousness of the impasse between the SPC and the Ministry of Public Security.

NPCSC interpretation reiterated three of the constitutive elements, as detailed in the SPC 2000 'Explanations', but it negated the constitutive element, requiring involvement of state functionaries.[41] This was accomplished with a somewhat disingenuous statement to the effect that, while state functionaries could be members of criminal organization, this was not a necessary element that determines the existence of such organization.[42]

The NPCSC's legislative interpretation may have broken the impasse in Chinese bureaucratic politics, but it created a new set of problems. The nullified constitutive element had originally provided a clear benchmark that helped to distinguish between what is a COWTN and what is 'ordinary criminal organization'.[43] However, there were several alternative elements that helped to insure this distinction. Chinese People's Public Security University Professors Li Wenyan and Tian Hongjie listed five other differences that included new emphasis on the geographical dimensions of organization and the ready resort to violence.

In the first place, a COWTN, as compared to 'ordinary criminal organization', has a much more complex and multi-tiered organizational structure. Second, its membership consists of at least 5 members, instead of the 3 required for the determination of 'ordinary criminal organization'. Third, its criminal activities primarily concern its financial interests. Fourth, the COWTN has stable, well-defined geographical boundaries within which it routinely carries on its criminal activities. And finally, the COWTN is more likely to carry out its criminal activities using weapons or threats of violence and terror.[44]

The serious implications of COWTN crime for public order and social stability prompted China's jurists to search for appropriate criminal law to defeat and suppress the COWTN. For instance, Li Wenyan and Tian Hongjie proposed that the NPC pass an 'Anti-Organized-Crime Act' that would target COWTN crime. They believed that CL97 Article 294 did not adequately cover all of the new COWTN crime.

Li and Tian proposed legislation to cover the crime of allying with foreign criminal syndicates and the crime of crossing state borders and carrying out the crimes of criminal syndicates. They proposed increasing the punishment for such crime to life imprisonment. They also wanted stipulated fines and the confiscation of property so as to broaden the punishment of offenders. They reiterated conventional theory to the effect that corrupt state officials ought to receive more severe punishment than ordinary citizens. To further their law-and-order agenda, Li and Tian lobbied for the creation of a national institution that would specialize in fighting triads and COWTN. They were sympathetic to Public Security, and they supported the granting of special powers to the police in the gathering of evidence.[45]

While fighting against COWTNs, the regime did not forget the threats of terrorist organizations (*kongbu zuzhi*) and their 'criminal activities'. The Chinese jurists believe that terrorist organizations have a close connection with both criminal triad organizations (*heishehui fanzui jituan*) and COWTNs. Terrorist organizations have received financial support from both organizational categories. And from a legal perspective, the three major categories of 'criminal organization' share many characteristics in their organizational structures and methods in carrying out their criminal activities.[46]

Terrorist organization as 'organized crime'

For the first time in Chinese criminal law, the CL97's Article 120 stipulated that persons organizing, leading, or actively participating in a terrorist organization could be punished with 3–10 years' imprisonment. Other participants in such organization could be punished with no more than 3 years' imprisonment, criminal detention, or supervisory control. This provision criminalized membership in terrorist organization. Given the tremendous loss of life, the disruption to property, and sometimes to national economy, China's lawmakers are inclined to regard terrorist organization as an extremely heinous category of criminal organization.

However, while the CL97 stipulated severe punishment for individuals belonging to terrorist organization, it failed to define 'terrorist organization'. Zhao Bingzhi and He Xingwang, in their monograph on the CL97, called for judicial interpretation that would clearly define such organization.[47] In fact, there has been a paucity of both legislative definition and judicial interpretation of this essential terminology.

Perhaps, it is ironic that jurists once attacked the criminal law's special provisions on counterrevolutionary crime because the scientific nature of law is unable to tolerate the vagaries of politics, but now some jurists are emphasizing that 'terrorist organization' must have 'political objectives' and to achieve the said objectives, its members must intend to use violence or the threat of violence. Professors Ye and Liu have added that a terrorist organization could be created out of financial interests or other social purposes.[48] They did not justify the analogical reference to 'other social purposes'.

These unofficial understandings roughly approximate the FBI's definition of 'terrorist organization' as organization that unlawfully uses 'force or violence against persons or property to intimidate or coerce a government, the civilian population, or any segment thereof, in furtherance of political or social objectives.'[49] China's jurists believe that terrorist crime requires a definition of the purposes or objectives of 'terrorist organization', but they have been unable to reach a consensus on the contents of this terminology.

Zhao Zuojun, of the Higher People's Court in Henan Province, has pointed out that the purposes or objectives of terrorism concern the criminal motivation of offenders and that motivation is difficult to pin down in a scientific manner. Instead, he suggests that related organization has to be identified with reference to specific terrorist activities. These activities could include assassination of foreign leaders, domestic leaders and dignitaries, and ordinary citizens, genocide, kidnapping, hijacking aircraft and other transportation, committing arson, breaching a dike, and spreading dangerous biological pathogens. However, other jurists have noted that these activities could also be carried out by other criminal organizations, such as the COWTN. For the moment, the clarification of the differences between 'terrorist 'and other criminal organization has been left to future research and interpretation.[50]

At the time of the making of the CL97, Chinese lawmakers were not only unclear about the question as to what is 'terrorist organization', they were reluctant to admit that such organization exists in China. Wang Hanbin, then Vice-President of the NPCSC, reported that '... some departments mentioned that China has already witnessed organized terrorist criminal activities and such activities are very harmful; and in order to combat these crimes, the provision on terrorist organizations has been enacted.'[51] But Wang did not acknowledge that such organization was commonplace. Some jurists have argued that the CL97 provision on terrorist organization merely anticipated the emergence of such organization. However, the terrorist attacks on the World Trade Center on September 11, 2001 lent credence to the threat of terrorism as a palpable reality that requires well-defined countermeasures.

Partly in response to 9/11, the NPC revised the CL97's stipulations on terrorist organizations and their activities on 29 December 2001. This revision affected eight extant articles. Also, several new crimes were added to the law. Articles 114, 115, 125, 127, and 291 covered crime involving the spreading, storage, stealing, and robbing of poisonous or contagious virus and radiated materials. Article 120 stipulated the crime of financially assisting terrorists and their activities. Article 191 covered several areas relating to the laundering of money obtained through terrorist activity, the crime of spreading fake poison and contagious virus and radiated materials, and the crime of manufacturing or spreading false information concerning terrorist activities so as to undermine public order. Article 121 increased the severity of the punishment for activity concerning the organizing and leading of terrorist organization from long-term imprisonment to life imprisonment.[52]

In 2002, the Bank of China created an anti-money laundering task force to cut off the financial sources of terrorist activity and several related anti-money laundering state regulations were issued.[53] This may suggest a certain level of political focus; however, it is hard to fathom why the NPCSC did not take advantage of the opportunity of amending the CL97 to provide once and for all a clear definition of 'terrorist organization'. The law has not caught up with the politics in this vital area. Seven years after the CL97's promulgation, and three years after the United States declared war on terrorists, the NPC, the SPC, and the SPP have yet to provide much needed definition.

On various occasions, the Chinese leaders have referred to the 'three evils', 'terrorism, splittism, and religious extremism', particularly as these concern China's borders and the stability of nearby Central Asia.[54] The linkage of terrorism with extremist and separatist movements in China after many years of weak criminal law stipulation on terrorist organization is regarded by some critics as a politically disturbing development.

There is a division of international opinion on this development. Denny Roy, for example, states that '...indeed, in the context of Central Asia this linkage has long made sense because the militant Muslim insurgencies at issue exhibit all three elements.'[55] On the other, there is critical Western comment on how the Chinese are using 'strike-hard' tactics against the Xinjiang separatist movement. During her visit to China in November 2001, Mary Robinson, UN High Commissioner for Human Rights, expressed concern that Chinese government might exploit the international struggle with terrorism to intensify its mistreatment of ethnic Uyghurs and Tibetans.[56] In light of such concern, any future Chinese definition of 'terrorist organization' is likely to spark a great deal of international interest.

In the meantime, the Chinese authorities have a number of alternative criminal law options that they can deploy against separatist movements. Much earlier, the CL79 had stipulated the death penalty for activities relating to separatism. CL97 Article 103 stipulated severe punishment for crime concerning organizing, participating in, and carrying out the activities of 'splitting' the country. In recent years, Article 103 has been used frequently to punish various criminal activities related to the separation movements in Tibet and Xinjiang. While this Article does not specifically criminalize membership in a separatist organization, this matter is moot as such organization has no chance of obtaining legal status in China. In the current international circumstances, CL97 Article 120's reference to the crimes of organizing, leading, or actively participating in a terrorist organization could also give the regime yet another 'weapon' with which to punish any individual who is convicted of involvement with separatist movements inside China.

As indicated earlier, punishment for a person who is affiliated with a terrorist activity can be severe, with a possible maximum sentence of ten years' imprisonment. Indeed, with the spread of organized crime and the different types of criminal organizations, there has been frequent resort to heavy punishment – this despite the 1996–7 commitment to reduce 'heavy-penalty-ism' in favour of 'the punishment must fit the crime'. The rationale for heavy penalties has always been the need to preserve public order through effective criminal law deterrence.

However, since the early 1980s heavy punishment has yet to produce a significant reduction to organized crime and criminal organization since the early 1980s.[57] In fact, Professor Kang Shuhuai, a leading criminologist at Beijing University, has observed that, in recent years, organized crime has penetrated into almost every developing area of profit-making criminal activity, including the selling and buying of women and children, smuggling, drug trafficking, prostitution, the smuggling of migrants, etc.[58] In effect, 'organized crime' has got the whole waterfront covered!

The following analysis highlights two of the most serious and widespread aspects of organized crime, namely, drug trafficking and the smuggling of emigrants. The proliferation of these crimes have particularly distressed China's political leaders as they serve as an unwanted reminder of the deepening angst in society, the spread of corruption, and the decline of Chinese morality. Also, these categories connect more directly with the dynamics of 'internationalization', or 'globalization'. Drug trafficking and the smuggling of illegal emigrants are developing into transnational crime, and the Chinese fight against such crime has been informed by a concern for China's 'good image' as well by the practical need for greater international criminal law cooperation.

Drug trafficking as 'organized crime'

Drug trafficking is a crime, which, by definition, is conducted by organized criminals. In recent years, the rapid rise in drug use has attracted a great deal of political concern. A June 2000 'Circular', issued by the Central Committee for Comprehensive Management of Public Order and the National Narcotics Control reported that narcotics consumption triggers other criminal activity, thus compounding this crime's impact on public order. In 1999, the number of registered drug addicts stood at 681,000. By 2003, this number jumped to 1.05 million. In this period, on average, 75 per cent of the registered drug addicts were young people under the age of 35.[59] One of the key addiction recovery measures used in China is 're-education through labor'. In 2003, 61,500 drug addicts received 'compulsory drug treatment' (qiangzhi jiedu) while undergoing 're-education'.[60]

Prevention of drug consumption and drug trafficking is a complex and multidimensional task. To promote the strict management of narcotics and psychotropic substances, China has issued through the 1980s and 1990s more than thirty relevant laws, statutes, and regulations.[61] Some provincial governments have also issued local drug control regulations dealing with specific problems and concerns in their respective jurisdictions.[62]

However, the real villain of drug addiction has been organized drug trafficking.

In modern Chinese revolutionary history, drug trafficking was a serious problem. Under the Nationalist government many corrupt government officials were, themselves, involved in, and/or profited from drug trafficking. In 1950 the new regime issued the 'Decrees Prohibiting Opium Trafficking'. Drug prohibition movements were initiated in 1952. Under the new regime, drug trafficking, together with drug consumption, was forcefully stamped out. In the period of 1954–79, drug-related crime was simply not a serious issue.[63] As a result, the CL79 only had one relevant article, which stipulated that a person involved in the manufacturing, selling, or transporting of opium, heroin, morphine, or other narcotics could be punished with a maximum sentence of fifteen years' imprisonment.

However, the early 1980s witnessed a rapid increase in drug trafficking, especially in southern provinces. The illegal drugs came into China mainly from two sources, the Golden Triangle (an area between Myanmar, Thailand, and Laos) and the Golden Crescent (an area near the borders of Afghanistan, Pakistan, and Iran).[64] The drugs that were shipped to China were not necessarily intended for domestic consumption. The drugs were processed in China's inland provinces and then the refined product was often smuggled into Hong Kong, via Guangdong, for worldwide distribution.[65]

In the early 1980s, NPC lawmakers assumed a correlation between the rapid increase in drug trafficking and the lack of available severe criminal law punishment in the CL79. To correct this situation, the NPCSC issued, in 1982, the 'Decision Regarding the Severe Punishment of Criminal Elements Who Seriously Undermine the Economy'. This 'Decision' over-corrected for the lack of deterrence in that it increased the maximum punishment for drug trafficking from fifteen years' imprisonment to the death penalty.[66] In 1988, the NPCSC issued the 'Supplementary Decision Regarding the Punishment for Smuggling', which extended the death penalty to drug smuggling.[67] The scope of related crime was expanded to include smuggling drugs by work units or legal persons and these agents could be punished along with individuals.[68]

However, even with severe punishment and the death penalty for drug traffickers, the drug traffic continued unabated. In 1990, the NPCSC issued the 'Decision on Drug Control', which further stipulated drug-related crimes and punishment. The SPC commented that the 1990 NPCSC 'Decision' was designed to respond to the recent proliferation of drug-related crimes and to related technical issues that had emerged over the course of judicial practice in the handling of substantive technical issues. The latter specifically included the calculation of the amount of drugs and the specific categories of drugs involved in drug-related crime.[69]

The 1990 NPCSC 'Decision' consisted of 16 articles stipulating 7 major new drug-related crimes concerning drug smuggling, trafficking, transporting, and manufacturing. The 'Decision' reinstated severe punishment for state functionaries who used their official positions to commit drug-related crimes.[70] The 'Decision' racheted upwards the stipulations for severe punishment. An offender caught smuggling, trafficking, transporting, or manufacturing 1,000 grams of opium, or 50 grams of heroin could become liable to the death penalty.

Regardless of the 1996–7 'balance of values', the 'Decision's' descriptions of crime and its heavy punishment provisions were directly incorporated into the CL97 without significant revision. CL97 Articles 347–57, for example, described drug-related crimes, including the crimes of smuggling, selling, transporting, and manufacturing drugs. Article 348 dealt with drug possession. Crimes relating to the harbouring of criminals engaged in the smuggling, selling, transporting, and the manufacturing of drugs were spelt out in Article 349. Article 350 detailed crimes relating to the violation of state regulations for the purposes of illegally transporting across borders acetic oxide, ethyl ether, chloroform, or other raw materials, or elixirs that are used in the making of drugs.

Article 351 covered the illegal cultivation of opium poppy, marijuana, or other kinds of plants, used in the manufacture of drugs. Article 352 stipulated the crime of illegally selling, buying, transporting, hand carrying, or possessing non-sterilized seeds or saplings of the opium poppy or other kinds of plants from which drugs are extracted. Article 353 specified crimes relating to the inducing, instigating, or tricking of others into taking or injecting drugs. Article 354 targeted crime relating to the harbouring of others and the injection of drugs. Article 355 sought to minimize collateral damages and regulated the appropriate production, transportation, and management of state-controlled narcotics for the treatment of those suffering from mental illness.

The CL97 had its own version of 'zero tolerance'. It provided the death penalty for those committing crime involving a large quantity of drugs (50 grams of heroin or 1,000 grams of opium). It also introduced severe punishment for state functionaries and repeat offenders who commit drug-related crimes. In order to deprive offenders of their illegal incomes and economic ability to repeat drug offences, the offenders' assets were exposed to confiscation. Fines could also be applied.

On the other hand, when compared with previous criminal law legislation, the CL97 introduced new detail concerning the adjudication of drug-related cases. However, serious gaps remained with respect to the consistent and accurate enforcement of the law. In 2000, the SPC resorted to new 'flexibility'! The SPC organized a workshop on adjudication. The workshop 'Minutes' explicitly acknowledged that due to the lack of detail in existing stipulations, there was inconsistency in the determination of related crime and punishment across the country. The SPC urged the courts at the lower levels to make use of the 'Minutes', as an interim guide to judicial practice until such time as the SPC issues a full judicial interpretation.

The 'Minutes' addressed five significant concerns in adjudicating drug-related criminal cases, including the determination of a joint crime, the proper calculation of the amount of drugs involved, collection of evidence and its validity, and the application of the law to cases concerning the stealing and robbing of drugs.[71]

The most contentious issue concerned the proper calculation of the amount of drugs involved in various crimes. In cases involving the trafficking and manufacturing of drugs, the amounts could ultimately determine the application of death penalty. CL97 Article 357 had indicated that 'the amounts of drugs refers to the officially verified amount of drugs smuggled, sold, transported, or manufactured, or the amounts illegally in possession'. Article 357 deliberately stipulated that the 'amount' should not be calculated with specific reference to the purity of the drugs.

Drug purity, however, became an issue. Prominent jurists like Zhao Bingzhi and He Xingwang contended that the calculation of the drugs involved could not be considered scientific unless drug purity was taken into account. The issue of purity speaks to the issue of 'social harmfulness'. In their opinion, a large amount of highly diluted drugs is arguably less harmful to an individuals' physical and psychological well-being than a small amount of highly concentrated drugs.[72]

The SPC 'Minutes' agreed with Professors Zhao and He, and these 'Minutes' deliberately ignored the CL97's reservation concerning drug purity. The SPC reasoning reiterated the importance of caution in dealing with crime that attracts the death penalty. In what can only be described as an extraordinary procedural move, the 'Minutes' required the postponement of the death penalty for offenders who had been caught with the prescribed 'amounts' of 50 grams of heroin or 1,000 grams of opium.[73]

In the name of judicial justice, and subscribing to the reform principle, 'the punishment must fit the crime', this judicial interpretation challenged the legislated stipulations of CL97 Article 357. Again, the SPC overstepped the conventional limits of judicial interpretation. Although in this case, perhaps the outcome was more 'just' than was the case with the prosecution of the members of the FLG.

However, while the SPC 'Minutes' seized the initiative on the issue of drug purity, they failed to address local protectionism in drug-related law enforcement. Deng Zhenlai, in his investigative report, revealed that the higher level of drug-related crimes in the areas of Guangdong, Yunnan, and Xinjiang provinces was partly the result of desultory enforcement of the anti-drug laws. The punishment for the crimes in these regions was far less severe compared to that for the same crimes in large urban cities, such as in Beijing. Deng reported that an offender who possesses illicit drug in Beijing could receive a sentence of five-year imprisonment; while in Yunnan, the same offender would likely escape criminal law punishment. Similarly, an offender who commits a drug-related offence could be sentenced to death in Beijing while an offender who had committed the same crime in Yunnan might easily get away with five-year imprisonment.[74]

Why are there such significant disparities in law enforcement? Local judicial personnel in Yunnan contended that the disparity partly originates in a local understanding of the unofficial criminal law principle of 'fabu zezhong' (punishment is not applied where law is popularly ignored). Punishment was usually less severe in the areas where a crime was committed frequently. The lack of rigorous enforcement also related to national minority politics. To avoid local unrest, the judicial authorities were deliberately forgiving in their application of criminal punishment to members of the national minorities.[75]

While the issue of inconsistent law enforcement has not been effectively addressed, the NPC has made considerable effort to insure the convergence of Chinese legislation with international treaty law on drug-related crime. For instance, traditionally, the possession of illegal drugs was not regarded as serious enough to warrant criminal punishment in China. However, the 1990 NPCSC 'Decision' and later, the CL97, criminalized illegal drug possession, bringing the relevant Chinese law in line with the relevant UN Convention on the prohibition of the illegal trafficking of narcotics and psychotropic substances. No doubt, China's leaders had their own domestic political reasons for targeting drug crime, but, at any rate, China, as a signatory to the UN Convention, was obliged to criminalize the possession of drugs.[76]

However, China's international reputation in these matters has been tarnished by the extensive use of heavy punishment. The Chinese criminal law control of drug-related crime has consistently relied on severe punishment, including the death penalty, and this conflicts with the 1996–7 emphases on human rights protection, based upon 'the punishment must fit the crime'. The irony in this was especially stark when the regime, on 26 June 2000, announced the execution of twelve drug traffickers to mark the International Anti-Drug Day.[77] The use of execution as a political marker on society's calendar has a long history in China, and, in this case, 'localism' directly challenged the rational synthesis of 'localization' and 'internationalization'.

In both areas of organized crime, drug smuggling and illegal emigration, there seems to be a comparable pattern of ill-timed ad-hockery and quick resort to heavy penalties. What law there is, is highly politicized in its stipulation, and follow-up regulation and interpretation often fails as the result of the lack of clearly defined terms in the law.

'Organized crime' and the smuggling of illegal emigrants

Similar to trafficking in drugs, the smuggling of human beings is also a transnational organized crime.[78] The latter has become 'a global problem' in the past decade, and China, as a major source of outward-bound illegal emigration, is right at the centre of this problem. In the past such smuggling moved in specific directions. In the mid-1990s, the primary destination was Japan. In recent years, the United States, Canada, and Australia, have increasingly become the preferred destinations partly because these countries have been comparatively favourable in their treatment of asylum seekers.[79] The receiving countries, however, are becoming increasingly concerned about the impact of illegal emigration on their own law enforcement, social order, and emigration and asylum policies.

While the problems concerning Chinese illegal emigrants have been studied by Western scholars, much of these studies have been primarily concerned with the personal profiles of the illegal emigrants and the 'snakeheads'.[80] There is a need for more research on the questions of how the Chinese regime has responded to organized criminal activities and whether this response is consistent with the 1996–7 judicial justice highlighting 'no crime and punishment without law' and the balancing of public order and human rights concerns.

The Border Defense Bureau, under the Ministry of Public Security, reported that since 1993, there has been an increasing trend in the organized smuggling of illegal emigrants.[81] This trend continued into the new century.[82] In October 2003, the Ministry of Public Security launched a 'strike-hard' campaign targeting human smuggling, especially in China's southern provinces.[83] In fact, the majority of the illegal emigrants came from the province of Fujian. There is a related historical tradition in Fujian. A family feels very proud and is respected if one of the sons can send back from overseas a large sum of money to help build a new house and/or sponsor a village banquet.[84] One might also note that outward-bound migration from Fujian relates more to a sense of relative deprivation rather than to real levels of poverty.[85]

Smuggling illegal emigrants has been carried out in many different ways. From the perspective of the Chinese legal authorities, human smuggling especially concerns the improper acquisition of travel documents and state border crossings. CL79 Articles 176 and 177 addressed the issue of illegal border crossings. But, in the early 1980s, the jurists complained that the CL79 stipulations were seriously inadequate. Again, the relevant punishments were overly lenient and the CL79 stipulations lacked the necessary detail to deal with the increasingly sophisticated and large-scale operations of 'organized crime'. In order to fight the criminal activities effectively the NPCSC issued, in March 1994, the 'Decision on Severe Punishment for Organizing and Transporting People Across State Borders'.[86]

This 'Decision's' eight articles featured stipulations concerning judicial practice and its response to specific crimes concerning illegal border crossings and related activities. The latter included the export of labour, the forging of passports and exit visas, and crime relating to the assistance of others to make illegal border crossings and to the abetting of illegal crossings by corrupt state functionaries. Compared to the CL79 stipulations, the 'Decision's' punishments were more severe. 'Organizers', for example, could expect life imprisonment, and persons who illegally crossed China's international borders could face two years' imprisonment. The stipulations in the 1994 'Decision' were subsequently incorporated into CL97 Articles 318–22.

CL97 Article 318 stipulated the crime of organizing illegal border crossings. Articles 319–21 detailed crimes concerning the aiding and abetting of such crossings, including the crime of using deceptive methods to obtain documents, the forging of travel documents, and the illegal transport of emigrants across the borders. However, the CL97 again failed to define key terms, such as 'organizing illegal border crossings' and 'grave circumstances'. This lack of clarity made it all the more difficult to maintain the principle, 'the punishment must fit the crime', and it fostered inconsistent judicial calculations of social harm as it correlates with the terms of punishment.

In an attempt to close this gap in law, the SPC issued in 2002 the 'Explanations for the Application of Laws in Adjudicating Cases of the Organizing, Transporting of Others for the Illegal Crossing of Borders'. The 'Explanations' defined 'organizers' as those who draw, induce, or introduce others into illegally crossing state borders. The organizers' specific liabilities related to the crime of 'organizing illegal state border crossing', and the stipulated punishment for such crime is seven years' imprisonment, and, in the event of repeat behaviour, life imprisonment. Clearly, this rather broad or 'liberal', interpretation of the term, 'organizers', was designed for the purpose of severely punishing as many 'criminals' as possible in the name of public order.[87] Moreover, there were problems in the calculation of correlated social harm and prison time. Under Article 1 of the 'Explanations', someone who 'draws in', 'induces', or 'makes introductions' could be sentenced to 7 years' imprisonment, while a person who actually commits the act of illegally crossing the border faces only 2 years' imprisonment. The punishment in this case seems to focus on the nefarious nature of organization rather than the nature of actual criminal acts by individuals.

Based on this judicial interpretation, the 'snake-heads' are identified as the organizers of human smuggling activities; their smuggling activity is a form of organized crime; and the snake-heads are regarded as members of criminal organization. This might help to explain why such crime is so persistent and widespread. Ko-lin Chin likely irritated his colleagues when he countered that not all smugglers are actually affiliated with criminal organizations. In some cases, human smuggling is alternatively carried out as 'a form of entrepreneurial activity' that is controlled by many otherwise legitimate groups working independently.

Kong Xiaoning, a journalist, at the *Renmin Ribao* (People's Daily), reiterated the official viewpoint, but he pointed to two additional factors concerning the difficulties in controlling illegal emigration. In the first place, the authorities were having difficulties in putting the 'snake-heads' behind bars because most of them resided and operated overseas, where the relevant punishments are comparatively lenient and the extradition of such criminals is more difficult. Second, in Kong's view, some destination countries were indirectly encouraging the trafficking of emigrants by allowing illegal emigrants to apply for political asylum.[88]

Apparently, Kong Xiaoning overlooked some obvious domestic social and political factors that closely correlate with the recent increase in illegal emigration, including China's increasingly weak social and border control, an increase in the number of privately owned boats, and growing official corruption among local police and government officials who either assist or abet illegal border crossings.

Conclusion

Human smuggling and drug trafficking are two of the more important types of 'organized crime' in China; however, in the past two decades, criminal organization has spread into all sorts of profit-making activities, including the trafficking of women and children, prostitution and gambling operations, armed robbery, automobile theft, etc. During the reform years, the NPC took on new responsibility for the creation of Deng Xiaoping's 'complete set of laws'. The NPC has often thrown itself into new law-making activity, and yet there is a continuing pattern of failure with regard to the comprehensive stipulation of clearly defined law.

Certainly, the intent was there to make greater use of the criminal law in controlling 'organized crime', but there was also the problem of the ill-timed coordination between legislation, interpretation, and the issuance of state regulation. Moreover, the *zhengfa* system continues to intervene within the criminal justice process with its emphases on 'strike-hard' campaigns and the coordination of the criminal law's response to new crime within a national strategy for the 'comprehensive management of public order'.[89] This 'management' has focused particularly on problems of official corruption and the rising crime rate among the rural migrants in the cities.

Also as part of this comprehensive strategy, new regulations have been issued to improve the accountability of banking and financial services so as to prevent money laundering. For the same reason, fines and the confiscation of offenders' property are playing a new role in related crime-fighting. The additional emphasis on fines and confiscation seems particularly appropriate as property and illegal earnings have served to finance organized criminal activity.

Chinese jurisprudence and legislation attempted to clarify the legal contents of organized crime with reference to a specific emphasis on the nature of criminal organization. The CL97 helped to establish the three different categories of criminal organization, namely, 'ordinary criminal organization', the COWTN, and 'terrorist organization'. The lawmakers and jurists struggled to establish the differences between these organizations in law. There was some progress. After considerable debate and discussion, the terms 'hooliganism' and 'hooligan criminal organization' were dropped from the law.[90]

On the other, there has been considerable confusion and very interesting controversy over the state functionary issue. In this case, the NPCSC nullified the SPC's position. The SPC was bruised, but not vanquished. The NPCSC, the SPC, the SPP, and the Ministry of Public Security continue to jockey for position, and the jurists are seriously searching for a universally accepted mechanism that can predictably deal with serious issues of competing jurisdiction.

What continuity there is in Chinese criminal law legislation favours a strong focus on the apparent necessity of deterrence and the creation of public order through extending the fields of 'criminal liability' and, most importantly, through the application of severe punishment. When compared with development in the West, the Chinese legal concept of 'organized crime' appears to be predicated in a deliberate and politically inspired ambiguity. At any rate, this concept is much more inclusive in its broad-guaged approach to the scope of criminal responsibility. These 'Chinese characteristics' directly reflect domestic politics. There has been a political preference for ambiguity that allows the authorities to cast a much bigger net in relation to organized crime. The Party and the NPC simply refused to recognize the development of 'typical' triads in China. Apparently, almost all of the new crime originates with the different forms of 'ordinary criminal organization' and with the COWTN.

Criminal syndicates or underground societies could only be called COWTN. The creative development of the 'COWTN' was politically expedient. The objective was to expand the scope of criminal law prosecution and punishment. In China, organized crime is severely punished not only because of its 'social harmfulness', but also because the spread of such crime calls into question the legitimacy of the regime. The latter has often responded by enhancing the 'Chinese characteristics' within the criminal justice system and pushing the law and the Party politics of morality more closely together. The extended scope of criminal liability, the focus on the nature of, and membership in, criminal organization, and the propensity to rely on 'heavy-penaltyism' all relate to the 'unscientific' vagaries of the *zhengfa* system.

5 Crime and human rights in cyber-space

Nowhere is the pace of new criminal development faster than in cyber-space. Certainly, the wide-ranging political, economic, and social implications of the revolution in internet technology are not lost on the CCP. Some Chinese research has contrasted the 'traditional' media, such as radio, television, newspapers, and magazines, as 'controllable media' (*kekuxing meijie*), with the internet and its various applications, as 'uncontrollable media' (*bukekuxing meijie*).[1] Apparently, the Party knows better. For the sake of public order, not to mention regime legitimacy, it has set out to control the 'uncontrollable media', and it has done so with only passing regard for the protection of human rights. This chapter examines the legal dimensions of the Party's strategy for control, and it will analyse the impact of this strategy on the post-1996–7 trend for criminal justice reform.

The CCP wants to oversee the transition to 'Digital China', but the Party leaders see in the spreading internet both the dangers and opportunities of globalization. The internet is, in their view, a social and political paradox that requires vigilant management. The internet is a powerful new revolutionary force that cannot be dismissed or abandoned for it holds the key to a knowledge-based society. It offers incredible new and tantalizing advantages in the areas of telecommunication, commercial development, advanced education, and scientific research. At the same time, however, the internet has given millions of ordinary Chinese unprecedented access to politically sensitive information from the West; it has facilitated the development of new platforms for political discussion and organization; and it has expedited an exponential development of new crime in cyber-space.[2] In their commentary on this same paradox, Chinese scholars have described emerging internet technology as a 'double edged sword' (*shuangmian jian*) – implying that the new information technology encompasses both 'good' causes and 'evil' purposes.[3]

For the first time in March 2001, the Chinese listed an industry as a separate item in the five year plan. Information technology was and still is hot. As one expert and member of the National Committee of the Chinese

People's Political Consultative Conference put it:

> An information-based society is not confined to the building of infra-
> structure for information technology or simply developing the IT
> industry,... the kernel for an information-based society is to change the
> ways of economic operation, social operation, government operation,
> and even the life of the ordinary people.[4]

While the CCP leadership has placed a very high priority on information
technology as a new key element in planning for national economic development, it has become intensely preoccupied with public order and
control over newly developing 'criminal liabilities' in cyber-space.
The government has attempted to achieve control through the rapid
development of related law and regulation. This new regulatory regime
has focused on the control of internet service providers (ISP) and internet
users. The Party-State has become deeply involved in the censorship of
online publications, e-mail exchange, and the content of domestic Chinese
chat rooms. In its attempt to block access to Western news sources and
pornographic materials, the Party-State has created what many derisively
refer to as 'the Great Fire Wall of China'.

While one might think that the revolution in information technology
would naturally support the 'rule of law economy', the Party has been
counterintuitive in its related consolidation of the controlling features of
its *zhengfa* system. As we have already seen in earlier chapters, the post-1999
leadership view, combining the rules of law and virtue, reflects the keen
political interest in preserving Chinese culture and morality *vis-à-vis*
Western decadence and Falungong heresy. But, the reduction in internet
crimes and popular exposure to Western information has been carried out
at the expense of the 1996–7 'balance of values' in human rights protection
and public order. The 2003 US State Department Report on human rights
in China has, for example, correlated internet control with the Chinese
government's violations of freedom of online expression and publication,
online correspondence, and rights for online privacy.[5]

Put these profound political issues within the real context of the
internet's phenomenal development. Currently, there are approximately
80 million internet users in China. This is more than any other country
except for the United States.[6] In China, the large-scale adaptation of
electronic communication networks only began in 1994.[7] But the spread
of internet use has been extraordinary. In 1997, there were only 250,000
internet users. Two years later, there were 3.5 million computers online
in China, more than 15,000 domestic Chinese-language sites, 1,000 internet content providers, nearly 600 e-commerce websites specialized in
online businesses such as ticket and hotel reservation, procurement and
shopping, and 300 ISPs. In the same year, China's first on-line auction
house was opened.[8] In 2000, internet users reached 20 million, and by

mid-2003 this number grew to 68 million and then to 80 million by mid-2004.[9]

In China, as in the West, the internet has become indispensable to many educational and scientific research institutions and to the daily personal activities of millions of ordinary people. In 2001, Jiang Zemin claimed that the internet would serve as the future foundation for economic prosperity, social progress, and development in China.[10]

Some reformers have even suggested that e-mail can be used to support improved governance in China. A 5 June 2001 Xinhua report gave a number of examples of how e-mail was affecting government law and policy. A farmer in the Northwest, for example, e-mailed the State Environmental Protection Agency (SEPA) to set up a special fund to assist in the rehabilitation of the degraded vegetation in the Hexi Corridor. His e-mail was supported by the flooding of the SEPA's mailbox. The same report hailed Zhao Yuhong of Heilongjiang Province for sending an e-mail to the NPCSC's website to propose that revisions to the Marriage Law forbid concubinage. The Xinhua report cited various experts to support the following conclusion: 'Under the market economic system, the change in interest relations stimulates people's willingness to participate in politics. And the internet provides [the] public with a rapid and cheap access to political affairs.'[11]

Keeping in mind that it is empirically difficult to establish both the quantitative and the qualitative dimensions of incipient e-governance in China, one can, by way of example, cite changes at the NPC. During the 2002 NPC, a large number of internet users reportedly participated in discussions of national affairs and government policy making. The official Xinhua News Agency commented that the extensive application of the internet in China might provide a short cut to democracy.[12]

Categorizing internet crime

Chinese jurists, like their Western counterparts, have defined 'cyber-crimes' (*jisuanji fanzui*) as crimes that are committed with the involvement of computer information technology.[13] Cyber-crimes in the PRC have been classified into two large categories: crimes directly targeting computer systems and information networks; and crimes committed through the use of computers and their related networks.

The former include a new series of criminal activities as indicated in the following breakdown: the unauthorized access to computer networks; interference with, or interruption of the operation of computer information systems; the deletion, alteration of, or the addition to the data or application programs, installed in, or processed and transmitted by the computer systems; and the creation and spread of viruses and other programs that interrupt the normal operation of computer systems. Chinese scholars dubbed such crime, 'pure computer crime' (*chunzhengde jisuanjifanzui*).

The second category of cyber-crime relates to use of computers in the commission of 'conventional' crime concerning, for example, financial fraud, theft, corruption, misappropriation of public funds, the stealing of state secrets, criminal harassment, the dissemination of pornography, extortion, sabotage, espionage, kidnapping, murder, etc. Chinese jurists have labelled such crime, 'computer-related conventional crime' (*sheji jisuanji fanzui*).[14]

In the United States, Canada, and Western European countries, criminal legislation on cyber-crime emerged in 1970s and accelerated rapidly in 1980s. But, in China, computer and information technology came later, and the first piece of legislation on cyber-crimes was only enacted in 1997. Professor Zhao Bingzhi of Chinese People's University and his colleague Yu Zhigang have acknowledged that before 1997, Chinese cyber-criminal legislation was slow in its response to new criminal phenomena and, as the result of the lack of due vigilance, would-be criminals were not appropriately assigned criminal liability and accordingly punished for their 'crimes' in cyber-space.[15]

There is a new generation of cyber-criminal legislation and internet-related government administrative regulation that is now beginning to address newly stipulated 'criminal liabilities'. The former concentrates on the punishment of serious computer-related criminal activities. The latter has been issued by the central government departments to control internet use, including internet gateway connections, internet service providing, and internet access. Ostensibly, this mixed strategy of law and regulation was designed to prevent cyber-crime and to preserve public order as well as Chinese morality and culture. However, this particular strategy has resulted in the CL97's excessive reliance on government regulation for key computer-related technical definitions and explanations.

Within the two categories of computer-related crime, the regime has focused particularly on three highly vexing types of crime. Such crime included category 1 crime undermining computer systems and networks as well as category 2 crime concerning the computer-based spread of information 'harmful' to national security, and crimes concerning online information 'harmful to social order and morality'. This chapter focuses on these particular types of crime and how related crime fighting has responded to the 1996–7 criminal justice reform as it relates to the ongoing effort to entrench the new balance of values on the basis of new rational strategy in favor of comprehensive stipulation and the principle of legality, namely, 'no crime, without law' and 'no punishment without law'.

In relation to the two categories of computer crime, what is the exact mix and range of remedies that has been used to assert control over the internet? Has the regime effectively used law and regulation to impose the state's strict and unqualified control over internet use? In what specific ways has such expansive and open-ended control affected the protection of individual human rights?

It may be that the CCP is not worrying about anything. The author of *China Dawn*, David Sheff, described the rise of China's own internet pioneers in the following terms: 'The story of *China Dawn* is really about idealistic visionaries who decided that they wanted to go back and continue the revolution that the students in Tiananmen Square began. Now these same people are in prominent positions.'[16] Since the 1997 elimination of counterrevolutionary crime, the regime has claimed that there is no such thing as 'political crime' in China. The situation is developing continuously, but this chapter will attempt to examine questions of internet dissent and the related critical distinctions between crimes, endangering national security, and 'political crime'.

Computer network security and Chinese cyber-legislation

In the late 1990s, vital operations of government departments, finance and banking industries, and the educational and scientific research institutions became increasingly dependent upon computer information systems and networks. Network hackers, or cyber-vandals (*heile*) tested the vulnerability of these new systems and networks.[17] In April 2000, for example, US-based hackers vandalized several hundred Chinese websites, including those belonging to the central and provincial governments.[18] A 2000 government survey also revealed that 44 per cent of the 300 Chinese internet firms surveyed had experienced tampering, while 40 per cent of firms' websites had been repeatedly attacked.[19] The highly computerized Chinese financial and banking institutions were especially vulnerable. In 1999, the majority of 908 network-related crimes filed for investigation by the public security departments concerned financial service network systems.[20] A large proportion of the serious network security-related crimes therein were committed by insiders, who were stealthily working from within their own companies and institutions.

The potential for great harm to national security, economic development, and prosperity was serious, and China's scholars have readily criticized the weak security features of Chinese systems. In 2000, Professor Xu Rongheng of the Chinese Academy of Social Sciences (CASS) went so far as to claim that China probably had the worst computer network security in the world.[21] In the same year, the Ministry of Public Security targeted foreign manufactured computer products, complaining that some of these products had been deliberately exported to China without the usual security features.

To protect the national interest and economic security, China's companies have been forbidden since 2000 to buy or to sell any products with encryption software designed in foreign countries. Alternatively, they were instructed to develop and produce 'self-controlled and self-implemented' (*zizhu zhangwo zizhu shishi*) network components and information security platforms to provide unified security interfacing for various applications of inter-connecting and internal networks.[22]

Indeed, both Chinese authorities and legal scholars agree that crimes against computer network system were particularly harmful to the society as they inflict huge economic losses and undermine social and political stability.[23] To protect China's computer networks and prevent network-security-related criminal activities, in addition to improving computer-network security and increasing state investment in network infrastructure, the regime has also been actively making network-related criminal-legislation and government regulations to punish the new generation of cyber criminals.

Laws and regulations on network security in the earlier 1990s

The network technology and its applications first appeared in China in late 1980s. But at that time, there was not much computer-related criminal activity. In the educational and scientific institutions, only very few researchers, who had capacity in the English language, were able to access the networks. However, internet use then spread like wildfire in the 1990s. Law and regulation were overtaken by new criminal development. The first Chinese computer-network-related provisions were drafted by the Ministry of Public Security's Computer Management and Inspection Bureau and issued by the State Council in 1994.[24]

The 1994 'PRC Provisions on the Protection of Computer Information System Security' provided the guidelines for managing the computer network system, and stipulated punishment, including criminal punishment, for spreading computer viruses. But the 'Provisions' failed to anticipate the many other network-related criminal activities that subsequently emerged. The Centre tried to play catchup. In 1996–8, there was a flurry of more than sixteen national regulations and ministerial notices addressing new problems of criminal responsibility, especially in the areas of China's domestic computer network connections to international computer networks and their security. In its great anxiety, the regime often, in a heavy-handed manner, emphasized social control and ignored the protection of human rights.

One of the critical network security issues was related to the control of network gateways connecting the domestic to the international networks. The 1996 'PRC Provisional Regulations on the Management of Connections of Chinese Domestic Computer Networks to International Networks' stipulated that all domestic computer systems could only be connected to international networks via the gateways established and managed by the Ministry of Post and Telecommunications. Other individuals and organizations were strictly prohibited from establishing domestic–international connections. Exemptions from this restriction required specific State Council approval.[25] These stipulations ignored related human rights issues and provided the State with a total technical and administrative monopoly over internet information access, online publication, and internet privacy.

Crimes concerning computer network security in the CL97

Rapid social and economic development in the early 1990s resulted in a large number of newly stipulated crimes, including network security-related crimes, for which there was no stipulation at all in the CL79. New provisions were, therefore, added to the CL97.[26] Up to a certain point, the CL97 was able to draw upon foregoing government regulation concerning the technical detail of the lawful use of the internet.

During the drafting of the CL97, the Ministry of Public Security lobbied hard for the inclusion in the newly revised law of heavy punishment for a wide range of network-security-related new crimes. In fact, the Ministry tried to push the law in its own preferred direction, drafting its own 'Proposal on Crimes Endangering Computer Information System Security'. If the Ministry is powerful, it is not always omnipotent. Its proposal was only partially adopted in the NPC's CL97. The NPC, however, chose not to exercise its full legislative authority, deferring a number of computer-related misdemeanours to future government regulation.[27]

New crimes concerning computer-networks were specifically stipulated in the CL97 Articles 285, 286, and 287. According to Professor Zhao Yanguang of Wuhan University and his colleagues, Articles 285 and 286 incorporated four different crimes that took the computer systems and networks as the 'object' of 'crime'. Article 285 covered unauthorized criminal access to computer-housed information concerning state affairs, national defense establishment facilities, and sophisticated science and technology.

Section One, Article 286 stipulated the crimes of deleting from, altering, adding to, and interfering with computer information systems, causing abnormal operations and 'grave consequences'. Section Three, Article 286 addressed the creation and spread of viruses and 'other' programming that interrupts normal operations and causes 'grave consequences'.[28] The crime in Article 285 attracted a sentence of less-than-3-year imprisonment, while the Article 286 crimes called for a sentence of less-than-5-year imprisonment, and 5–20-year imprisonment if the circumstances are 'grave'. In an important area relating to human rights protection, Article 287 resorted to analogy. It covered crimes concerning the use of a computer to carry out financial fraud, stealing, embezzlement, the appropriation of public funds, the stealing of state secrets, and *'other'* like criminal activities.

The CL97 stipulations covered a wide new range of cyber criminal liability and punishment, but many Chinese jurists were generally dissatisfied with the state of related national legislation, and they were particularly critical of CL97 Articles 285 and 286.[29] At Renda (the Chinese People's University), Yu Zhigang argued that Articles 285 and 286 were ineffective as they lacked stipulations for enforcement; hence they were dependent upon state regulation that was in constant flux. He explained that one of the constitutive elements of the cyber-crime, stipulated in these two articles was that the action of a criminal suspect must actually 'violate state regulations' (*weifan guojia guiding*). For Yu and his colleagues, the related state regulations specifically referred to the regulations, notices, and opinions issued by the State Council and its relevant ministries.

The original CL97 reference to state regulation not only tolerated, but encouraged 'flexibility'. The reference was rationalized as the means by which to avoid long and complicated technical explanations of various cyber-criminal activities, which have partially been described in various administrative regulations.[30] However, Liu Jiachen, Vice President of the PRC Supreme People's Court, explained that the term 'state regulations' was never intended to refer to state regulations in general. The CL97 anticipated instead specific reference to the 1994 'PRC Regulations on the Protection of Computer Security'.[31] In either case, the NPC never attempted comprehensive stipulation and the new CL97 provisions on computer network security deferred to future State Council regulation to determine important points of law.

In this area of growing criminality China's jurists were not concerned with the 1996–7 reform strategy calling for the reduction of 'heavy-penalty-ism'. They were more concerned whether the CL97 stipulations could effectively protect critical computer networks systems that serviced the financial and banking sectors, medical research and service institutions, and internet-content providers.[32] They argued that the stipulated punishments in law failed to correlate proportionately with the tremendous social harm caused in such sectors.[33]

Researchers at the Criminal Law Research Unit of the NPCSC's Legal Work Committee seemed to agree and yet they argued that CL Article 284 was sufficient to punish appropriately such behaviour. However, this Article's connection with network security behaviour was tangential at best. The Article refers to: '...whoever illegally uses *special monitoring or photographing equipment* and causes grave consequences is to be sentenced to not more than two years of fixed-term imprisonment, criminal detention, or control.'[34] Moreover, such opinion did not address the key dilemma, namely, that the deference to state regulation in the absence of legal clarity and the failure to stipulate clearly all the related categories of crime on the basis of principle of legality threatened to undermine the struggle for the rule of law with the 'flexible' development of pre-emptive state regulation.

The scholars found yet another gaping hole in criminal legislation. The CL97 had not dealt with the criminal liabilities of a legal person involved in cyber-crime. The issue of whether a legal person is criminally liable and punishable had been hotly debated in the CL97 drafting process.[35] CL97 Article 30 actually does stipulate that a legal person could be criminally liable, however, only in the circumstances where the law has a specific stipulation with regard to a specific criminal act.

The CL97, however, contains no stipulation that a legal person shall be liable for the network-security-related criminal activities, as described in Articles 285–87. A legal person who commits a network security crime is, therefore, not criminally liable under the CL97. The point is hardly moot, as some corporations and business entities have conducted well-planned attacks on the computer network systems of their business rivals. Professor Yu has recommended the revision of the CL97 so as to insure criminal responsibility and punishment for legal persons that engage in such criminal practice.[36]

The trend to expanded and more heavy penalties was reflected in debate concerning Article 285. Critics noted that Article 285, relating to unauthorized access, carries a light sentence of less than three years of imprisonment. However, they have cited international convention concerning extradition, noting that a three-year prison sentence is not sufficiently serious as to warrant extradition. They contend that this loophole originates with an inappropriately light sentencing that allows offenders to escape proper punishment.[37]

In order to emphasize the importance of appropriate punishment in relation to the harm caused by network security crime, some jurists recommend that such new crime be shifted from CL97 chapter 6, 'Crimes Disrupting the Order of Social Administration' to CL97 chapter 2 pertaining to 'Crimes Endangering Public Security'. In the world of Chinese criminal law, such re-location is no small technical matter.

The stipulation of specific criminal activities are conventionally organized into thematic chapters, such as crime against property, and crime against persons. However, at the same time, chapters on specific crimes are also arranged in a descending order reflecting the different levels of severity in social harmfulness, and, in theory, if not always in practice, these different levels are hierarchically connected to the different degrees of severe punishment. In sum, the scholars flagged the importance of the social harm relating to computer-related new crime, when they advocated the shift from the chapter on social administration so as to take advantage of the more severe punishments stipulated in the chapter on public security.[38] The latter is placed second in the law's hierarchy only in relation to the first category of crime regarding national security. To a certain extent, the issue is a politically symbolic matter of deterrence. Both CL97 chapters carry 5 articles requiring the death penalty and 7 articles stipulating life imprisonment. The hierarchical dimension in this specific pattern of punishment is obscured in the easy resort to severe punishment for non-violent crime.

To elevate further the significance of cyber-crime, Yu Zhigang proposed that the NPC draft a law specifically concerning such crime. The proposed law was to address many of the problems originating in the lack of clear definition of key technical terminology. Such a law could also respond to the problem of light punishment and extradition. Furthermore, such a new law could deal with the growing inconsistency of state regulation and its substitution of 'flexibility' for clear definition in NPC law. Yu also envisaged what he regarded as a rational division between criminal and administrative punishment. His proposed law would deal with major crime warranting severe criminal law punishment whereas punishment for minor computer-related crime could be dealt with under the 1986 'Provisions on Administrative Punishment Concerning the Management of Public Security'.[39]

Indeed, several steps have already been taken in light of the inconsistency of state regulation and the weakness of the CL97 provisions on cyber-crime. Beginning in 1996, 'The Provisions for the Security Protection and Management of Computer Networks and International Networks' were issued by the Ministry of Public Security. In 2000, 'The Administrative Measures for Security Information Networks and Internet', and 'The Measures for the Prevention and Control of Computer Viruses', were issued. When taken together these sets of provisions focus on the circulation of state secrets in domestic systems as they connect directly or indirectly with international networks.[40]

This policy was further enhanced in several other ministerial notices including 'The Provisional Regulations on the Management of State Secrets on Computer Information Networks', issued by the State Secrecy Bureau, and 'The Notice on Website Management for the Purpose of Preventing Incidence of Releasing Confidential Information on the Internet', issued by the Ministry of Personnel.[41] The leaking of state secrets and national security were identified as principal 'objects' in the regime's legal struggle for control over internet crime.[42]

The domestic critics have recognized that lax network security not only relates to the problems concerning the appropriate mix of law-making and state regulation, but also to the failure to earmark adequate resources and funding to enhance security and to the lack of focused attention on the part of industry and all related levels of government. China's micro-electronics industry still functions at a lower standard of performance, hence there are also related technical difficulties concerning cryptography, digital signatures, identity authentication, and firewall and monitoring systems.[43]

The regime, in its focus on network security, is adapting to the same kind of combined 'societal' and 'jural' tactics that inform its overall struggle to achieve the 'comprehensive management of public order'. To mobilize other forces for network security protection, the regime has even turned to market mechanisms to promote network security. In 2000, 'The Guidelines for Assessing Security Protection of Computer

Information Systems', issued jointly by the Ministry of Public Security and the State Bureau of Quality and Technology Control, outlined five criteria for evaluating computer network security protection that concerned user privacy, system auditing, security mark protection, structural protection, and visitor verification.[44] These 'Guidelines' essentially provided the security information for internet users to make the necessary informed decisions so as to select secure ISPs. At the same time, the Guidelines also required ISPs to produce secured internet products; and they provided the Public Security authorities with the security standards by which to supervise and assess ISP security risks.[45]

At the beginning of this analysis the question was asked: Has the regime effectively used law and regulation to impose the state's strict and unqualified control over internet use? Despite the 1996–7 commitment to comprehensive stipulation the regime continues to deploy analogy, and it has demonstrated an over-reliance on administrative regulation. The timed mix of law-making and state regulation is out of sync. CL97 dependence on administrative regulations poses another vexing problem relating to 'flexibility'. The commitment to the protection of human rights parallels the commitment to the principle of legality. 'Flexibility', while in some cases may be justified on the basis of the need to respond to an immediate crisis, often diminishes the 'rule of law' commitment to the protection of human rights, based on 'no crime without law' and 'no punishment without law'.

Since 1997, only some of the elements of cyber-crime have been stipulated on the basis of the NPC's legislative power and the approval of the CL97. The State Council and its ministries have, in effect, been allowed to fill in the blanks left by legislation. Such generous deference to state agencies gives rise to the scenario whereby the definition of 'crimes' could be altered and/or prejudiced by the administrative branches of the central government without going through the NPC legislative process. Coupled with the problems of 'undefined critical terms' in the legislation, this kind of 'flexibility' may well encourage the regime to focus on state regulation to suppress political opposition in the name of protecting social stability and public order.

Moreover, the determination of the 'object' of computer-related crime reveals a much stronger political focus on 'conventional computer-related crime' (i.e. crime using computer systems and the internet as an instrument of criminal activities) rather than on 'pure computer crime', *per se*. This is confirmed, for example, in the organization and contents of the NPC 2000 'Decision on Safeguarding Internet Security'.

The 'Decision' places cyber crime within six categories, which for the most part focus on 'conventional computer-related crime': (1) crimes disrupting the safe operation of computer networks (this reiterates CL97 Articles 285 and 286); (2) crimes of using the internet to fabricate and disseminate information harmful to national security and social stability; (3) crimes of using the internet to disrupt the socialist market economic order and the management of social order; (4) crimes of using the internet to violate personal, property, and other legal rights of individuals, legal entities, and other organizations; (5) illegal acts, using the internet, that are not serious enough to warrant CL97 punishment, but could be alternatively punished under the 1986 'Provisions on Administrative Punishment concerning the Management of Public Security'; and (6) civil infringement and liability committed while using the internet that are not serious enough to be punished according to either the CL97 or the 1986 'Provisions'.[46]

Except for the first category, the 'Decision' was mainly concerned with the politically sensitive use of the internet to challenge public order and regime legitimacy. The rest of this chapter's analysis focuses on the two categories of 'conventional computer-related crime' concerning (a) the use of the internet to disseminate information that is considered 'harmful to national security' and (b) the internet dissemination of information that is considered 'harmful' to public order, social stability, and Chinese morality. It is in these areas that one might anticipate the most egregious demonstration of the *zhengfa* system's unqualified use of 'flexibility'.

Crimes against national security or political crime?

Philip Sohmen has observed that 'while recognizing the considerable growth potential of the internet, China has remained preoccupied with the risk to security and political control.'[47] In fact, such concern was expressed even before the NPC's approval of the CL97 in a notice issued by the Ministry of Public Security. This 1996 'Notice on Strengthening the Security of International Computer Network Connections' addressed several national security-related internet activities, including those of using the internet to undermine Chinese sovereignty and territorial integrity; to undermine national security; to instigate separation of the country; and to undermine the unity of China's different ethnic groups.[48]

The CL97 did not exactly spell out content such as internet-related crime endangering national security. Article 287 generally referred to 'using a computer to carry out financial fraud, stealing, embezzlement, appropriation of public funds, stealing state secrets, and other criminal activities shall be punished according to this law.' Despite or perhaps because of its great policy significance, the reference to national security had to rely on analogical reference to 'other criminal activities'.

However, the later NPC 2000 'Decision' did stipulate the crime of using the internet to fabricate and disseminate information harmful to national security. In fact, the 2000 'Decision' listed the following specific crimes: (1) crime using the internet to fabricate rumors, slander and defame others, to publish and disseminate harmful information, to instigate the overthrow of the regime, and the socialist system, or to instigate splitting of the country, and undermining state unity; (2) crime using the internet to steal or to leak state and military secrets; (3) crime using the internet to instigate ethnic hatred and discrimination, and to undermine ethnic unity. However, from within the politics of the Chinese criminal justice system, it is not easy to establish legal clarity based upon comprehensive stipulation. The 'Decision' also failed to offer any legal clarity as to the definition of very important terms such as 'information harmful to the national security,' 'information used to overthrow the regime and socialist system,' and 'state and military secrets'.[49]

Within the confines of the traditional *zhengfa* system, the lack of definition of key terms was often simply rationalized as acceptable 'flexibility'. In pre-1997 criminal law making, flexible stipulations without clear definitions of legal terms were self-consciously justified as necessary to the suppression of 'class enemies'. However, the contemporary adaptation to such 'flexibility' conflicts with 'no crime, without law and no punishment without law'. Supposedly, 'flexibility' has been discredited in the reform era. Supposedly, the application of the CL97 is to be carried out on the more favourable basis of new constitutional reference to 'running the country according to the rule of law' and 'establishing a rule of law economy.' It now appears, however, that analogy continues to play a supporting role in determining the contents of crime and punishment. In short, the death of analogy in 1997 was greatly exaggerated!

Not only has analogy returned from the grave, but, with respect to the development of the law on the internet, there is a paucity of necessary defining detail. It would seem that the devil really is in the details. Based on the current criminal law, internet use to further the subversion of state power, or to overthrow the socialist system, or to incite the splitting of the country can be punished with life imprisonment. In cases that require severe punishment, the legal system is supposed to act more deliberately and cautiously. Clearly, in the enforcement of such stipulations, undefined critical terms, such as 'state secrets', 'rumors or slander', and 'harmful information', could easily erode judicial justice and related fundamental human rights.

Moreover, there is a pattern whereby the key criteria in determining crime and punishment – 'social harmfulness' – have been extended to cover politically sensitive issues concerning the protection of China's culture and morality. Some Chinese scholars have claimed that the specific domestic focus on 'social harm' (*shehui weihai*), connecting law to Chinese society and culture, is legitimate 'localization'. Others have attempted to leverage 'internationalization'. They have attacked 'social harm' as a 'Chinese exceptionalism' that overemphasizes the harmful social consequences of specific 'criminal' behaviour at the expense of the scientific definition of 'crime'. As we have seen, many of China's jurists have been alarmed by what they perceive as the great harm caused by cyber crime, and this may have exacerbated the fundamental problem of the timed relation between clearly defined law and flexible state regulation. The lack of clear and comprehensive stipulation has opened the door to open-ended interpretations of available, but weak stipulation.

Within this context, the independence of law is more likely to be overtaken by politics. Take, for example, the posting of opinion on social and political issues as the 'subversion of state power'. In 1999, Lin Hai was sentenced to two years' imprisonment for instigating the overthrow of state power through the internet. In fact, the 'subversion' in this case rested precariously upon the fact that Lin shared 30,000 e-mail addresses with anti-China magazines that then turned around and disseminated into China information, criticizing government leaders and some police officials.[50] Did Lin receive the full benefit of judicial justice based upon 'the punishment must fit the crime'?

On 2 January 2001, the Chengdu City Procuratorate accused Huang Qi, a local computer engineer, of violating CL97 Articles 103 and 105. Under Article 103, Huang was accused of 'subverting state power', and under Article 105, he was accused of 'organizing national separatism and destroying national unity'. Allegedly, he had used his website, 'Tianwang Missing Persons Website' to post material on democracy, the Xinjiang independence movement, the FLG, and demands to reverse the Party position on the 1989 Tiananmen Square 'turmoil'.[51] Similarly, in 2001, Guo Qinghai, a bank employee in the city of Cangzhou near Beijing, was accused and convicted of inciting subversion to overthrow the government because of his posting of pro-democratic articles on overseas websites.[52]

In November 2003, four internet dissidents in Beijing received harsh prison sentences for posting online reform essays concerning social inequality. For this, they were accused of 'subverting' state power! Xu Wei and Jin Haike received 10-year prison terms while Yang Zili and Zhang Honghai received 8-year terms.[53] In September 2003, Li Zhi, a 32-year-old finance official in Sichuan Province, was also charged with 'conspiracy to subvert state power' for expressing his subversive views on internet bulletin boards and chat rooms and for communicating online with overseas dissidents.[54]

All of these cases suggest the prejudicial nature of the unclear stipulations set out in both the CL97 and the 2000 NPC Decision. The 1997 elimination of the criminal law category of 'counterrevolutionary crime' was rationalized as a 'scientific' prerequisite for the development of fair procedure. It was publicly acknowledged that the law was unable to handle the unscientific and constantly shifting requirements of politics. Since 1997, in its anxiety to tame the internet, the government, under the Party's leadership, appears to have created a new generation of political crime on the basis of 'flexibility'. This seriously contradicts the reform thrust of the 1996–7 strategy criminal justice reform, based upon transparent and comprehensive stipulation so as to ensure both public order and human rights protection.

There is an ongoing international debate as to whether the internet can serve as an agency of democracy and human rights. Alternatively, the internet might possibly be used for the negative purposes of disinformation and the furtherance of the agendas of extreme nationalism. Western and Chinese observers have speculated on the political implications of the accelerated development of the Chinese internet. At the Rand Corporation, Nina Hachigian has argued that while Chinese internet use may not immediately trigger drastic political change, political changes may not be that far away. Hachigian explained:

> In the near term, the internet's effects will not threaten the CCP's power because the party's management tactics are effective, because only a small proportion of the population is on-line, and because few care to challenge the ruling regime during the present period of economic and political stability. But perhaps five years hence, when one in ten Chinese citizens will have internet access and virtually everyone will know someone with an account, the shift in information control and communication will have the potential to undermine CCP rule. Exposure to new ideas, new perspectives on government actions, and events in China will have grown. Economic independence from the state will have increased. Connections between citizens will have multiplied. A political or economic crisis in this wired China of the future would unfold differently than it would today.[55]

For Philip Sohmen, in the long run, although change seems likely, there is not necessarily a direct correlation between political change and internet use in China:

> While the government has attempted to maintain strict control over the internet, the nature of the technology means that it is likely to remain one step behind. In the long-term, the internet will be one of the factors that contribute to the erosion of the state's political control. To suggest that it will become an instrument of widespread dissent and a tool for subversion, as the government seems to fear, is unlikely. Change is more likely to come through the increasingly tight links with the outside world that the internet forges, and through its contribution to economic growth. In the short term, the government will be able to maintain its strict control of both online and offline expression, not through regulation but through its ability to use force to scare dissenters into submission.[56]

For our purposes here, however, the recent proliferation of internet use has occasioned the creation of a new generation of criminal liabilities on the basis of a revised criminal justice strategy that has qualified comprehensive stipulation and related human rights protection with increased reference to 'flexibility' and 'heavy-penalty-ism'.

Crimes concerning information harmful to society

The CL97 did not comprehensively stipulate specific crimes concerning the production and dissemination of harmful information, including anti-government commentary, 'evil-cult' publication, and Western 'distortions' of the news, not to mention the dissemination of Western pornographic materials on the internet. The 2000 NPC 'Decision' helped to launch this process. Over the past decade the State Council and its ministries have tried to fill in the blanks of the CL97 with a bewildering array of state regulations and notices defining information-related cyber-criminal activities.

As Mao would have attested, in order to overthrow a regime, one must first create an adverse opinion, and to insure the proper subversive effect of such an opinion, there is the need for media control as a fundamental aspect of political power. The present-day internet has extensive communication capacity that is accessible to millions of ordinary citizens in real time. Historically, the CCP has acted to ensure complete control over the media, and arguably this control has served the Party well since 1949.[57]

The majority of the internet-related regulations and notices, issued by the State Council and its ministries, reiterate the same concerns about public order and regime stability. In sum, these regulations have identified nine categories of information that could be deemed 'harmful to society'. Any one of the following categories might require criminal punishment based upon the mix of state regulations and CL97 articles. In order to qualify as 'harmful' internet-based information, information must:

1   conflict with the principles in the Constitution;
2   endanger state security, containing state secrets subversive to the socialist regime and undermining state unity;
3   undermine the honor and interests of the state;
4   instigate hatred among different ethnic groups be racially discriminating, undermine ethnic harmony;
5   undermine state policy on religion, promoting evil cults and feudal superstitions;
6   create rumors, disturbing the public order, and undermining social stability;
7   relate to sex, gambling, violence, killing, terrorism, and methods of committing crimes;
8   libel and slander others, violating others' rights and interests;
9   relate to any other content prohibited by other state laws and regulations.

One could drive an eighteen-wheel transport truck through the holes left in some of this language. What is meant by the 'state's honor'? What qualifies as 'hatred'? How is an 'evil cult' defined in law. Moreover, anology rears its head in the final category. 'Fabricating' and 'disseminating' of any of the loosely stipulated information, listed above, can be easily treated as a criminal offence. In order to eliminate these criminal activities, the government has attempted to achieve monopoly control over both ISPs and gateway access, as well as internet and website content.

State control of internet providers and access

In the early 1990s, state regulations sequentially focused on control over the internet gateways and regulation of ISPs. In 2000, the State Council, for the first time, addressed ISP issues in 'The Methods of Managing Internet Service Providing Businesses'. Article 3 of 'The Methods' classified Chinese ISPs into profit and non-profit providers. 'The Methods' and subsequent regulations required the collection of information, concerning users' online time, account numbers, home addresses, domain names, and home phone numbers.

Article 14 of 'The Methods' required that the related information be kept for sixty days and that it be made available to public security departments upon their request. Article 15 stipulated that the ISPs were prohibited from making, duplicating, transmitting, and disseminating any of the information described in the above nine categories. Under Article 16, the ISPs also had to report to relevant government organization any user transmission of proscribed information. Article 19 stipulated that failure to comply could result either in the cancellation of the operating permit of delinquent ISPs or fines ranging from 100,000 to 1,000,000 yuan (US$12,500–125,000).[58] Obviously, the regime was hoping to turn the ISP business managers into state informants.

Once an ISP starts operating, the next critical issue is control over access to 'harmful' information. The regime has responded by placing restrictions on the number and type of users who can gain access to the internet, and from where, as well as in the content and types of websites these users can visit. The use and purchase of personal computers among urban families has grown 40 per cent each year since the late 1990s, but the majority of internet users still log on to the net from cybercafés (*wangba*) that are located throughout urban and rural municipalities.[59] Thus, regulating cybercafés has become the focus of Chinese control of popular access to both the internet and websites.

Many internet users prefer to access the net from a café computer, instead of from home computers. Logging on to the internet from a café is cheaper. Also, the cafés provide a sense of anonymity within a congenial social setting. When a computer accesses the internet, the system's IP number is transmitted to the website visited. When a computer in a café is used, it is the café computer's IP address, and not the user's, that is transmitted.[60]

The government, however, sought to remedy the security and informational problems associated with anonymity. A 2001 State Council 'Notice on Strengthening the Management of Internet Service Providers on Business Premises' warned that cybercafé anonymity facilitates user access to information harmful to society, such as information regarding sexual violence and superstition.[61] That same year, the Ministries of the Information Industry, Public Security, Culture, and the State Administration of Industry and Trade, jointly issued the first cybercafé-related regulation – 'Management Methods concerning Internet Service Providers on Business Premises'.

Compared to those issued later, the 2001 'Management Methods' were relatively moderate in terms of restricting access to the cafés and the degrees of punishment for violations of the regulations. The CCP leadership was extremely upset about youth's increasing exposure to pornography on the net. Many in the Party found this morally repugnant. Article 10 of the 2001 'Methods' required that any youth, aged 14 or under, could only enter the cafés and use the internet facilities in the company of an adult. Article 12 stipulated that the cafés could not be used to make, duplicate, search for, transmit, and disseminate information relating to the nine categories. Under Article 18, the violation of these management methods could result in a 'rectification' of the business, concerned.

The nature of the problem and the need for 'comprehensiveness' required a combined 'societal'–'jural' strategy. In 2001, the same Ministries and the State Administration of Industry and Trade jointly issued a notice to tighten up the 2001 'Methods' provisions for implementation and punishment. The 'Notice' reintroduced the importance of self-censorship or self-regulation of business activities for the purpose of providing better services for their consumers. Philip Sohmen speculated that this resort to self-censorship indicated the authorities' failure to achieve direct control as well as an important shift in strategy, from physically blocking and screening all foreign and domestic websites with objectionable materials to a policy of deterrence, shutting down businesses, levying heavy fines and imposing self-censorship.[62] However, the CCP has historically brought together different types of organizational control, and the new reference to 'self-censorship' is not that surprising as it converges with the mass-line practices associated with socio-legal strategies promoting the 'comprehensive management of public order'.

In May 2002, in order to promote self-censorship and self-discipline of internet-related businesses, the Internet Society of China was established.[63] This move also suggests reliance on the corporatist tradition of integrating mass associations with the Party's organizational agenda. Article 6 of the Charter of the Internet Society of China explicitly referred to the Association's need to promote sector covenants of self-discipline and to advance state information security. 'The Internet Society of China's Covenant of Self-Discipline' was subsequently released in December 2001.[64] The 'Covenant' basically converged with the content of the 2001 'The Management Methods Concerning Internet Service Providers on Businesses Premises'.

However, the emphasis on self-censorship was not enough to stem the tide of cybercafé 'crime'. Beijing undercover inspections of cybercafés in 2002 reported widespread problems. Of the sixty-one cafés, inspected, 47 per cent had been operating without proper licences. The majority did not have fire extinguishers on the premises. The report also concluded that youth were able to surf online pornography and play online games without much restriction.[65] In yet another report, internet addiction was closely correlated with an increasing rate in school dropouts in Jiangsu province.[66] This information,[67] as well as the political storm over the Beijing Lanjisu Cybercafé incident, where twenty-four young people were killed by fire in 2002, provided the regime with a politically convenient justification to tighten further the State's control over the cybercafés. In August 2002, a national 'Cybercafe Rectification Campaign'was launched with the State Council's approval of 'The Provisions for the Management of Internet Service Providing Businesses'.

The 'Provisions' focused on issues of fire safety and café internet activity. While sharing many similarities with the 2001 'Management Methods', the 2002 'Provisions' provided more detail to limit 'illegal' cybercafé activities and to ensure heavier penalties for offenders. These 'Provisions' reiterated the importance of self-censorship. At the same time, they attempted to fill in the blanks left by legislation, detailing prohibited internet activities, including the activities of making, downloading, copying, searching for, and disseminating the nine categories of information.

'Provision' Articles 14, 15, 17, and 18 stipulated new crimes, including the making and disseminating of computer viruses, unauthorized access to computer networks to damage their operations and storage of information, and online illegal activities such as online gambling. Article 23 once again required cybercafé owners to check and to record their clients' identification cards and their online activities. Under Article 19, owners were obliged to report to the public security departments any occurrence of prohibited internet activities on their premises. Under Article 21, youths, under the age of 14, were absolutely forbidden to use the cybercafé internet. Article 24 required the owners to implement a number of fire safety measures. Article 9 stipulated that the cafés must be at least 200 metres away from schools and residential buildings.

At the same time, the 'Provisions' used thirteen articles, for the first time, to provide rather detailed explanations on the enforcement and punishment of violations. The state functionaries who were directly involved in the enforcement of this regulation are prohibited from participating in internet service providing businesses, and fines are extensively used to punish the business owners and internet users who violate the 'Provisions'. For instance, fines of up to 15,000 yuan were stipulated for owners who either failed to check their users' identification cards and internet activity or who allowed under-aged users on to their premises. In serious cases, the relevant businesses could be shut down.[68]

Direct control over the internet, such as the blocking and screening of objectionable web content and flow of information, had proved inadequate. Policy and law moved inexorably in the direction of censorship and severe punishment. These strategies, for the control of internet use and the related flow of information, are having serious repercussions for the protection of human rights. These strategies contradict the 1996–7 'balance of values', based upon a comprehensive stipulation of law and the reduction of heavy punishments so as to insure a new rational correlation between the nature of the crime and punishment.

Moreover, the State is having some success in controlling the information flow from and to the international communities even in this era of globalization and information revolution. Also, state regulations have been crafted in such a way as to seriously trench on the human rights of ordinary citizens, concerning online expression and publication, the freedom of online access to information and the right to online privacy.

State censorship of website content and online publication

No doubt the authorities are extremely anxious about what they consider to be socially harmful information posted on the internet and websites. They recognize that the internet is a critically important popular medium, the particular development of which has a bearing on the life of the regime. The Party's strategy for control, however, has relied on the flexible creation of successive provisional state regulations.

In his analysis, Philip Sohmen concluded that

> the internet becomes a serious threat to government traditional control of mass media because of the internet's global spread and open nature. The internet brings access to much that the government has attempted to insulate China from, whether independent news, pornography, or anarchic discussions.[69]

The Chinese authorities have sought a monopoly over internet news censoring content concerning anti-government remarks, unofficial news, pornographic and 'superstitious' materials. Reportedly, there are 30,000 internet police engaged in the monitoring of the internet.[70] In 2003, the information concerning SARS came under the same interdiction. The strategy for control depended upon the application of 'provisional' state regulations. In 2000, the State Council and the Ministry of Information Industry jointly issued 'The Provisional Regulations for the Management of Website News Posting'. In the same year, the State Council issued 'The Methods for Managing Website Content Providers'.

Articles 6–8 of these 'Methods' stipulated that all internet and website content could only be produced and/or disseminated by internet service businesses and organizations that were holding operation permits obtained from the Post and Communication Management Departments under local governments. Article 15 reiterated the blackout of any of items concerning the nine categories of information, and Article 20 provided that related violations would result in severe punishment, including either fines or imprisonment according to the requirements of the CL97.[71]

Apparently, the only *bona fide* news was the official news reporting on government websites, such as those belonging to the Xinhua News Agency and the *Renmin Ribao* (People's Daily).[72] Article 7 of the 'Provisions' specified that internet organization could not cite the foreign news media. The approval of the State Council's News Media Office was required for any 'lawful' citation of foreign news. According to the CL97, offenders could be punished with a wide range of penalties including the loss of website operation permits and/or fines, and fixed term imprisonment. [73]

Publishers and internet news companies protested. They argued that these measures would burden the development of China's internet industries and reduce their competitiveness in the global market. The government's response was incredulous. The stricter regulation of net content would help prevent news abuse, reduce the violations of intellectual property rights, and serve to increase global competitiveness through the protection of patents on technology, communications, and publications. [74]

The government established a special one-billion yuan fund, dedicated to the enhanced development of the official news media.[75] The purported goal of this project and similar other projects concerning China's publishing houses is not only to control and sponsor the growth of the internet websites through the increase in flow of state-censored information, but also ostensibly to increase China's capacity for trade, e-commerce, and global competitiveness.[76]

In 2002, the State Press and Publication Administration Bureau and the Ministry of Information Industry moved to tighten further government controls, jointly issuing 'The Provisional Regulations on the Management of Online Publications'.[77] The 'Provisional Regulations' stipulated that all online publications must be inspected and approved by the local departments of the Ministry of Information Industry and the State Press and Publication Administration Bureau.

Domestic reformers have argued that these 'Provisional Regulations' contradict the PRC's 1982 State Constitution and its provisions guaranteeing the freedom of expression and correspondence. Wang Yi warned of this, and he contended that the 'Provisional Regulations' used the term, 'publications' in such a sweeping way that almost all online materials and publications posted under jurisdiction of the 'Provisional Regulations' could be placed in jeopardy. The use of vague and improperly defined legal terms such as 'publications' exemplifies the government's approach to internet reporting on increasingly complicated social issues and provides the authorities with the requisite flexibility to manage unanticipated situations in internet development.[78] In effect, this constitutes a politically inspired lack of clarity that promotes flexibility at the expense of the comprehensive stipulation of clearly defined law.

The growth of websites and popular internet use has facilitated the increased availability of pornographic materials in Chinese popular culture. Former President Jiang Zemin condemned the internet's spread of 'socially detestable phenomena' on the internet.[79] The Party had long abominated pornography as a sign of moral degeneration, and it believes that pornography promotes obscenity, crime, and violence, even murder. And it is of course the political concern for the protection of Chinese morality and social stability that explains the CCP's adoption of the 'combined rules of law and virtue'.

Chinese strategies for eliminating internet pornography range from moral and economic persuasion to criminal law punishment. The government believes that website pornography can often be traced to overseas internet providers. Large long distance phone bills, therefore, attract the attention of those monitoring internet content. The authorities warned their citizens of the 'moral and economic peril' in visiting such sites. Not only does such antisocial behaviour result in immoral social interaction, but the government also points to the wasted resources that constitute a drag on the GDP. [80]

While Canada and the United States have focused on criminalizing the production and possession of child pornography, China has taken a broad-gauged approach that covers all the material that the government thinks is pornographic. According to CL97 Articles 363–67, the production, duplication, publication, selling, and dissemination of such materials could be punished with life imprisonment. Indeed, such heavy punishment has been used in recent years.

There is, for example, the case of Bu Xinghua. A mother wrote to her Municipal Party Committee complaining of pornography's deleterious effects on her son, who had been secretly watching laser disks. As the Deputy General Manager of Suzhou Baodie – the company that made the disks – Bu was sentenced to seventeen years in prison for the creation and dissemination of 'spiritual poison'.[81] This was an extraordinary extension of second-hand criminal liability, and, in such cases, 'the punishment must fit the crime' is dishonoured in concept and practice.

The escalating rhetoric concerning the need to establish a 'rule of virtue' originated in part with the political and legal campaign against the FLG. The Party has sought to outlaw websites with religious and politically sensitive content. 'Heretical cults', 'illegal' political groups, and internet dissidents have all attracted the special attention of the internet monitors. The suppression of related websites has been pursued through various types of regulations, surveillance, the confiscation of equipment, the use of informants, and, in serious cases, criminal punishment.[82]

Using the same techniques, used by the hackers and dissidents, government officials have even logged online to criticize dissidents on both the official news and BBS sites.[83] They have also acted to shut down dissident websites in China, using ICMT packet flooding.[84] Whenever they have discovered suspect foreign websites with objectionable materials, the officials have blocked these websites. However, due to the lack of clear and consistent definition of 'objectionable material', such blocking is often uneven, if not quixotic.[85]

The story of the government's control of the internet suggests that in this economically important and politically sensitive sphere of activity, there is a low tolerance for new crime. The protection of individual human rights is for the most part lost in the flurry of provisional regulation that is designed to insure appropriately moral public order. The Party can claim to act in the name of protecting society from unacceptably immoral behaviour, but its great interest in social stability is transparently self-interested. Finally, the 'flexibility' of the *zhengfa* system has been enlisted in this moral struggle. There has been a profligate reliance on provisional regulation that conflicts with reform attempts to insure clear and predictable law, based upon comprehensive stipulation.

Conclusion

In the new sphere of cyber-crime, there is a definite imbalance of public order in relation to the protection of human rights. In the absence of clear law, provisional state regulation has proliferated, and this proliferation is eroding the 1996–7 principles of legality. In line with a 'societal' tradition that politically relies on 'flexibility', the legal control of cyber-crime was combined with the mass-line, socio-jural approach to the 'comprehensive management of public order'.

While the State Council and its ministries generated a plethora of provisional regulation that threatened offenders with criminal law sanctions, internet users, and business owners were made legally responsible for self-censorship. In effect, the ISPs were required to play the role of informant at the expense of online privacy, and the freedom of online expression and publication has been routinely violated. At the same time, internet dissidents were selectively accused and convicted for 'subverting state power', and this suggests that in Chinese cyber-space, 'political crime' exists despite the formal elimination of the criminal law's special provisions on 'counterrevolutionary' crime in 1997.

While there has been an extended development of provisional state regulation that only tentatively connects with stipulated criminal law, serious problems of enforcement have come to light. The problem of enforcement originates to some degree in enhanced bureaucratic politics and the confusion of overlapping state jurisdictions. The State Council and its Ministries of Culture, Information Industry, Public Security, Post and Communication, and the State Administration of Industry and Trade have all been involved in the proliferation of provisional administrative regulation.[86] This overlapping of jurisdictions has encouraged bureaucratic infighting over regulatory power in a new area where technology is affecting a wide range of government functions.[87]

Nina Hachigian has reviewed the problem of overlap and regulatory inconsistency and its cost to the making of a rule of law in China:

> These intra-governmental squabbles are producing a growing thicket of regulations.... The substantial body of laws that has resulted – many of which are either never enforced, enforced selectively, or actually in conflict with one another – is inconsistent with China's stated desire to promote the rule of law and creates a nebulous legal environment that scares off investors. But the uncoordinated rush to regulation does serve the government's control agenda: the resulting rules create the maximum possible scope of official authority.[88]

Philip Sohmen also commented on the problem of enforcement:

> [This is] because it is impossible to censor the internet in a comprehensive manner. The quantity of information passing over it is vast – monitoring communication through e-mail, instant messaging, and the other channels that the internet enables is in itself an enormous and ever-expanding task. Moreover, rapid technological development, combined with the ingenuity of hackers, means that methods of circumventing controls are produced as quickly as officials can devise them.[89]

At the same time, the difficulties of enforcement increasingly relate to the complex impact of 'internationalization' on China. China is becoming increasingly more susceptible to the influence of international communities. For example, during the 2001 Association of Petroleum Exporting Countries (APEC) conference in Shanghai, the 'great firewall' was lifted to allow foreign conference participants as well as Chinese internet users access to the *Los Angeles Times*, the *Washington Post*, the *New York Times*, the *Voice of America*, and *USA Today*.[90] China's induction into the WTO may further complicate the government's efforts to block foreign internet influence. Already, the WTO has lobbied for the removal of censorship from its websites, and those of other international organizations. The stated purpose for this is the spread of ideas and economic change, including the ways in which China may become more competitive in the global economy.[91]

Although the law and regulations have not been enforced across the board, the regime's control over internet use is extraordinarily tight. Internet use may not bring immediate drastic political change in China. But, its rapid development has already had profound effects on other aspects of Chinese society. As a result of the recent proliferation of internet use, a new class of criminal liabilities in cyberspace has emerged, including crimes concerning computer network security, using computer networks to carry out undermining of financial order, and crimes of producing and disseminating information harmful to national security and social order, and morality, and crimes concerning online pornographic materials. Although recognizing the internet's potential to fillip social and economic development, China's Party-State has attempted a blanket control over internet use. Tight internet control has also been justified on the basis of maintaining Chinese culture and morality and elimination of 'unhealthy' Western influence, and the political focus on immorality informs the leadership interest in combining the rules of law and virtue.

Control over gateways and network security was initially asserted through new provisional state regulations and their weak and tangential reference to criminal law. Then control was asserted over website access. In this process two significant problems emerged. In the first place, many critical terms in the relevant legislation had been left undefined. This created significant opportunities for 'flexibility'. Extended interpretation of law and provisional administrative regulations challenged 'no crime, without law and no punishment without law'. Second, the related management of unanticipated social and political crisis neglected the new emphasis on the protection of human rights.

In drafting the CL97, the NPC failed to stipulate clearly the new elements of cyber-crime, and the State Council and its Ministries effectively co-opted the process of comprehensive stipulation through extended interpretation and the often premature issuance of provisional, and sometimes inconsistent, or repetitive regulation. In effect, in order to pursue its own political agenda the regime has conveniently tolerated weak legislation.

For many reform scholars and jurists, the 1996–7 confirmation of the 'balance of values' was, to date, the most important achievement of Chinese criminal justice reform. The balancing of public order and human rights protection was to reflect the new CL97 principles of equality before the law, the punishment must fit the crime and no crime, without law. The new balance of values in law was to be operationalized on the basis of comprehensive stipulation. The State's post-1996–7 approach to new cyber-crime has regularly sacrificed human rights protection to the politicized priorities of national security, social order and Chinese morality, and these priorities have been encouraged on the basis of unqualified 'flexibility' rather than on the basis of the clear and comprehensive stipulation of the law.

6 Squaring the circles of criminal justice reform?

In March 1997, Xiao Yang, the Minister of Justice, commented on the progressive nature of China's newly revised criminal law. Reviewing the past seventeen years since the passage of the CL79 he noted: '... the political, economic and social life of China and people's ideas and concepts have changed with each passing day. In the new era, new crimes which were never seen before have cropped up....'[1] This observation concerning the depth and rate of change might apply to an even greater degree to the post-1996–7 period of criminal justice reform.

The notion of balancing public order and human rights protection is complex, and it is not easily accomplished within the China's particular political-legal, or *zhengfa* system. Large bureaucracies jealously cling to 'customary practices'; they do not easily change course to embrace new ideas, especially if these ideas are unfamiliar and explicitly contrary to well-established local practice. The sheer magnitude of Chinese criminal justice operations and the lack of well-trained and well-disposed personnel impose limitations on change.

One must also take into account the basic political fact that change is hard. Mao Zedong wanted great change, but he never found it easy to master change. In terms of Mao's formal thinking to push forward there must be a complex synthesis of qualitative and quantitative change. Mao's dialectics, in fact, recommended two propositions, namely that qualitative change can lead to quantitative change and that quantitative change can result in qualitative change. To put this in terms of contemporary legal reform one might argue that the 1996–7 reform represented an extraordinary qualitative change that has yet to be consolidated in the quantitative dimensions of praxis.[2]

According to State Council reporting in the year, 2003, public security agencies handled 2.341 million criminal cases relating to gang-related crimes, homicide, robbery, rape, kidnapping, and other serious violent crimes. Of this total, 57,505 cases related to activity jeopardizing public security; 184,018 cases involved the violation of the personal and democratic rights of citizens; and 278,969 cases involved property crime. In the newly recognized area of 'extended detention', the cases involved

25,736 people, and cases of illegal detention numbered 259. There were only 29 cases involving illegal search, 52 cases concerning confession under torture, and 32 relating to the abuse of prisoners, or detainees.[3] While the numbers for the categories of extended detention down through the abuse of prisoners seem inconsequential, they represent the beginnings of an important change in judicial justice or procedural practice.[4]

Is the law now sufficiently comprehensive to deal with proliferating new crime? How many more 'new crimes' have emerged since the great revision of 1996–7? Has the criminal justice strategy that informs and supports this reform yielded important results? The competing detail and trends, as described in the foregoing chapters, suggest that the post-1996–7 ledger of criminal justice reform has produced mixed results. Despite the good intentions of 1996–7 to create a modern criminal justice system, subsequent events have revealed that the related codification of the criminal and criminal procedural laws was not nearly as comprehensive as some reformers had thought at the time. Moreover, after the reform of 1996–7, the criminal justice system had little choice but to accept a mixed strategy of less than systematic stipulation and 'flexibility'. Criminal procedure has made some progress, but the criminal procedural law, itself, still has a long way to go to achieve equality with the criminal law.

Within such an enormously complex transitional context one might even argue that success is harder to explain than failure. In the first place, there have been extraordinary reform successes as, for example, in the elimination of 'custody and investigation' and 'custody and repatriation'. Such success may yet lead to a major procedural reform of the system of administrative detention. Jurists have to negotiate from within the changing parameters of the *zhengfa* system, but, with the right kind of political connections, they have sometimes made a great difference at the right time and in the right place.

Second, while the direction of current major reform to criminal procedural law is becoming increasingly clear, the practical shift from an inquisitorial to an adversarial court process involves an uphill battle to modify what the chief of the SPC called 'customary practices'. This shift is a work in progress that includes the reduction of more familiar principles of the Continental Tradition in favour of adaptation to an unfamiliar and sometimes ideologically suspect US system of due process.

Third, there has been extraordinary failure such as in the FLG case where extremes of the Party's *zhengfa* system were re-asserted so as to achieve state-enforced morality based upon 'flexibility'. Despite the promise of 1996–7, in some cases, analogy survived the new principle of legality. 'Flexibility' has proven to be multifaceted, but it is especially evident in the frequent resort to 'extended judicial interpretation'. This trend was all too apparent in the new strategy to deal with fast developing 'pure computer crime' and 'computer-related conventional crime'.

Also, in order to achieve 'flexibility', the legal aspect of internet control permitted CL97 dependence upon provisional state regulation.

In the context of the 1996–7 reform, the jurists were able to persuade the Party to adopt new principles and procedures for the sake of China's 'good image' and to better achieve the modern goals of domestic stability and economic development through reform and the open door. Few could have predicted the impact of the 'Falungong problem'. Responding to what it regarded as a clear threat to the 'socialist' regime, the Party responded with an aggravated fixation on public order, democratic centralism, and the top-down manipulation of the 'comprehensive management of public order' at the expense of rule-of-law making. The new 1996–7 dimensions of 'jural development' still had to deal with the 'societal' dimensions of the *zhengfa* system.

The study of the success and failure of the post-1996–7 strategy for criminal justice reform has to be interdisciplinary and multifaceted. It must cover the qualified and deliberate adaptation to and the sponsorship of unfamiliar international norms and new jurisprudence as the basis for the law's response to new crime. It also involves the changing of the structural relations within the *zhengfa* system. While the conventional relations between the various actors have had some affect on the implementation of new procedure, the CPL96 and CL97 may have helped to precipitate new patterns of interaction between the SPC, SPP, and the Ministry of Public Security. Each of these agencies have had to take into account new law that affects their respective functional responsibilities. Also, each has an equal power to interpret the law, and this often encouraged a pattern of inter-agency competition that requires a new mechanism of final arbitration. Some would argue that such arbitration should be based upon a more routine legislative interpretation of the law.

The partial adaptation to the adversarial rather than the inquisitorial trial format, as featured in the CPL96, is likely to have the greatest impact on the operations of Public Security. Sometimes Public Security has been able to resist the application of reform principles, and sometimes not. In order to placate the Ministry of Public Security, for example, the NPC extended the period of custody in return for the Ministry's acquiescence in the elimination of 'custody for investigation'.

There is an uneven consciousness within the different bureaucratic parts of the justice system as to the contents of rights and the related enforcement of the law. As Chen Xingliang, Deputy Director, Law School, Beijing University, has explained, when mapping potential support for adaptation to the international standards of judicial justice, there is a very rough spectrum of support wherein the jurists and the Ministry of Justice are most advanced in the advocacy of human rights and procedural reform and are more likely to make common cause.

Procuratorial organization, on the other hand, is more hesitant, but it is, at least, partially interested in the introduction and application of reform principles, and there are increasing examples of SPC–SPP cooperation in matters concerning judicial interpretation. Lastly, public security organization is more often than not recalcitrant, as it occupies the conservative end of this political spectrum. At this end of the spectrum, there is the traditional exclusive emphasis on public order. Perhaps, it is not uncommon in many jurisdictions for the police to complain about the excessive resort to due process to protect the rights of the accused seemingly at the expense of meritorious police efforts to prove guilt and to insure public order through the certain punishment of the guilty.

In China, Public Security has traditionally regarded the criminal law as a 'weapon' to be used decisively and without qualification against the 'waves' of criminal behaviour. Chen Xingliang has pointed out that the inter-agency politics over the course of reform have recently become more problematic in that the Minister of Public Security is a Politbureau member, and this gives him precedence over the Presidents of both the SPC and SPP. Protocol requires that the Presidents of the SPC and SPP report to the Minister.[5]

Chen Xingliang argues that real reform needs popular support and the right political conditions. He cited, by way of example, the recent case of Liu Yong, who was a kingpin in a case regarding 'organized crime with a triad nature'. Advocates for procedural justice such as those at the Peking University's Law School vigorously argued that procedural justice is especially necessary in cases involving the death penalty. However, the application of procedural justice in Liu's case was engulfed in political sensationalism when a group of disgruntled public security officers revealed that the accused had been tortured.

Liu's forced confession immediately raised jurist concerns over the application of reform principles and the integrity of the trial of first instance that had resulted in a death sentence. In light of new information concerning illegally acquired evidence, the accused, in the trial of second instance, was spared immediate execution and given a sentence, peculiar to the Chinese system, namely, the death penalty with a two-year reprieve. The Peking University Law School was then inundated with e-mails from irate citizens who condemned the School's meddling scholars for having perverted the natural course of justice at the second trial.

An unassuaged public demanded an immediate death penalty. Such demands are still taken seriously in China and jurists will cite the principle, 'if you do not execute, you will not satisfy the people's anger' (*busha, buzu yi ping minfen*).[6] The public uproar was so strident that, in a rare and controversial move, the SPC, in December 2003, forced an extraordinary third trial under its own jurisdiction. The SPC reinstated the original death sentence that was immediately carried out. This third exercise contradicted the stipulation in Article 10 of the CPL96, which designated the determination of the trial of second instance as final. For some frustrated jurists, the whole affair suggested that a 'distorted image of the rule of law' (*fazhi luanxiang*) had been created in China.[7]

The above case, notwithstanding, the SPC, as compared to the SPP, is often, but not always, more likely to narrow the scope of criminal liability and to restrict the use of heavy penalties in criminal law. Chapter 4 on 'organized crime' provided one of the most significant examples of such an inter-agency split. The definition of 'organized crime with a triad nature' in the SPC's interpretation required a controversial third constitutive element of such 'crime', involving the identification of complicit state functionaries. The SPP was more eager to cast the criminal law's net wide so as to identify and prosecute more criminals. The SPC's extra functionary requirement element was regarded as a drag on the effective criminal law approach to public order. SPP believed that the SPC was making it harder to catch the criminals. The SPC and SPP were at loggerheads. In a very rare move, they appealed to the NPCSC to provide one last interpretation that would settle the issue. The law-and-order instincts of the NPCSC prevailed as its interpretation dropped the element of state functionary identification as prerequisite to the establishing of criminal liability.

The SPC lost yet another engagement with the NPCSC as the latter, in the face of public opinion, has often preferred to expand the terms of reference of 'criminal liability'. In its provisions criminalizing the 'misappropriation' of public funds, CL97 had not provided sufficient clarification on the issue of designated purpose. Crime relating to the diversion of public funds, as malfeasance, needed explanation as to the specific purpose underlying the alleged illegal diversion of public funding. SPC interpretation addressed this gap in the law by specifically relating the act of misappropriation to the diversion of state funds by individual functionaries for their own personal use. The NPCSC, however, countermanded the Court's narrow interpretation so as to include not only the diversion of funding for self-aggrandizement, but also the unauthorized bureaucratic diversion of funding from one public purpose to another.[8]

The formation of reform alliances seems opportunistic, depending on the nature of the issue, and the prevailing politics at the time. Some reformers have suggested, however, that the rising pattern of conflicted interpretations requires regular reference to the NPCSC for legislative interpretation and that such a mechanism, as compared, for example, with amendment to the CL97, is a quick and efficient means for dealing with the proliferation of new crime within society.[9]

Competing strategies for criminal justice reform

The 1996–7 strategy for criminal justice called for the correction of wide-spread 'customary practices' in the justice system, that were more or less exclusively predicated in the unqualified importance of public order. The attempts to strike a balance between public order and the protection of human rights has, in fact, often been influenced by competing strategies for the rough and ready implementation of criminal justice reform so as to protect society from rapidly developing new crime.

At times, in the name of a comprehensive management approach to rising crime rates, the Party has asserted the vital importance of public order, and the Party accordingly has waged 'strike hard' and 'crime prevention' campaigns that draw on updated principles of mass-line politics and organization. 'Prevention' tends generally to highlight 'social countermeasures'; for example, one enthusiastic jurist argued that the campaign against 'organized crime' would require extensive social measures that would, at the macro-level, draw on the positive aspects of democracy, market reform, moral reconstruction, and the comprehensive management of public order.[10]

Such campaigning is, nevertheless, an obviously highly politicized exercise that often challenges the deliberate and more sedate and impersonal operation of the 'rule of law'. The law, despite its 'supreme authority' has sometimes been placed within the wider political framework of the 'comprehensive management of public order'. In the launching of the Spring 2001 campaign to 'strike hard' against the harmful rise in crimes concerning explosion, homicide, robbery, kidnapping, and poisoning, Jiang Zemin's 'three represents' were enlisted in a mass campaign 'giving equal emphasis on two fronts and doing well in both'. The latter called on Party and government cadres to 'correctly handle the relationship between reform, development, and stability, and to keep a firm grasp on, and do a good job in, public order'.[11]

In such a comprehensive public order context of mobilization and education, the law is forced closer to the red-hot core of Chinese politics. Once culture and morality are heavily politicized, the political leadership, in its anxiety over social stability and declining morality, is likely to care less about the 'balance of values'. The protection of human rights receives much less precedence than public order, and the limits of stipulated punishment are sometimes exceeded in the strike-hard emphasis on severe punishment.[12] The primacy of public order is even reflected in reform argument that often puts a spin on human rights protection as a means to support social stability and public order.

The following *Liaowang* 16 April 2001 editorial commentary reiterates Jiang Zemin's 26 December 2000 comment on the vital political importance of 'public feelings'. It almost exclusively highlights the importance of public order based upon 'comprehensive management' and the law's capacity for severe and swift punishment:

> Doing a good job in public order is a major social issue, and a major political issue as well. It has a bearing on the fundamental interests of the masses of the people, the prolonged political stability of the state, the governing status of our party, and the implementation of our party's basic line. If our public order is poor, the people's lives and

property cannot be guaranteed. This will affect not only the image of the party and the government in the people's eyes but also the overall interests of reform, development and stability.[13]

For those interested in the development of the 'rule of law' in China, the above comment is blunt, if not confused. The law is 'supreme'. It cannot brook any one's interference, and yet the law must still accommodate 'public feeling'. As a 'weapon' to fight crime, the law must subordinate itself to Party-led coordination within the comprehensive dimensions of the updated mass-line approach to rising crime. One will not, for example, find in the following viewpoint even a *pro forma* reference to the impersonal application of principles of legality under the 'supremacy of law'. Instead there is sonorous reference to a single imperative, emphasizing political mobilization and education so as 'to exterminate evil':

> It is necessary to exterminate evil thoroughly, and remove the cause of future trouble. It is necessary to persist in integrating special organs with the mass line; extensively conduct social mobilization, fully mobilize the masses of the people, encourage them to join in the 'strike hard' campaign, develop a social atmosphere in which the criminals 'are chased after by all,' as well as powerful momentum, so that the criminals are stricken to death while the masses of the people can hold their heads high.[14]

One might well wonder how the law, as it is predicated in a 'scientific' treatment of the facts and legality, can cope with 'stern' 'vigilante' activity or 'sorting out' by masses who hold their heads high. The 2001 'strike hard' campaign in Jinan city offers some perspective on this problem:

> Jinan city recently held a gathering for lenient and stern treatment in the struggle to 'strike hard' and sort things out. The gathering publicly dealt with 20 suspects involved in 112 cases; 10 of these people were dealt with sternly according to law for going head-on (*ding feng*) in committing crime, while the other 10 were dealt with leniently and not held accountable because they had turned themselves in and made a clean breast of things.[15]

Over the two years of this 'strike hard' campaigning, state officials from the Minister of Justice on down referred to the importance of psychologically compelling momentum so as to break the back of criminal activity. 'Accuracy' was mentioned, but it seemed as if it were an afterthought. The masses had to be aroused to directly participate in strike hard campaigning. A close insistence on the letter of the law might conceivably dampen the masses' enthusiasm, and yet the campaigning is somehow to respect a fair understanding of criminal activity. CPL97 Article 2 affirms that the 'aim' of procedural justice is 'to ensure accurate and timely ascertainment of facts about crimes' (*baozheng zhunque, ji shide chaming fanzui shishi*).[16]

CPL96 Article 6 – that is the same one that endorses 'equality before the law' – explicitly requires 'reliance' on the masses. It reads: 'In conducting criminal proceedings, the People's Courts, the People's Procuratorates, and the public security organs *must rely on the masses*, base themselves on facts and take law as the criterion. The law applies equally to all citizens and no privilege whatsoever is permissible before the law.'[17]

Perhaps it was pure coincidence that the 20 Jinan City suspects divided so evenly into two neat groups of 10. Certainly, it is worth arguing whether the highly charged political dynamics of such a gathering is likely to accommodate a sober consideration of the finer points of judicial justice. Awe-inspiring momentum in the heat of struggle does not square particularly well with the evidentiary rules of pedestrian procedural justice, as they are rooted in CPL96 reference to 'using facts as the basis and the law as the yardstick'.[18] Indeed one might well ask whether, in this case, 'Chinese characteristics' square with the core meaning of Randall Peerenboom's 'thin' let alone 'thick' 'rule of law'.

The 'comprehensive management of public order' presumes extraordinary social involvement in dealing with the proliferation of deviant behaviour, and it has two big functions. It supports 'strike hard' campaigns, but it also focuses on prevention, including not only education to prevent crime but also applied social policy to address the conditions that give rise to crime through a coordinated community approach that draws together state and social organization.

Feng Shuliang Professor and former Deputy Director of the Institute for Crime Prevention at the Ministry of Justice explains the contemporary mass-line dynamic as it represents the continuation of 'Mao's Mass Line':

> China's experience has proved that it is necessary to rely on social forces to combat crime in a systematic way. Preventive measures should form a network in all areas, ranging from a community to a city to a country. Crime prevention is a system consisting of interrelated social forces. The basic structure of such a system includes prevention by the mass movement, by professionals, and by technical measures. The targets of prevention are the general population, major types of crimes, and special populations at high crime risk. Prevention should be implemented in social institutions and organizations such as family, schools, community, and work units.[19]

Originally, the mass line was formally conceptualized as a two-way process, whereby the masses, under the Party's 'proper leadership', were engaged in the creation and implementation of policy in a top-to-bottom and bottom-to-top dynamic. In theory, the mass line offered a new and even rational empirical solution to China's specific problems.

In coping with such an enormous landmass and population, governance and law was expected to respect the local differences of time and space, hence the mass-line slogan, 'suit measures according to local conditions' (*yin di zhiyi*). It was this same reasoning that originally justified the jurisprudential principle of 'flexibility'. On one level, such reasoning made perfect sense. Law would eventually emerge out of policy practice and social experiment. The 'law' would, itself, 'squat at key points'. Local practical experimentation with regulations in new areas of criminal activity could inform subsequent national legislation that would 'scientifically' benefit from related local trials. In the crafting of the 4 September 1991 Law on the Protection of Minors, for example, the NPC drafters drew on the practical experience related to the Shanghai municipal regulations concerning the protection of youth.

To take from Chapter 3 yet another example of bottom-to-top mass-line dynamics and the creation of national law, in February 2000, the Liaoning Provincial Court, Public Security Office, Office of the Committee for Comprehensive Management of Public Order and the provincial branch of the Women's Federation created regulations which included the definition of 'domestic violence'. The subsequent revision to the Marriage Law criminalized domestic violence, and the SPC, in the second part of its interpretation of the Marriage Law, dated 24 December 2001, already had a benchmark in the widely accepted detail of provincial experience.

On the other hand, the recent reform period has witnessed the spread of 'local protectionism'. This phenomenon was different from 'localization' in that it ignored and sometimes even actively resisted the implementation of the new norms and procedures embedded in national legislation. It was the mass line having gone astray. When he was President of the SPC, Xiao Yang acknowledged that protectionism by lower courts had resulted in 'a chronic lack of enforcement of verdicts' as well as 'a rise in violence against the police'.[20]

Also, 'local protectionism' has, at times, spurred the law's commodification at the expense of its uniform and just application. Professor Dan Wei of the SPP Research Institute of Procuratorial Theory spent seven years investigating human trafficking in China's southern provinces. Dan has suggested that local government was increasingly interested in levying fines and to lesser extent imposing administrative detention as compared to correctly and consistently imposing criminal law punishment on the organizers of human trafficking.[21]

It seems that the fines became more important than the deterrence as the functioning of the criminal law was subordinated to the pressing requirements of local budgets. This was the case despite the strong emphasis at the centre on severe punishment for such 'evil' crimes. This 'localism', was fanned in the local scramble for resources and in the increasingly expanding discretion of local judges. Moreover, from place to place there was an extraordinary range of fines for the exact same categories of crime. All of this suggested how 'local protectionism' was misappropriating the principle, 'act according to local conditions'. The latter had always formally required that local regulation and organization was to comply with central policy and law.

One could argue that (a) the mass line is the natural ally of 'flexibility', and that (b) the mass line wants the law to conform to its 'societal' organizational and political priorities. These assumptions, however, militate against the supremacy of law. The latter had been justified as it was assumed that the Party would 'respect the law as the mature outcome of its own policy response to the will of the masses'.[22] Law, in the Chinese context, may well have been developed and generalized on the basis of local practice, but the new 'rule of law' theory assumed that once law is legislated, it must inform state regulation and judicial and administrative interpretation. In battling new crime, however, the State has often moved ahead of the law, proliferating provisional administrative regulations without the benefit of the clear definition of basic concepts in law.

The 1996–7 strategy for criminal justice reform prematurely presumed that 'flexibility' could be easily restricted in accordance with the modern requirements of rational legal development. Too much was made of analogy as the single mode of 'flexibility'. And there was subsequently a lack of clear focus on the diverse range of factors that constitute 'flexibility'. Post-1996–7 practice has certainly revealed that 'flexibility' involves more than just subscription to analogy.

Since 1997, the SPC and SPP have issued more than eighty judicial interpretations.[23] 'Flexibility' was in fact structurally built into the judicial and legislative interpretation of law that was sometimes extended to the point where interpretation substituted itself for law and became a necessary practical component of codification. The *zhengfa* system underwrote such flexibility in its deliberate rejection of the Western notion of the 'separation of powers'. This system has continuously supported a more extensive and popular-oriented interpretation of the law by an unusual range of different and increasingly competing agencies.

'Flexibility' versus 'comprehensive stipulation'?

The 1996–7 strategy that centred on comprehensive stipulation assumed that for society and the economy to get the most out of the rule of law, the law had to provide clarity and predictability that could serve as the new functional basis for stability and the mediation between, and adjustment of, competing 'newly emerging' interests in China's increasingly competitive context. In 1996–7, criminal justice reform may have over invested in the potential of a comprehensive stipulation of law that could anticipate changing criminal activity in a transitional societal and economic context. The need for flexibility was expected to go down with the final creation of a complete set of laws and increasing recognition of the supremacy of law. All manner of competing state regulation would then be guided by a consistent reference to clear standards that had been pre-established in stipulated law.

However, significant problems arose when China's 'relatively complete' legal system of 1996–7 ran up against the rapid metamorphosis of criminal liability. Stipulation could not keep up with new crime. In this difficult context, flexible interpretation of law by several agencies, such as the SPC, SPP, NPCSC, State Council, Ministries of Civil Affairs and Public Security, etc., seemed necessary to stopgap the lack of clear definition in national legislation.

The increased use of judicial and legislative interpretation precipitated jurist debate over the relation between NPC legislation and the many administrative agencies involved in the law's interpretation. Some jurists argued that the extensive use of judicial interpretation is a positive and legitimate feature of China's criminal justice system.[24] Some argued that, in effect, there is both good and bad flexibility. The CL97 did not abolish flexibility, it tried to abolish analogy. Not only did analogy come back but other forms of 'flexibility' assumed growing practical importance.

The subscription to 'no crime, without a law' and 'no punishment with a law' was important in principle, but it did not always offer immediate solution to pressing societal and economic developments. As the law, itself, could not foresee all circumstances, interpretation apparently had no choice but to step in and serve as a secondary form of criminal codification. At times extended interpretations trenched on the exclusive legislative powers of the NPC, but what if the SPC, as was the case with 'rape in marriage', circulates immediately needed interpretation that acts to resolve a human rights dilemma? Particularly, in light of the persisting difficulties of the *zhengfa* system and its exclusive focus on public order should any opportunity for progress be seized? Does the substance of human rights protection require an activist state that is ready to deploy flexibility in a good cause?

Even from within the Byzantine labyrinth of bureaucratic politics, jurists have on occasion found influential allies within the Party, itself, and within the bureaucracies of state justice so as to push the envelope of criminal procedural reform. Indeed, the rule-of-law making process in China is a very explicit and complicated political process, but it is important to discern what political assumptions are at work at any given time.

'Chinese characteristics' might be incorporated within a rational synthesis that brings together 'internationalization' and 'localization'. On the other hand, an inspired definition of these 'characteristics' could just as easily be conscripted within a conservative morality that prefers the moral certainties of the old *zhengfa* system. As was discussed in Chapter 3, reform jurists were able to promote the activist state's intervention within the family to protect the rights of individual family members. On the other hand, as was described in Chapter 2, the jurists were unable to debate the legal treatment of FLG members. In the latter case, the state politically co-opted the SPC and readily deployed the *zhengfa* system's principle of flexibility to deal arbitrarily with the FLG.

And yet one can also point to occasions when the jurists successfully deployed the synthesis of 'internationalization' and 'localization' to create a successful political argument for criminal justice reform that seemingly promotes the cause of domestic stability and economic reform. In the first place, the law, in its attempts to guarantee rights and interests of the people, is to help to promote social stability and the 'good image' of the Party and government among the people in the context of transition and proliferating crime.

Second, the local adaptation to international human rights norms helps to promote China's 'good image' abroad. For the reformers, the latter is a politically convenient matter of the Party and the state self-consciously identifying with modernity and civilization. Ostensibly, the rule of law, as it counts on procedural justice and the protection of rights, constitutes a new rationality that is important to China's modern development. Hence Song Yinghui, in his original justification for the CPL97, draws on the 'balance of values' and the synthesis of 'internationalization' and 'localization':

> The truth of the matter is that due process, crime control and human rights protection are values pursued in the criminal procedure of all countries. They are also aspects of the frequent conflict of interests throughout the criminal procedure. Whether or not to recognize the principle of non-self-incrimination and the consequent right to remain silent is a concentrated expression of the value orientation in choosing between these conflicting interests in a country's criminal procedure.[25]

The reformers in the post-1996–7 era have sometimes made headway. As has been discussed 'custody and investigation' was eliminated, but at some cost to the reform of the rules of arrest and detention. More recently, 'custody and repatriation' was replaced by 'The Measures for Assisting and Managing Urban Vagrants and Beggars with No Means of Livelihood'. Compulsory detention and return of vagrants to their place of origin has been replaced by a new voluntary programme whereby the Ministry of Civil Affairs is to provide temporary housing for the homeless.

In 2003, the SPC, the SPP, and the Ministry of Public Security issued a joint circular, 'Notice on the Strict Enforcement of the Criminal Procedure Law and on the Conscientious Prevention and Correction of Extended Detention'. Reformers are even now discussing legislation to provide compensation to the victims of extended administrative detention. Moreover, the latest State Council report on China's human rights achievements has included a new section on the judicial guarantee of human rights. According to this report, in 2003, in what was the 'most extensive' and 'biggest' operation in the guaranteeing of human rights, 25,736 individual cases relating to the illegal extension of detention were corrected.[26]

However, the qualitative analytical detail in the previous chapters suggests that the 1996–7 strategy for criminal justice reform was predicated in a number of overly optimistic assumptions. At the time of the drafting of the CPL97 and CL96, reformers took to heart Deng Xiaoping's instruction that China needed a complete set of laws. There was a feeling that as the reform process deepened the CL79 and CPL79 were increasingly outstripped by events. As it turns out, however, the CPL96 and CL97 have also been outstripped by events. In 1996–7, who could have predicted the advent of SARS, the proliferation of cyber-crime, and the Party's nationwide campaign against the FLG.

In hindsight, it would seem that the reform jurists overestimated the possibility of the comprehensive stipulation of the law to deal with the development of prospective new crime within China's rapidly developing socio-economic context. Also, it could be argued that not only is comprehensive stipulation impossible in such a fast-changing environment, but the reduction of the flexibility that had characterized the *zhengfa* system was based too exclusively on the single issue of analogy.

The 1996–7 strategy did not do a good job in anticipating the range of future new crime. Furthermore, the NPC, itself, has been conflicted about changes in China's social environment. The spread of new criminal activity outpaced the NPC's legislative agenda. In fast-developing areas relating for example to cyberspace, there was a political rush to deal with major new categories of computer-related crime. State ministries issued a range of new regulations so as to regain the commanding heights of public order, but they did so without the benefit of pre-established NPC law and without the law's clear definition of key constructs that captured the essential contents of new crime.

The tension between post-1996–7 comprehensive stipulation and flexibility, as it is reflected in a wide-gauged process of judicial and legislative interpretation of the law, is well illustrated in the CCP's legal strategy to arrest the frightening spread of SARS in the Spring of 2003. In this instructive case, the government was quite prepared, at least in the short term, to tolerate a marked imbalance of public order with human rights protection.

Law, politics, and SARS

One of China's leading experts on criminal procedural law once said that the most profound dilemma relating to the development of judicial justice concerns the balance in legal stipulation between punishing specific criminal acts and the protection of individual rights. In the particular context of national emergency Chen Guangzhong of the Chinese University of

Law and Politics ultimately was also prepared to give priority to the protection of society, as distinguished from the protection of individual rights. Chen readily acknowledged that at times it would be necessary in the context of serious challenge to social stability and public order to take away the freedom of citizens.[27] At the same time, he noted that it is especially important in China to give more attention to the human rights of individuals.

One could argue that the litmus test of human rights commitment is in a state's response to national emergency. If ever there was a case for flexibility in the name of public order, SARS is that case. In fact a review of this case draws together some of the main issues that have so far informed our discussion of the post-1996–7 struggle for criminal justice reform. In light of the rapid spread of SARS, China's new premier, Wen Jiabao stressed the law's importance, saying that 'we must stress heavily the importance of using legal methods and bring fully into play legal weapons to win the war in preventing SARS.'[28] The government, however, was primarily concerned about the use of the criminal law as a 'weapon' in the struggle to maintain public order and safety. In fact there was negligible reference to the rights of the accused or for that matter the rights of victims. Given the limitations of week national legislation on infectious disease there was built-in pressure to rely on the necessary flexibility inherent in 'the extended explanatory role' (*kuoda jieshi zuoyong*) of legislative and judicial interpretation.[29]

China's political leadership quickly discovered that there was insufficient criminal law stipulation with which to deal with the rapidly unfolding dimensions of a national health crisis like that of SARS. The latter threatened to outpace the organizational capacity of the state. Originally, the CL79 offered only one potentially relevant article, Article 178. The latter, however, was very narrow in its focus on specific infectious disease control at international border crossings.

The authorities did have in place the 1989 Law on Infectious Disease Prevention and Control. This law distinguished between infectious disease categories, 'A', 'B', and 'C'. 'A' covered the plague and cholera whereas 'B' and 'C' included less virulent diseases such as the measles, polio, and types of hepatitis.[30] This 1989 Law, however, took as its main reference point in criminal law, the now superseded CL79. Once SARS became a critical issue, there was serious concern that the 1989 Law, in its dependence on the CL79, provided very little concrete procedural and organizational guidance for the government and its public health personnel in dealing with such a national health crisis.

The only real backstop that officials in 2003 had in the criminal law was the new set of CL97 Articles 330–37 under 'Section 5: Crimes of Impairing Public Health'. Although still incomplete, the CL97, as compared with the CL79 was more serious in its legal approach to public health crisis. However, in terms of the hierarchical categories of the criminal code,

CL97 Articles 330–37 lacked priority. They had been placed deliberately in the chapter on crimes concerning 'disrupting the order of social administration'. Moreover, while the CL97 had indeed made a new start in defining related criminal liabilities, this was insufficient in meeting the SARS challenge to public order.

Wang Zuofu has suggested that the CL97 Article 115 might serve as a practical basis for dealing with accused charged with spreading radiated material or infectious virus. However, Article 115, specifically mentions only crimes concerning arson, explosions, the breaching of dikes, and the spread of poison. The deliberate spread of infectious disease within a population could only be inferred on the unstipulated basis of analogy. Article 115 refers to inflicting serious injury or death on people 'by other dangerous means'.[31] This article provides a range of punishment depending on the degree of social harm, and this range includes the death penalty in Section One. The application of the death penalty on the basis of analogical reference to 'other dangerous means', however, was problematic in light of frequent legislative and jurisprudential emphasis on upholding the strictest procedural standards in relation to cases involving the death penalty.

The CL provisions specifically referenced the 1989 Law in Article 330. The latter confirmed that the scope of Class 'A' disease would in future be determined on the basis of the 1989 Law and 'the relevant regulations of the State Council'. In other words, national criminal legislation, itself, invited the State Council to take on responsibility for the stipulation of extended law on crime and punishment. This, in fact, has been part of a wider pattern of controversial reference to the State Council. As for example in Chapter 5 of this book, the State Council defined elements of cybercrime in the absence of critical definitions in NPC legislation.

In May 2003, the State Council issued 'The Emergency Provisions in Dealing with Public Health Crises'.[32] These provisions started to fill in the blanks left in 1979 and 1989. Eight of the 54 articles were used to stipulate 'criminal liabilities', requiring a new range of criminal law and administrative law punishment. Even so, in the midst of the SARS crisis, the authorities were still fearful of what they saw as a serious lack of provisions, facilitating public order through the decisive enforcement of the law based on severe punishment. The 1996–7 strategy for comprehensive stipulation of the law was unable to expedite the fast-developing policy response to SARS. On 14 May 2003, the SPC and SPP stepped into the fray issuing 'The Explanations Concerning the Issues in the Application of Law Regarding Criminal Cases on the Prevention and Control of Outbreaks of Infectious Diseases'.[33]

The 18-article 'Explanations' connected with 26 specific articles in the CL97. However, the 'Explanations' constituted 'extended judicial interpretation'. The SPC and SPP went beyond interpreting the available provisions of stipulated law to create new law to deal with new crime.

The 'Explanations', for example created the new crime of 'deliberate spreading of infectious disease pathogens or virus and endangering public security.' Commission of such crime invited the application of CL97 Article 115, which, as we have seen, includes the possibility of the death penalty. Moreover, the SPC and SPP had acted to elevate the status of such crime. Related issues were previously dealt with under the less serious criminal liabilities of the CL97 section on the disruption of social administration.

The 'Explanations', however, placed the crime of deliberately spreading infectious disease pathogens under the more serious heading of 'crime endangering public security'. Some jurists, nonetheless, argued that such 'extension' was necessary. The emergency conditions of SARS apparently immediately required more severe penalties so as to achieve social control based upon maximum deterrence.[34] The preoccupation with public order was also clear in Article 1 of the 'Explanations' that stipulated that persons suspected of having the virus who refuse examination, quarantine, and treatment and who then spread the virus unintentionally are subject to 3–7 years' imprisonment as stipulated in the CL97, Article 115, Section Two. The World Health Organization (WHO), in fact, was critical of this particular interpretation for fear that it might discourage persons with the disease from going to hospital.

The 'Explanations' also attempted to anticipate a bewildering and unfamiliar array of criminal activities that would require the bolstering of criminal law deterrence so as to secure public order. In Chengdu, in May 2003, for example, six people were convicted of public disorder in the People's Court of Dujiangyan. Apparently, they had spread rumours, damaged health facilities, caused traffic jams, and mobilized hundreds of people to stop the building of a quarantine area in a local hospital. The 'Explanations' required that any person convicted of spreading rumours about infectious disease for the purpose of promoting national disunity and separation or to overthrow the socialist state and system became liable to no less than five years in prison. This jumped to fifteen years in severe cases, as described in CL97 Articles 103 and 105 under the chapter concerning crimes endangering national security. Also, those persons found guilty of making and selling fake or adulterated drugs were liable to fifteen years' imprisonment. With 'severe circumstances', punishment for this crime could attract the death penalty, as indicated in Article 2 of the 'Explanations'.

The question of public order during a national health crisis became even more politically sensitive when it converged with the ongoing campaign to suppress the FLG. This took the politics of flexibility to new heights. During the suppression campaign in 2000, there were accusations to the effect that FLG members had deliberately harmed their own members' 'human rights' by foisting on them FLG canon. This canon purportedly served as a magic bullet in treating serious illness, and the authorities claimed that the FLG criminally programmed their members against alternative treatment at local hospitals.[35] A much more serious criminal law issue emerged in the context of SARS in 2003. The FLG leadership was accused of conspiracy to exacerbate the SARS crisis and cause political turmoil. Followers were accused of trying to get to hospitals where they would contract SARS for the purpose of spreading the disease.[36] FLG followers were also accused of violating Article 1 of the 'Explanations' in that they had allegedly refused examination and treatment and deliberately sought to spread the disease to the wider public.[37]

The above discussion highlights the problem of achieving a balance between rights protection and public order in the context of national emergency. The SARS crisis provided the opportunity to go with 'flexibility', especially in light of the gaps in stipulated law. At the time, China's political leadership did not believe that comprehensive stipulation offered a real solution to the immediate problems of public order. The SARS case shows how it is possible within the *zhengfa* system to have extended interpretation that actually substitutes for law. This may not be as bad in Mao's day when policy often substituted for law, but, it, nonetheless, conflicts with the NPC's exclusive legislative power.

The SARS crisis also demonstrated how difficult it is to maintain any significant focus on the protection of rights in the middle of a fast-developing crisis. Initially, China's government had lost valuable time in treating the disease. Flexibility was then suddenly applied wholesale to achieve public order and the protection of society. This issue of rights and emergency extends beyond SARS.

These issues of appropriate legislated response were not confined to the SARS context. In the 1999 Shanghai 'Methods for the Prevention of AIDS', anyone entering or exiting from Shanghai who was suspected of having Acquired Immunodeficiency Syndrome (AIDS) was required to undergo a Human Immunodeficiency Virus (HIV) test. However, the 'Methods' also declared that people are not to discriminate against AIDS patients and their right to medical services, employment, and education. That same year, the Health Ministry issued an order urging the protection of the rights and interests of AIDS patients.[38] At the March 2004 meeting of the NPC, delegates called for a new law on the prevention and control of AIDS. They argued that the central and the local authorities had 'fallen short of the requirements of the new situation and some regulations are in fact conflicting with each other'.

Commenting on the NPC debate, Zhang Kong, Vice President of the CHINA VD and HIV/AIDS Control Association brought the balance of values into the legislative equation. He stated:

We have to find a balance between the protection of [the] right[s] of person and the protection of public health. While striking hard at those [who] deliberately spread AIDS, it is necessary to protect the basic human rights of AIDS patients, such as the right to health, medical treatment, residence, employment, education, privacy, marriage and travel.[39]

Comprehensive stipulation based on well thought out legislation might possibly go further in developing the balance between public order and the protection of rights. Although comprehensive stipulation within the *zhengfa* system during an acute national emergency might focus on heavy criminal penalties, there is at least some modest possibility that with NPC debate more attention might be paid to the 'balance of values'.

In Taiwan, there was a different legislative approach to SARS. The Legislative Yuan was able to pass on 5 June 2003 the SARS Prevention and Relief Statute at a point where the disease started to loose steam. This approach placed more reliance on fines. Concealing a recent history of exposure to the SARS virus, for example, can attract fines of between US$288 and US$3322. While circulating groundless rumours about SARS to the people's detriment could result in a jail term in the PRC, in Taiwan it could attract a fine of up to US$14,409.[40]

While the original PRC approach to SARS demonstrated the regime's willingness to substitute the flexibility of state regulation and judicial and administrative interpretation for stipulated law, the issue has developed further suggesting the possibility of post-SARS correction. The NPCSC has passed amendments to the 1989 Law on the Prevention and Control of Infectious Disease that include the elimination of those provisions enabling the State Council to determine, on its own cognizance, the categories of disease. The amendments also address key financial aspects of the SARS health crisis. NPC delegates focused on how to finance the treatment of the poor and how to support local government in its response to crisis.[41]

Future prospects for criminal justice reform

As was previously pointed out, Chen Guangzhong raised the issue of the derogation of rights in the context of national emergency. However, as one of the lead drafters of the original CPL96, Chen has also given a great deal of attention as to how criminal procedural law reflects progress made towards the 'rule of law'. He has argued in favour of the revision of Article 1 of the CPL96, changing the emphasis from 'punish crimes and protect people' to 'punish crime and protect human rights'.[42] This might possibly address the lack of consistency between criminal and constitutional law as they have offered different definitions of 'equality before the law'. The former had focused on a principle of equal punishment for everyone no matter what their standing, or status. State constitutional law, on the other hand, had focused on the equal protection of everyone's rights.

Chen is also concerned that the CPL96 Article 1 narrowly referred to criminal procedural law supporting substantive justice, as in the criminal law. He is urging that Article 1 be re-worked so as to include a more progressive reference to the importance of judicial justice, itself.

Chen has also objected to opinion that places efficiency above justice, and he has warned that injustice will actually reduce 'efficiency'.[43] Chen generally drew attention to the lack of appropriate judicial practice in China, and he has focused on the CPL96's convergence with the key principles enunciated in the UN International Convention on Civil and Political Rights, including the presumption of innocence, forbidding the use of torture, *habeas corpus*, fair and independent trial, and the right to defence.[44]

A great deal of the detail in the foregoing chapters suggests that reform is an uneven process that can produce either extraordinary success or failure. Also it is clear that China's criminal justice system is undergoing a profound transition that involves a rapidly developing process of 'internationalization'. The 1996–7 reform represented a significant start to this process of transition, particularly in its new CL97 emphasis on the three principles, 'equality before the law', 'the punishment must fit the crime', and 'no punishment without a law' and with the self-conscious focus on a new and equal relationship between the criminal law and criminal procedural law.

Unfortunately, procedural law still does not enjoy equality with the criminal law, and the practical application of the three key principles has been uneven and weak. However, the 1996–7 reform did mark the beginnings of a paradigm shift requiring a major change from the inquisitorial to the adversarial trial systems. This process involves resisting the worst features of the *zhengfa* system, and it involves moving away from established institutional and organizational biases that exclusively favour public order based upon 'heavy-penalty-ism'.

Under the *zhengfa* system, even the actual physical layout of the court reflects an 'umbrella model' (*san xing*), highlighting the hierarchical cooperation between all the players except the defence. Apparently, there is no room for the defence under this 'umbrella'. The judge, in this system, not only moderates issues of trial procedure, but also actively seeks the 'truth' in the case. The judge can jump over the defence, make investigations, and examine witnesses. The defendant all the while is unable to claim the right to silence, is unable to call and cross-examine a full range of witnesses, and is subjected to rounds of questioning from the judge, the public prosecutor as well as from the victim. The Procurator, on the other hand, not only prosecutes the defendant, but she/he is also responsible for the integrity of trial procedure. This is not to mention the practice whereby the procuratorate deliberately fails to provide the defence with full disclosure of the evidence. The plight of the hapless defendant is physically demonstrated in the court seating which separates the accused from his/her own lawyer.

The CPL96 took a significant step towards a new 'triangular model' (*sanjiao xing*) that deliberately reinforces the impartiality of trial proceedings and the equality between the defence and the procuratorate. This model largely conforms with the underlying assumptions of the US model of adversarial proceedings, but such reform is still tentative and incomplete. It has not fully addressed the tradition of 'judicial integration' (*sifa yi tihua*).[45] And some jurists have suggested that the related research that went into the CPL96 was too rushed.[46]

Adaptation to an adversarial system requires reconsideration of procedures and structures that had developed more in line with the Continental assumptions of the inquisitorial system, and such adaptation requires significant 'localization' of a new set of international norms. Even at the time of the NPC's 1996 approval of the amendments to the criminal procedural law and the administrative punishment law, there was editorial commentary to the effect that the Chinese notion of a collegial panel, including 2 judges and 1 people's assessor, is superior to the Western jury system where there is less latitude for legal expertise. The Pro-PRC Hong Kong paper, *Wen Wei Po* went so far as to conclude: 'It is an irrefutable fact that compared with certain countries (such as the United States) China's citizens enjoy more practical and extensive rights and interests in accordance with the law.'[47]

Some reformers are now arguing that criminal justice reform ought to include more differentiation in the trial system and that a labour intensive panel of 2 judges and 1 assessor is not always needed to deal with more simple cases where there is a clear and ready admission of guilt. A single judge might alternatively preside in cases where the accused is prepared to plead guilty.[48] Perhaps this particular efficiency is not so threatening as its differentiated approach to justice is still roughly consistent with 'the punishment must fit the crime'.

In China, however, there is a predisposition to emphasize the absolute character of justice. The unfamiliar American notion of plea-bargaining (*bianhu jiaoyi zhidu*), for example, has often been criticized for its casual subordination of justice to bureaucratic efficiency. Plea-bargaining favours a judicial process that modulates justice so as to facilitate the efficient use of court proceedings. Law professors, Zhu Yuling and Si Lantao, for example, have endorsed differentiated trial procedures for the sake of simplifying criminal litigation, but they 'turned the tables' on their colleagues in the United States claiming that plea-bargaining diminishes the principles of 'every one is equal before the law' and 'the punishment must fit the crime'. In their view, plea-bargaining distorts the correct relationship between social harm and criminal liability. Zhu and Si were worried that plea-bargaining could result in the determination of different qualitative degrees of criminal liability for the commission of the same crime by different people.[49]

Given the incompleteness of the transition to the adversarial system and the complex dynamic of 'internationalization' and 'localization' what are the likely stages of criminal justice reform in China? The 1996–7 major revisions to the criminal law and criminal procedural law proceeded more or less in tandem as had also been the case in 1979. The potential development of judicial justice may have been filliped in the NPC 17 March 2004 amendment to the State Constitution. Among the 14 revisions, there were 2 new key clauses, supporting the protection of human rights and the protection of lawful private property.[50]

Presently, however, there is not much jurist/legislative activity to indicate that a major revision to the criminal law is in the offing. There is little political support for it, and it appears that change in this sector will likely take place on the incremental basis of closely targeted amendments.[51] Apparently, the particular criminal law issue of punishment is politically hot in that it raises public concerns about China's distinctive morality and culture. While enflamed public opinion often demands severe punishments, procedural change may invite less public scrutiny.

At least within the legal community, there is a rising concern that the CPL96 was too hurried as well as incomplete. Again with the senior experts at the Chinese University of Law and Politics in the lead, the Criminal Procedural Law is slated for a major revision over the next 3–5 years.[52] And this process has new cache thanks to the March 2004 State Constitutional reference to the protection of human rights.

The argument for procedural reform sounds quite familiar to the Western observer. Chinese scholars contend that the accused is in a comparative position of weakness before the powerful state and that the defendant's human right to a fair trial has to depend upon the improvement of the procedural rights associated with criminal defence.[53] This issue of fairness informs the continuing advocacy for inclusion of the 'presumption of innocence' within the coming revision. These same scholars discount as overly sanguine any suggestion that the protection of the defendant's rights can be guaranteed in the purported disinterest and self-restriction of the judicial agencies.

Chen Guangzhong and Song Yinghui, as key players in the currently planned revision to the CPL96, have argued, for example, that the review of arrest has to be transferred from the jurisdiction of the procuratorate to that of the court. They want judges to approve arrest.[54] When it comes to the discrete prospects for reform of criminal procedural justice this is more likely to happen where the synthesis of 'localization' and 'internationalization' is more innocuous and less politically threatening to the Party's legitimacy as it correlates with upholding Chinese morality.

To revise or to abolish the death penalty

There is, for example, bedrock support for the death penalty among the general population, the Party, and even among many in the reform legal circles. Furthermore, there is no reason to presume that a ruling Party that is so seriously concerned about its own legitimacy would place itself in opposition to such sentiment for the sake of international opinion. Apparently, American opinion on this point is seen as especially hypo-critical given the increased use of the death penalty in the United States.

Moreover, many jurists, themselves, see the issue as intractable. They believe that the origins of modern 'heavy penalty-ism' lie deep in Chinese history and culture. While few are prepared to tackle the issue dead-on, some jurists are revisiting the CL97's expanded provision for the death penalty particularly in cases dealing with non-violent crime. Reformers have made the case that practically no other country applies the death penalty in cases of non-violent economic crime. Their argument for its restriction is, in effect, part of the process of 'internationalization' and the domestic political concern for China's 'good image'.

Especially in light of what Zhao Bingzhi refers to as the 'long-lasting retributive psychology of the public', the trend is toward the restriction of rather than the abolition of the death penalty. Zhao Bingzhi, Director of the Research Center of Criminal Jurisprudence, People's University, Beijing has called for a more cautious application of this penalty in light of the reform commitment to the 'balance of values':

> The judicial [personnel] should evaluate the criminal's personality in an objective and comprehensive manner through the concrete facts in the cases, and carefully consider the conditions of applying [the] death penalty, not only for safeguarding social order and public benefits but also for the criminals' basic human rights and the reformation (*sic*), and firmly carry out the criminal policy of 'the death penalty should be carefully and cautiously applied'.[55]

Zhao saw 'heavy penalty-ism' as in contradiction with the socialist 'rule of law'. He argued that the death penalty is not exclusively a matter of deterrence and that it should only be confirmed in cases of extreme social harm. He added his qualification that if alternative punishment

> is enough to eliminate the criminal's capability of recommitting the crime, and enough to achieve the purpose of commonly and specially preventing crime from happening, [the] death penalty should not be considered as a necessary means for awing those potential criminals.[56]

The emphasis on rehabilitation is not at all new, but Zhao deployed this commonly accepted theme to pursue a new contemporary purpose, namely, the restriction of the death penalty to violent crime.

In light of continued public subscription to the domestic principle 'severe punishment against the crimes committed by public officials', Zhao Bingzhi believed that the application of the death penalty in relation to crimes of corruption and bribery would likely have to wait for a change in political circumstances. On the other hand, Zhao thought that for non-violent crimes jeopardizing public security, where there is no direct harm to society, the death penalty provision could be relaxed in the near future.

On the procedural side of this issue is the substantive issue of appeal. At least in the mind of some reformers, the 1996–7 revision, while it had declared that the 'punishment must fit the crime', it did not, itself, consistently address the issue of heavy-penalty-ism, particularly as it concerned the application of the death penalty for non-violent economic crime. Article 10 of the CPL96 declares, without qualification, that the trial of 'second instance' is final. Due to rising crime rates and the issue of public stability, the 1996–7 revision did not address the outstanding reform requirement of appeal to the SPC in all cases of the death penalty.[57]

The Chinese aphorism, 'human life connects with heaven' (*renming guan tian*) may reflect an inherent cultural preference for more exhaustive process in cases involving the state's taking of a human life. Prior to 1983 all those sentenced to death had the right to appeal the sentence to the SPC. Subsequently, those sentenced to death were only guaranteed the right to appeal to a court at the next highest level, and this was not the SPC in all cases. The process has at times stopped at the Higher Court. Prospective revision to the CPL96 is likely to require SPC approval in all cases relating to the death penalty.[58]

The issue of SPC approval was recently highlighted in the case of a teenager, Gao Pan. On 28 May 2002, the Baoding city Intermediate People's Court sentenced Gao to death for the aggravated murder of a neighbour with scissors. In a trial of the second instance, Luo appealed to the Provincial People's Higher Intermediate Court. The appeal was premised in CL97 Article 49 that exempts youth under the age of 18 from the death penalty. Gao claimed that he was under 18 at the time of the crime, but he, nonetheless, lost his appeal and was summarily executed. The case sparked some interest, and Tong Lihua, Director, Commission for the Protection of Minors, Chinese Lawyers Association, submitted a letter of proposal to the NPC asking that it posthumously re-examine Gao Pan's case and that it amend the current system of death penalty approval.[59]

The changing commitment to due process

On a number of points concerning due process, there will be resistance to the revision to the CPL96, and this resistance suggests the difficulties of Chinese jurists in dealing with law that is always expected to manifest 'Chinese characteristics'. A new law on evidence is in the works.[60] As was discussed in Chapter 1, the US principle regarding the exclusion of illegally acquired evidence is the subject of contemporary debate. Domestic critics, who oppose the importance of such principle, tend to focus alternatively on the importance of criminal liability, and are not as mindful of reform argument to the effect that there is an unequal relation between the accused and the state. They, therefore, reject the proposed shift from the Chinese traditional model, based upon a self-professed 'neutral' understanding of punishment as 'functionalism' (*zhinengzhuyi*) towards an American model that focuses on the protection of the accused on the basis of 'agent doctrine' (*dangshirenzhuyi*).[61]

Opponents also argue that a wholesale change in this area would trip the proper Chinese balance between emphases on punishment and protection. Exclusion of illegal oral confession is seen as a necessary adaptation to the UN Covenant on Civil and Political Rights, but there is continuing dispute over a law of exclusion that specifically excludes written confession and the 'illegal' collection of material evidence. Public Security of course argues that at the end of the day it must have the tools to fight crime and that unlike in the United States, police work in China's vast hinterland does not have the advantage of the technology such as the lie detector test.[62]

Reformers appear to be making some headway in arguing for revisions that will insure the defendant's excess to a lawyer during the investigation phase, carried out by Public Security. And also, there is concern that the present law has not really accommodated the defence ability to call the full range of witnesses. The CPL96 does not mention the 'right to remain silent'. Article 11 of the CPL96 did affirm: 'A defendant shall have the right to defence' (*bei gao you quanhuo de bianhu*). However, this did not specifically uphold the right to remain silent.[63] Various reform jurists are campaigning for this right as well as a clear statement on the 'presumption of innocence' (*wuzui tuiding*). Predictably, Public Security is resisting such amendment, arguing that it is already hamstrung by so many similar changes and that this will give too much precedence to protection at the expense of justice and public order.[64]

Conclusion

To re-work one of Mao Zedong's favourite metaphors, criminal justice reform is not a clean sheet of paper upon which one can write pristine Chinese characters. Instead, contemporary criminal justice reform might be likened to a messy palimpsest where old characters are only partially erased and new characters are scribbled over the remnants of still visible old characters. Also, there is no reason to assume that the synthesis of 'localization' and 'internationalization' will be a consistently neat process. Tradition still informs China's legal culture, particularly as it insists on an immediate correlation between law and culture. And the *zhengfa* system has shown a great deal of resilience in its socio-legal approach to new crime. If there is a paradigm shift in criminal justice reform that is underway, its outlines are only just taking shape. Randall Peerenboom, in a recent analysis of the prospects for a major improvement in criminal justice, noted: 'Any improvements will be piecemeal, gradual, and come about only as a result of a long struggle to educate the public, change citizen's attitudes and strengthen institutions.'[65]

If there is both continuity and discontinuity in the struggle to insure the 'Chinese characteristics' of criminal justice system, it is also clear that, at key points, China's jurists and their political supporters have been able to leverage the process of 'internationalization' in their struggle for reform. Notwithstanding the counterintuitive increase in heavy penalties in the sphere of cyber-crime, traditional 'heavy-penalty-ism', and its challenge to modern principles such as 'the punishment must fit the crime' has been brought out into the open.

Furthermore, extended detention has come under attack as an inappropriate 'flexibility' that challenges the new principle, 'no punishment without a law'. Such detention reportedly conflicts with the NPC's legislative integrity and the related 1996–7 strategy for comprehensive stipulation. Regulations concerning 'custody and investigation' and 'custody and repatriation' have actually been eliminated. The death penalty for non-violent crime is under increasing scrutiny. The right to silence and the presumption of innocence may well be included in the next round of procedural revision.

All the actors in this piece are engaged in an extraordinary transition that involves new and complicated bureaucratic politics. It would be easy to say that post-1996–7 criminal justice reform has only had a minimal impact on China's political and social reality, but the conceptual and structural biases of the *zhengfa* system are not easily overcome. This transition's basic terms of reference are in constant flux. And no doubt the outcome of criminal justice reform will impact 'tens of thousands of households'. While the durability and resistance of the *zhengfa* system seems quite strong, the scope and nature of legal reform is truly extraordinary, if not unprecedented, in modern Chinese legal history. The relationship between the *zhengfa* system and the struggle for the rule of law would appear to be a two-way proposition. The former has on occasion affected the development of the latter. On the other hand, the *zhengfa* system is not the same closed monolithic system that it once was. It is no longer self-contained, and if it influences the 'rule of law', the latter also influences it.

Those conservatives who advocate the unqualified extension of the *zhengfa* system have now to contend politically with a real and not easily controlled synthesis of 'internationalization' and 'localization'. This correlation has affected the State Constitution and the passage of new procedural law. It even has set in motion a reform process supporting adaptation to adversarial court proceedings. At the same time, local culture does matter as jurists, legislators, and politicians seek practical ways of adapting international legal norms and expectations to local conditions. To some extent one can argue that 'localization' is legitimate. In the West, it is not uncommon to hear the aphorism, 'the law is local'.

Certainly, criminal justice reform has had to negotiate the realities of politics and morality within Chinese society. The NPC, for example, moved forward to protect the rights of individual family members, responding to international human rights concerns and China's own revolutionary commitment to gender equality as against the persistence of a 'patriarchal' society. On the other hand, the NPC, in its revisions to the Marriage Law did not go so far as to challenge frontally the contemporary insistence on Chinese morality. It decided to criminalize 'domestic violence', but it stuck to a narrow understanding of 'domestic violence' as physical abuse, and it passed over the issue of sexual harassment.

It is, in the end, hard to avoid the conclusion that the 1996–7 strategy for criminal justice reform was too exclusively predicated in 'comprehensive stipulation' as opposed to extended 'flexibility'. This strategy had to be significantly supplemented with administrative regulation and judicial and legislative interpretation given the seemingly exponential development of post-1996–7 new crime. While stipulation will hopefully continue, it would seem that some reserved element of flexibility, if not 'extended flexibility', is still necessary to insure public order and social stability, not to mention the state's own legitimacy as it relates to public order, justice, and the protection of public and individual rights.

Despite the persisting structural features of the *zhengfa* system and the mass-line attempts to co-opt the law within the 'comprehensive management of public order', the record will show that there have been important victories in the cause of reform since 1996–7. Nonetheless, the CPL96 was too rushed and criminal procedural law still has a long way to go before it achieves its equality with substantive criminal law.

As for rights protection, there is an important new developing formal, if uneven and hesitant practical reference to the balance of values in the criminal justice reform. The essential importance of such new reference or conceptual articulation may be suggested in the persistent resistance of astonished and distressed public security organization. The latter is not used to having to deal with procedural restraints, and it must now devote its attention and resources within a newly defined bureaucratic struggle. Public Security often protests judicial reform as it wants the unfettered use of the law as a 'weapon' against new crime. The formal development of procedural law, despite the problems of lagging practice, is critically necessary as a political precondition to self-consciously progressive change.

In the absence of complete regime change what reform is possible? In the absence of regime change Stanley Lubman has argued that China cannot even claim to have a legal system, while Randall Peerenboom has argued that the regime is changing and that reform can make an important practical difference.[66] Even if some of the post-1996–7 failures have been spectacular, such as in the FLG case, this has not negated progress in every corner of the criminal justice system. An appreciation of the magnitude and complexity of China's changing legal reality and adaptation to the bewildering spread of 'new crime' may encourage analysis that focuses on the steady and increasing articulation of human justice and its possible realization at key points in practice.

In 1996–7, China's legal reformers had a plan. Perhaps, the plan was more noble than feasible. In the first place, it was assumed that it would be possible to achieve the comprehensive stipulation of law and that this stipulation could easily incorporate new concepts, based upon a new balance of public order and human rights protection. Furthermore, the new balance would neatly reflect the synthesis of 'globalization' and 'localization'. Second, it was assumed that over time these new concepts could be effectively deployed against persisting 'customary practices'. However, in the unpredictable course of events that followed upon the 1996–7 revisions, there was a resurgence of 'flexibility' that was enlisted in political attempts to preserve public order as against the proliferation of new crime.

In 1996–7, there was a real anxiety to move in haste towards a new system of criminal justice, but the true extent and resilient nature of the *zhengfa* system, as it promotes the Party's conventional socio-legal strategy and the 'comprehensive management of public order', may not then have been fully appreciated. While recognizing the prodigious and progressive efforts of China's legal community since 1996–7, it would seem that what is needed now is the old-fashioned Chinese virtue of patience. Any quick judgment as to the slow and conflicted progress of Chinese criminal justice reform ought to be offset against a well informed and deep understanding of what is possible from the point of view of those Chinese actors and organizations, who are engaged in the very difficult, but incredibly meaningful task of balancing public order with human rights.

Select glossary of Chinese criminal justice terms

Abducting and selling humans   *guaimai renkou*
拐卖人口

Act according to law   *yifa banshi*
依法办事

Administrative detention   *xingzheng juliu*
行政拘留

Agent doctrine   *dangshiren zhuyi*
当事人主义

Anti-money laundering regulations   *fan xiqian guiding*
反洗钱规定

As for leniency and severity,
  take severity as primary   *qingqing zhongzhong, yizhong
   weizhu*
轻轻重重, 以重为主

Balance of values   *jiazhi pingheng*
价值平衡

Bigamy   *chonghunzui*
重婚罪

Causing death by negligence   *guoshi sharen*
过失杀人

Civil infringement   *minshi qinhai*
民事侵害

Civil liability   *minshi zeren*
民事责任

Coercive indecent act   *qiangzhi weixie xingwei*
强制猥亵行为

Cohabitation   *tongju*
同居

Combining decorum and law   *lifa jiehe*
礼法结合

Comprehensive management of
  public order   *shehui zhi'an zonghe zhili*
社会治安综合治理

Compulsory drug treatment   *qiangzhi jiedu*
强制戒毒

Computer-related conventional crime	*sheji jisuanji fanzui* 涉及计算机犯罪
Concubinage	*feifa tongju* 非法同居
Controlled media	*kekongxing meijie* 可控型媒介
Counterrevolutionary crime	*fan geming zui* 反革命罪
Crime committed by a work unit	*danwei fanzui* 单位犯罪
Crime committed by organized populace	*juzhong fanzui* 聚众犯罪
Crime endangering public security	*weihai gonggong an'quanzui* 危害公共安全罪
Crime of abuse	*nuedaizui* 虐待罪
Crime of 'indecency'	*weixiezui* 猥亵罪
Crime of rape	*qiangjianzui* 强奸罪
Crime prevention	*yufang fanzui* 预防犯罪
Criminal accessories or accomplices	*congfan* 从犯
Criminal act	*xingshi fa'an* 刑事法案
Criminal behaviour	*fanzui xingwei* 犯罪行为
Criminal detention	*xingshi juliu* 刑事拘留
Criminal gang	*fanzui tuanhuo* 犯罪团伙
Criminal instigators	*jiaosuofan* 教唆犯
Criminal jurisprudence	*xingfa falixue* 刑法法理学
Criminal justice	*xingshi zhengyi* 刑事正义
Criminal law	*xingfa* 刑法
Criminal law's rule of law	*xingshi fazhi* 刑事法治
Criminal liability	*xingshi zeren* 刑事责任
Criminal organization	*fanzui jituan* 犯罪集团

Criminal organizations with a triad nature (COWTN)	*heishehui xingzhi zuzhi* 黑社会性质组织
Criminal procedural law	*xingshi chengxufa* 刑事程序法
Criminal prosecution	*xingshi qisu* 刑事起诉
Criminal punishment	*xingshi chengfa* 刑事惩罚
Criminal syndicate	*heishehui fanzui zuzhi* 黑社会犯罪组织
Criminalization	*xingshihua* 刑事化
Cultural relativism	*wenhua xiangdui zhuyi* 文化相对主义
Custody for investigation	*shourong shencha* 收容审查
Custody for repatriation	*shourong qiansong* 收容遣送
Customary law	*xiguanfa* 习惯法
Customary practices	*xiguan zuofa* 习惯做法
Cyber-crime	*jisuanji fanzui* 计算机犯罪
Cyber-criminal legislation	*jisuanji xingshi lifa* 计算机刑事立法
Cyber-vandals	*heike* 黑客
Cybercafé	*wangba* 网吧
Death penalty	*sixing* 死刑
Demonstration	*shiwei* 示威
Discrimination against women	*qishi funu* 歧视妇女
Domestic violence	*jiating baoli* 家庭暴力
Drug trafficking	*fanmai dupin* 贩卖毒品
Dual purposes theory	*shuangchong mudi lilun* 双重目的理论
Ensuing accurate and timely ascertainment of facts of the crimes	*baozheng zhunque jishi de chaming fanzui shishi* 保证准确及时地查明犯罪事实

Equality before the law	*falu mianqian renren pingdeng* 法律面前人人平等
Extended judicial interpretation	*kuodajieshi* 扩大解释
Fair and independent trial	*gongping duli de shenpan* 公平独立的审判
Falungong	*falungong* 法轮功
Functionalism	*zhineng zhuyi* 职能主义
Gender equality	*xingbie pingdeng* 性别平等
Habeas corpus	*renshen baohuquan* 人身保护权
Heavy penalty-ism	*zhongxingzhuyi* 重刑主义
Heretical cult	*xiejiao* 邪教
Hooligan activities	*liumang xingwei* 流氓行为
Hooligan criminal organization	*liumang fanzui jituan* 流氓犯罪集团
Hooligan gangs	*liumang tuanhuo* 流氓团伙
Human rights protection	*renquan baohu* 人权保护
If you don't execute, you will not satisfy the people's anger	*busha bu zuyi ping minfen* 不杀不足以平民愤
Illegal earnings	*feifa shouru* 非法收入
Illegal emigrants	*feifa yimin* 非法移民
Independent purposes theory	*duli mudi lilun* 独立目的理论
Individuals without identifications, jobs, and permanent residence	*sanwu renyuan* 三无人员
Institutionalized management	*fazhihua guanli* 法制化管理

International Covenant on Civil and
  Political Rights
	*gongmin he zhengzhi quanli guoji
	  gongyue*
	公民和政治权利国际公约

Internationalization	*guojihua* 国际化
Internet privacy	*wangluo yinsi* 网络隐私

Joint crime	*gongtong fanzui* 共同犯罪
Judicial independence	*sifa duli* 司法独立
Judicial integration	*sifa yitihua* 司法一体化
Judicial interpretation	*sifa jieshi* 司法解释
Jurisprudence	*falixue* 法理学
Law enforcement	*falu zhixing* 法律执行
Legal institutionalism	*falu zhidu zhuyi* 法律制度主义
Legal nihilism	*falu xuwu zhuyi* 法律虚无主义
Legalization	*faluhua* 法律化
Life imprisonment	*wuqi tuxing* 无期徒刑
Local protectionism	*difang baohu zhuyi* 地方保护主义
Localization	*bentuhua* 本土化
Maltreatment	*nuedai* 虐待
Marriage law	*hunyin fa* 婚姻法
Mercenary marriage	*maimai hunyin* 买卖婚姻
No crime without law	*fa wu mingwen guiding bu weizui* 法无明文规定不为罪
No punishment without a law	*fa wu mingwen guiding bu shoufa* 法无明文规定不受罚
Non-penalization	*fei xingfahua* 非刑罚化
Offenders who are coerced or induced to participate in a joint crime	*xiecongfan* 协从犯
One hundred households	*baojia* 保甲
Ordinary criminal organization	*putong fanzui jituan* 普通犯罪集团
Organized crime	*you zuzhi fanzui* 有组织犯罪

Organized hooligan activities

you zuzhi liumang huodong
有组织流氓活动

Organizing the populace to commit crime

juzhong fanzui
聚众犯罪

Plea-bargaining

bianhu jiaoyi zhidu
辩护交易制度

Police professionalism

jingcha zhuanye zhuyi
警察专业主义

Police wanted list

jingfang tongji mingdan
警方通缉名单

Policy is the soul of law

zhengce shi falu de linghun
政策是法律的灵魂

Political–legal system

zhengfa xitong
政法系统

Presumption of innocence

wuzui tuiding
无罪推定

Principal offenders

zhufan
主犯

Procedural justice

chengxu zhengyi
程序正义

Procuratorial power

qianchaquan
检察权

Protection of society

shehui baohu
社会保护

Public order

gonggong zhixu
公共秩序

Public safety (public security)

gonggong anquan
公共安全

Punishment fits the crime

zuixing yizhi
罪刑一致

Punishment is not applied when law is popularly ignored

fa bu zezhong
法不责众

Pure computer crime

chunzhengde jisuanjifanzui
纯正的计算机犯罪

Rape in marriage

hunnei qiangjian
婚内强奸

Re-education through labour

laodong jiaoyang zhidu
劳动教养制度

Remedial measures

bujiu cuoshi
补救措施

Right to defence

bianhuquan
辩护权

Right to keep silent

chenmoquan
沉默权

Right to request	*youquan tichu qingqiu* 有权提出请求
Rights and interests	*quanyi* 权益
Rule of law (nomocracy)	*fazhi* 法治
Rule of law economy	*fazhi jingji* 法治经济
Rule of man	*renzhi* 人治
Rule of virtue	*dezhi* 德治
Self-censorship	*ziwo shencha zhidu* 自我审查制度
Self-control and self-implementation	*zizhu zhangwo zizhu shishi* 自主掌握,自主实施
Severe punishment	*congzhong chufa* 从重处罚
Sexual abuse	*xing nuedai* 性虐待
Sexual harassment	*xing saorao* 性骚扰
Smuggling	*zousi* 走私
Snakeheads	*shetou* 蛇头
Social harm	*shehui weihai* 社会危害
Special provisions	*tebie tiaokuan* 特别条款
State censorship	*guojia shencha zhidu* 国家审查制度
Strike-hard	*yanda* 严打
Subversion of state power	*dianfu guojia quanli* 颠覆国家权力
Suit measures according to local conditions	*yindi zhiyi* 因地制宜
Supremacy of law	*fa de zhigao wushang xing* 法的至高无上性
Supreme people's court (SPC)	*zuigao renmin fayuan* 最高人民法院
Supreme people's procuratorate (SPP)	*zuigao renmin jianchayuan* 最高人民检察院

System of monogamy	*yifuyiqizhi* 一夫一妻制
Taking policy as a substitute for law	*yi zhengce daiti falu* 以政策代替法律
Ten abominations	*shijie* 十诫
Terrorist criminal organization	*kongbu fanzui jituan* 恐怖犯罪集团
Third party	*disanzhe* 第三者
'Three evils' (splittism, terrorism, and extremism)	*sangu shili (fenliezhuyi, kong buzhuyi he jiduanzhuyi)* 三股势力(分裂主义, 恐怖主义和极端主义)
Triad organizations	*heishehui fanzui zuzhi* 黑社会犯罪组织
Trial	*shenpan* 审判
Triangular model	*sanjiaoxing* 三角型
Umbrella model	*sanxing* 伞型
Uncontrolled media	*bu kekongxing meijie* 不可控型媒介
Underworld societies	*heisheui* 黑社会
Vagrants	*mangliu* 盲流
Violation of state regulations	*weifan guojia guiding* 违反国家规定

Notes

1 New crime, human rights protection, and public order

1 For related generalization see the entry under 'criminal law' in David Robertson, *The Routledge Dictionary of Politics*, 3rd edition, London and New York: Routledge, 2002, p. 126.

2 For insightful discussion of how stability is prized in the comparative development of the 'rule of law' in different countries and legal traditions see Randall Peerenboom, 'Competing Conceptions of the Rule of Law in China', in Randall Peerenboom (ed.), *Asian Discourses of Rule of Law*, London and New York: Routledge, Taylor & Francis Group, 2004, p. 124.

3 Zhang Sutang and Wang Jinfu, 'A Milestone in the Legislation History of China – Written on the Occasion of the Adoption of the Amended Criminal Law of the People's Republic of China', Xinhuashe, in *Daily Report*, FBIS-CHI-97-051, 14 March 1997, p. 1.

4 See the comments of Li Lin and Li Buyun as discussed in Ronald C. Keith, ' "Internationalization" and "Localization" in the Chinese Pursuit of Human Justice', in Sheeren Ismael (ed.), *Globalization, Policies, Challenges and Responses*, Calgary: Detselig, 1999, p. 143.

5 Pitman Potter, *The Chinese Legal System: Globalization and Local Legal Culture*, London and New York: Routledge, 2001, p. 15. Potter updates his discussion of 'selective adaptation' suggesting that '…the performance of China's emerging legal system will continue to challenge the expectations and experience of the liberal models upon which it appears to draw.' See Pitman Potter, 'Legal Reform in China: Institutions, Culture and Selective Adaptation', *Law and Social Inquiry*, vol. 29, no. 2, Spring 2004, p. 487.

6 Zhang Sutang and Wang Jinfu, 'A Milestone in the Legislation History of China – Written on the Occasion of the Adoption of the Amended "Criminal Law of the People's Republic of China" ', *Xinhua*, Beijing, 14 March 1997, in FBIS-CHI-97-051, 14 March 1997, p. 5.

7 Su Ning, 'PRC: Ren Jianxin, Wang Hanbin on Amended Criminal Procedure Law', *Xinhua*, Beijing, 19 April 1996 in FBIS-CHI-96-078, 22 April 1996, p. 38.

8 See, for example, Chen Guangzhong and Zheng Xu, 'Xingshi susong faxue ershe nian' (Twenty Years in the Legal Study of Criminal Procedural Law), *Zhongguo faxue* (Chinese Legal Studies), no. 4, 1998, p. 16.

9 See Bryan A. Garner (ed.), *A Dictionary of Modern Legal Usage*, 2nd edition, Oxford and New York: Oxford University Press, 1995, pp. 604 and 605 for related commentary on both principles, 'no crime, without a law' and 'no punishment without a law'.

10 Zhang Sutang and Wang Jinfu, 'A Milestone in the Legislation History of China', in 'China Minister, Others Discuss New Criminal Code', FBIS-CHI-97-051, 14 March 1997, p. 3.

11 Ni Siyi, 'Commentary: Important Measure Adopted by China to Perfect Its Judicial System – Written at the Time of China's Promulgation of the New Criminal Law', Beijing Xinhua, Hong Kong Service, 14 March 1997.

12 Zhang Sutang and Wang Jinfu, 'A Milestone in the Legislation History of China', p. 2.

13 Potter, *The Chinese Legal System*, p. 11.

14 Ibid., p. 107.

15 For jurist debate on the 'balance of values' see Ronald C. Keith and Zhiqiu Lin, *Law and Justice in China's New Marketplace*, London: Palgrave, 2001, pp. 25–27.

16 Sometimes the literature refers to *fa ren tong zhi*, roughly 'rule of man and rule of law together'. For an example of the new monographs on the subject see Shanghai tanhuang wenhua yanjiuhui (ed.), *Fazhi yu dezhi* (Rule of Law and Rule of Virtue), Beijing: Zhongguo jiancha chubanshe, 2001, *passim*.

17 You Guanghui and Shi Yan'an, 'Falu quanqiuhuazhongde xingfa xiandaihua' (The Modernization of Criminal Law in the Context of Legal Globalization), *Xingshi faxue* (Criminal Law), no. 5, 2003, p. 4.

18 Jiang Zemin, 'Issues to Be Correctly Handled in Current Economic Work', in *On the 'Three Represents'*, Beijing: Foreign Languages Press, 2001, pp. 109–10.

19 Li Xihai and Yan Xinggui, 'Quanqiuhua, WTO yu gongan fazhi', (Globalization, WTO and the Rule of Law in Public Security) *Susong faxue, sifa zhidu* (Procedural Law and Judicial System), no. 1, 2003, pp. 44–49.

20 Changchun People's Procuratorate Research Group, *Jiancha jiguan yingdui rushi wenti yanjiu* (Procuratorial Work after China's Entry into the WTO), *Susong faxue, sifa zhidu*, no. 1, 2003, pp. 35–42.

21 'On the Drive to Eliminate Pornography, Cracking Illegal Publications', *Renmin Ribao* (People's Daily) Beijing, 14 June 2000, p. 1, in FBIS-CHI-2000-0614, 30 June 2000.

22 Beijing Interview with Cui Min, 15 October, 2001. Cui Min was one of several key drafters of the CPL96. The Chinese University of Politics and Law took the lead in the early drafting of this law.

23 Jiang Zemin, 'Promote the Development of the Party's Work Style, the Building of Clean Government, and the Fight Against Corruption', 26 December 2000, in Jiang Zemin, *On the 'Three Represents'*, p. 135.

24 Jiang Zemin, 'Speech at the National Conference of Directors of Publicity Departments', 10 January 2001, *On the 'Three Represents'*, p. 155.

25 Xin Ren, *Tradition of the Law and Law of the Tradition: Law, State and Social Control in China*, Westport, CT and London: Greenwood Press, 1997, p. 10. In his interpretation Xin draws from the well known study of Qing case law, Derk Bodde and Clarence Morris, *Law in Imperial China*, Philadelphia, PA: University of Pennsylvania, 1973.

26 Xin Ren, *Tradition of Law*, p. 23.

27 Geoffrey MacCormack, *Traditional Chinese Penal Law*, Edinburgh: Edinburgh University Press, 1990, p. 38.

28 Ibid., p. 62.

29 See, for example, Song Sibei, *Zhongguo gudai xingfadiande tili he jiegou tedian* (The Style, Compilation and the Structural features of China's Ancient Penal Code), *Falixue, fashixue* (Jurisprudence and the History of Laws), no. 10, 2003, p. 51.

30 Ibid., p. 55.

31 Deng Xiaoping, 'The Present Situation and the Tasks before Us', *Selected Works of Deng Xiaoping (1975–1982)*, Beijing: Foreign Languages Press, 1984, p. 227.

32 Deng Xiaoping, 'Implement the Policy of Readjustment, Ensure Stability and Unity' (25 December 1980), *Selected Works of Deng Xiaoping (1975–1982)*, Beijing: Foreign Languages Press, 1984, p. 352.
33 Deng, 'The Present Situation and the Tasks Before Us', *Selected Works*, 1984, pp. 238–39.
34 Shao-chuan Leng and Hungdah Chiu, *Criminal Justice in Post-Mao China: Analysis and Documents*, Albany, NY: State University of New York Press, 1985, pp. 7, 13. The jural and societal models correlate with how one understands the relationship between state and society. With qualified application of Migdal's theoretical distinction between 'society with a weak state' and 'society with a strong state', Xin Ren explores the distinction between the 'socialist-internalized model of social control' and 'individualistic model of external social control'. In the former the state achieves a blanket social control over everyone in society for the purpose of achieving a state controlled internalized uniformity of thought and action. In the latter case the law is to a degree liberated from the state so that it can independently serve individual interests. In this latter case, Xin Ren suggests on pp. 5–6 that '...social conformity no longer means conformity to socially accepted standards of right and wrong but only obedience to legally enforced rules.' See Xin Ren, *Tradition of the Law*.
35 For political debate about this see Ronald C. Keith, *China's Struggle for the Rule of Law*, London and New York: Macmillan Ltd. and St. Martin's Press, 1994, p. 42.
36 Deng Xiaoping, 'Reform the Political Structure and Strengthen the People's Sense of Legality', *Fundamental Issues in Present-Day China*, Beijing: Foreign Languages Press, 1987, p. 145.
37 Keith, *China's Struggle for the Rule of Law*, pp. 11–15.
38 Ronald C. Keith and Zhiqiu Lin, 'To Revise or not to Revise China's Law on Counterrevolution', *China Information*, vol. 5, no. 4, Spring 1991, pp. 26–28.
39 *The Criminal Law and the Criminal Procedural Law of China* (English and Chinese), Beijing: Foreign Languages Press, 1984, p. 32.
40 Beijing People's University interview with Wang Zuofu, 16 October 2001.
41 See the explanation of 'comprehensive management of public order' in Tian Pingan *et al.*, *Dangdai fa chexue yanjiu yu shensuo* (Research and Inquiry on the Contemporary Philosophy of Law), Beijing: Falu chubanshe, 2000, pp. 502–03.
42 See Kang Damin, *Gongan lun* (On Public Security), Beijing: Qunchong chubanshe, 1998, p. 482.
43 *Penal Regulations of the PRC for the Comprehensive Management of Public Order*, Beijing: Zhongguo fazhi chubanshe, 1997, p. 15.
44 '1999nian quanguo shehui zhian zonghe zhili gongzuo yaodian' (Main Points of the Work in 1999 for the National Comprehensive Management of Public Order), *Xingshi faxue* (Criminal Legal Studies), no. 4, 1999, pp. 87–88.
45 'Luo Gan, Zhou Yongkang Discuss Comprehensive Management of Public Security', *Xinhua*, Beijing, 12 April 2004, FBIS-CHI-2004-0412, AFS Document No.: CPP200404412000094, p. 1.
46 See Keith and Lin, *Law and Justice in China's New Marketplace*, pp. 27–39 and also Zuo Zeyuan, *Fazhi fanlun* (On the Rule of Law), Beijing: Falu chubanshe, 2001, p. 61.
47 In their edited overview of the last fifty years of criminal law study, Gao Mingxuan and Zhao Bingzhi identify the balancing of these two concepts as seminal to the twenty-first-century development of China's criminal law. See Gao Mingxuan and Zhao Bingzhi, *Xin Zhongguo xingfaxue wushi nian* (Fifty Years of New China's Criminal Law Studies), vol. 1, Beijing: Zhongguo fangzheng chubanshe, 2000, pp. 35–36.

48 Jiang Zemin, 'Speech at the Publicity Directors' Conference', *On the 'Three Represents'*, p. 16.
49 Wen Xiaoli, 'Shijian zhexue shiyezhongde "fazhi" yu "dezhi" ' (The Real Practical Implications of the Distinction between 'Rule of Law' and 'Rule of Virtue'), *Falixue, fashixue* (Jurisprudence and the History of Laws), no. 7, 2003, p. 34.
50 Zhang Chunsheng and A Xi, 'Zhunque bawo fazhide hanyi' (Correctly Understanding the Meaning of the Rule of Law), *Zhongguo Faxue* (Chinese Legal Science), no. 5, 1998, pp. 3–7.
51 For example, this was the mid-1980's position of Zhang Guohua, President of the Chinese Legal History Association. See Keith, *China's Struggle for the Rule of Law*, pp. 15, 51.
52 For example, see Ying Feihu and Dai Jinsong, 'Fazhi yu dezhi' (The Rule of Law and the Rule of Virtue), *Falixue, fashixue* (Jurisprudence and the History of Laws), no. 9, 2001, pp. 34–41.
53 There is some agreement between Western and Chinese viewpoint on this political question of 'instrumentalism'. Gao Mingxuan and Zhao Bingzhi note that prior to recent reforms, there was a traditional viewpoint apparent in jurisprudential theory relating to 'instrumental criminal law, means-to-an-end criminal law' *(gongju faxing, shouduan xingfa)*. See Gao Mingxuan and Zhao Bingzhi (eds), *Xin Zhongguo xingfaxue wushi nian*, p. 35.
54 Keith and Lin, *Law and Justice in China's New Marketplace*, p. 183.
55 Beijing People's University interview with Wang Zuofu, 16 October 2001.
56 Keith and Lin, *Law and Justice in China's New Marketplace*, pp. 202–14.
57 See Fan Wen, 'The Conflict between Legal and Social Harmfulness Definitions regarding how to Determine a Crime', *Xingshi faxue* (Criminal Law), no. 4, 1999, pp. 19–21.
58 Zhou Zhengxiao, 'Fanxui dingyi xin biaoshu' (A New Description of Crime), *Xingshi faxue* (Criminal Law), no. 4, 2001, pp. 25–29.
59 Zhao Tingguan, 'Zuixing Junhenglunde xingshuai yu zuizexing jun-henglunde queli' (The Rise and Fall of the Theoretical Balance of Crime and Punishment and Establishing the Theoretical Balance of Crime, Liability and Punishment), *Xingshi faxue* (Criminal Law), no. 10, 2003, pp. 22–27. The related Article 5 reads: 'The severity of punishment must be commensurate with the crime committed by an offender and the criminal responsibility he bears.' For this translated text of the amended Criminal Law see *Daily Report*, FBIS-CHI-97-056, 17 March 1997.
60 See, for example, Zhang Jianwei, 'Zhengju faxuede lilun jichu' (The Theoretical Foundations of the Jurisprudence on Evidence), *Susong faxue, sifa zhidu* (Procedural Law and Judicial System), no. 8, 2002, p. 10.
61 See, for example, Fan Peigen, 'Woguo buyi zhizhi "Meishi" feifa zhengju paichu chuize' (China Cannot Use 'American Rules' Excluding Illegal Evidence), *Susong faxue, sifa zhidu* (Procedural Law and Judicial System), no. 8, 2003, p. 65.
62 Gao Minigxuan, 'Ershi nian lai woguo xingshi lifade huigu yu zhanwang' (Reviewing the Past Twenty Years of China's Criminal Law Legislation), *Zhongguo faxue* (Chinese Legal Science), no. 6, 1998, p. 29. For traditional Confucian and Legalist views on 'heavy penalty-ism' see Xu Famin, *Fawenhua yu xingfa xiandaihua yanjiu* (The Study of Legal Culture and the Modernization of the Criminal Law), Beijing: Zhongguo fangzheng zhubanshe, 2001, p. 224.
63 Beijing Interview with Cui Min, October 15, 2001.
64 See, for example, Liang Genlin, 'Feixingfahua – dangdai xingfa gaigede zhuti' (Non-penalization – the Mainstream of Reform in Criminal Law in the Modern World), *Xingshi faxue* (Criminal Law), no. 3, 2001, pp. 19–23. There are

also issues surrounding 'de-criminalization' and 'victimless crime'. See Da Gushi, 'Fanzuihua he feifanzuihua' (Criminalization and Decriminalization), in Chen Guangliang (ed.), *Xingshifa pinglun* (Criminal Law Review), Beijing: Zhongguo zhengfa daxue chubanshe, vol. 6, 2000, pp. 421–22.

65 You Wei and Liu Jianhong, 'Lun xingfashangde "zong chong chufa"' (On 'Severe Punishment' in the Criminal Law), *Xingshi faxue* (Criminal Law), no. 2, 2001, p. 16.
66 Liu Yanhong, 'Xingfa leixinghua gannian yu fazhiguo yuanze zhi zheli' (Categorizing Criminal Law Concepts and the Theoretical Principles of a Rule of Law Country), *Xingshi faxue*, no. 9, 2003, pp. 37–38.
67 Donald C. Clarke and James Feinerman, 'Antagonistic Contradictions: Criminal Law and Human Rights in China', *China Quarterly*, no. 141, March 1995, p. 137.
68 As discussed in Stanley Lubman's introduction to Pitman Potter (ed.), *Domestic Law Reforms in Post-Mao China*, Armonck, NY: M.E. Sharpe, 1999, p. 5.
69 Carlos Wing-hung Lo, *Legal Awakening: Legal Theory and Criminal Justice in Deng's Era*, Hong Kong: Hong Kong University Press, 1995. Pitman Potter's review in *Modern China Journal*, 1999, pp. 184–87. This book was also reviewed by Gregg Benjamin, 'How to Look for Autonomous Law in China, or Elsewhere', *Review of Central and East European Law*, 1997, vol. 23, no. 2, p. 165.
70 Jonathan Hecht, *Opening to Reform? An Analysis of China's Revised Criminal Procedure Law*, New York: Lawyers Committee for Human Rights, October, 1996, p. 30.
71 David Lanham, 'The Chinese Criminal Procedure Law – A Comparative Review', *Global Journal on Crime and Criminal Law*, vol. 4, no. 1, 1997, p. 37.
72 Pamella Seay, 'Law, Crime and Punishment in the People's Republic of China: A Comparative Introduction to the Criminal Justice and Legal System of the PRC', *Indiana International and Comparative Law*, vol. 9, no. 1, 1998, pp. 43–54.
73 Linda Chelan Li, 'The "Rule of Law" Policy in Guangdong: Continuity or Departure? Meaning, Significance and Processes', *The China Quarterly*, September 2000, p. 199. For 'law as an instrument theory' (*falu gongju lun*) in internal Chinese debate see Zuo Zeyuan, *Fazhi fanlun*, 2001, pp. 8–11.
74 Stanley Lubman, *Bird in a Cage: Legal Reform in China After Mao*, Stanford, CA: Stanford University Press, 1999, p. 3.
75 See, for example, Sun Qian, 'Lun daibu yu renquan baozhang' (Arrest and Human Rights Protection), *Susong faxue, sifa zhidu* (Procedural Law and Judicial System), no. 1, 2001, pp. 2–12.
76 Keith and Lin, *Law and Justice in China's New Marketplace*, pp. 189–90.
77 Beijing interview with Cui Min, 15 October 2001.
78 See Keith and Lin, *Law and Justice in China's New Marketplace*, p. 196.
79 'China Chapter', in the 1999 US Department of State, *Country Reports on Human Rights Practices*, http://www.state.gov/global/human rights/1999_hhrp_report/china/html
80 This approximates an explanation given to the authors during discussion with Chen Xingliang in Beijing on 11 June 2004.
81 Information Office, State Council of the PRC, 'Reform through Labor', *Zhongguo zhengfu baipi shu* (White Papers of the Chinese Government), Beijing: Foreign Languages Press, pp. 144–45.
82 Ibid., 154.
83 Beijing interview with Cui Min, 15 October 2001.
84 For example, the entire no. 6, 2001 issue of the *Zhongwai faxue* (Peking University Law Journal) focuses on issues surrounding the system of labour education and rehabilitation.

85 'PRC: Internet User Opposes CPPCC Motion to Abolish Reeducation Through Labor', *Renmin wang* (People's Outlook), Beijing, 15 September 2003 in FBIS-CHI-2003-0921, AFS Document No.: CPP20030921000057.

86 Randall Peerenboom, 'Out of the Pan and into the Fire: Well-Intentioned but Misguided Recommendations to Eliminate All Forms of Administrative Detention in China', *Northwestern University Law Review*, vol. 98, no. 3, 2004, p. 1000.

87 Peerenboom, 'Out of the Pan and into the Fire', p. 1012.

88 Beijing interview with Cui Min, October 2001.

89 John Pomfret, 'China Voids Rule on Jailing Vagrants', *Washington Post*, 19 June 2003.

90 Amnesty International Press Release, AI Index: ASA 17:/028/2003 (Public) News Service 155, 27 June 2003.

91 Reform of the labour and education system is, for example, discussed in all nine of the articles, appearing in *Zhongwai faxue* (Peking University Law Journal), no. 6, 2001.

92 Wang Taixian and Ai Ming, *Fazhide lilian yu fanglue* (The Concept and Summary of Nomocracy), Beijing: Zhongguo jingcha chubanshe, 2001, *passim*.

93 For discussion of Chinese 'human rights' viewpoint on the importance of top-down state activism to compensate for the 'deficit in society and popular consciousness' see Keith and Lin, *Law and Justice in China's New Marketplace*, p. 244.

94 Some reformers have stressed their commitment to the correlation of civil society and the rule of law; for example, Liu Wanghong proposes a 'rule of law society' (*fazhi shehui*) in which society is governed according to law and in which society challenges the illegal interventions of state power. See Liu Wanghong, 'Guojia yu shehui: quanli gongzhide falixue sikao' (State and Society: Authority and Control in Legal Terms), *Falixue, fashixue* (Jurisprudence and the History of Laws), no. 1, 1999, pp. 15–20.

95 Beijing People's University interview with Wang Zuofu, 16 October 2001.

96 'PRC Fourth Five-Year Plan for Education in Legal System', FBIS-CHI-2002-0527, 27 May, 2001, p. 2.

97 Ibid., p. 3.

98 Keith and Lin, *Law and Justice in China's New Marketplace*, pp. 57–61.

99 'NPC Official Urges Resolving Problems in Implementing Criminal Procedure Law', FBIS-CHI-2000-1228, 28 December 2000, p. 2.

100 Ibid., p. 2.

101 Zhao Bingzhi (ed.), *Xin xingfadiande chuangzhi* (The Making of the New Criminal Code), Beijing: Falu chubanshe, 1997, p. 334.

102 'Guangdong Survey: 54.8% Advocate Criminal Penalties for Affairs, Concubines', 15 June 2000, *Xinhua*, in FBIS-CHI-2000-0615, 16 June 2000.

103 'Need for Sexual Harassment Law Stressed', *Xinhua*, Beijing, in English, 5 July 1998, FBIS-CHI-98-185, 7 July 1998.

104 See Zhao Bingzhi (ed.), *Xin xingfadiande chuangzhi*, p. 380 and 'Article Defines "Triad Crimes"', *Renmin Ribao*, Overseas edition in Chinese, 16 August 1997, p. 5. Gao Jinghong, 'Crimes of a Triad Nature', FBIS-CHI-197-246, 09 April 1997.

105 Keith and Lin, *Law and Justice in China's New Marketplace*, pp. 219–22.

106 For an example concerning the use of e-mail lobbying for environmental protection see 'Chinese Citizens Increase Use of Internet to Dialogue with Government', *Xinhua*, 5 June 2001, in FBIS-CHI-2001-0605, pp. 1–2.

107 'China Jails First Cyber-Dissident for Pro-Democracy Essay', Hong Kong AFP, 27 April 2001 in FBIS-CHI-2001-0427, pp. 1–2.

2 The 'Falungong problem' and the prospects for criminal justice reform

1 The following discussion follows very closely on the analysis provided in Ronald C. Keith and Zhiqiu Lin, ' "Falungong Problem": Politics and the Struggle for the Rule of Law in China', *The China Quarterly*, no. 175, September 2003, pp. 623–42.

2 Pitman Potter discusses this in *The Chinese Legal System: Globalization and Local Legal Culture*, London and New York: Routledge, 2001, p. 161.

3 On the distinction between 'law' and 'policy' as it relates to Party leadership, see the analysis of the views of Zhang Yongming and Li Buyun, in Ronald C. Keith, *China's Struggle for the Rule of Law*, London and New York: Macmillan and St. Martin's, 1994, p. 13.

4 The authors are grateful for a historian's view on this, namely, that of Dr Luke Kwong, Department of History, Lethbridge University. There is a great deal of literature on secret societies in the imperial context and the following serve only as selected examples of the literature: Susan Naquin, *Shangtung Rebellion: The Wang Lun Uprising of 1774*, Yale, 1981; Naquin, *Millenarian Rebellion in China: The Eight Trigrams Uprising of 1813*, Yale, 1976, Naquin and E. Rawski, *Chinese Society in the Eighteenth Century*, Yale, 1987; Joseph Esherick, *The Origins of the Boxer Uprising*, California, 1987, etc.

5 Mao Zedong, 'The Chinese Revolution and the Communist Party', *Selected Works of Mao Zedong*, vol. 11, Beijing: Foreign Languages Press, 1965, p. 308.

6 Gao Mingxuan, *Xingfaxue* (Criminal Law Science), Beijing: Falu chubanshe, 1984, p. 343.

7 Ezra Vogel, *Canton Under Communism: Programs and Politics in a Provincial Capital, 1949–1968*, New York: Harper & Row, Harper Torchbooks, 1970, p. 65.

8 Theodore H.E. Chen (ed.), *The Chinese Communist Regime: Documents and Commentary*, New York: Frederick A. Praeger Publishers, 1976, p. 294.

9 Ibid., p. 297.

10 NPC, PRC, *Zhonghua renmin gongheguo xianfa* (Constitution of the People's Republic of China), Beijing: Renmin chubanhe, 1975, pp. 15–16.

11 NPC, PRC, *The Constitution of the People's Republic of China*, Beijing: Foreign Languages Press, 1978, p. 35.

12 NPC, PRC, *The Constitution of the People's Republic of China*, Beijing: Foreign Languages Press, 1983, p. 32.

13 Richard Baum and Frederick C. Teiwes, *Ssu-Ch'ing: The Socialist Education Movement of 1962–1966*, Berkeley, CA: Center for Chinese Studies, University of Berkeley, 1968, Appendix B, p. 61.

14 Ronald C. Keith and Zhiqiu Lin, 'To Revise or not to Revise China's Law on Counterrevolution', *China Information*, vol. 5, no. 4, Spring, 1991, p. 30.

15 Gao Mingxuan, *Zhonghua remin gongheguo xingfa de yunyu he dansheng* (The Conception and Birth of the Criminal Code of the People's Republic of China), Beijing: Falu chubanshe, 1980, p. 144.

16 See 'Decision of the National People's Congress Standing Committee on the Severe Punishment of Criminal Elements who Severely Endanger Public Security', in *The Criminal Law and Criminal Procedure Law of China*, p. 241. Also see See Zhiqiu Lin and Ronald C. Keith, 'The Changing Substantive Principles of Chinese Criminal Law', *China Information*, vol. xiii: no. 1, Summer 1998, p. 81.

17 Heilongjiang Politics and Law Management College, comp., 'Guanyu chuli fandong huidaomen gongzuozhong youguan wentide tongzhi' (Circular Regarding Issues in the Handling of Counterrevolutionary Secret Societies),

Xingshi fagui huibian (Collection of Criminal Law Regulations and Law), Harbin: Heilongjiang chubanshe, 1990, p. 634.

18 Deng Xiaoping, 'Talk at a Meeting of the Standing Committee of the Political Bureau of the Central Committee', *Fundamental Issues in Present-Day China*, Beijing: Foreign Language Press, 1987, pp. 137–38.

19 Deng Xiaoping, 'Reform the Political Structure and Strengthen the People's Sense of Legality', *Fundamental Issues in Present-Day China*, p. 145.

20 Keith, *China's Struggle for the Rule of Law*, p. 168.

21 Keith and Lin, 'To Revise or not to Revise China's Law on Counterrevolution', *China Information*, p. 26.

22 Based upon his discussion with James Seymour, Danny Schechter, *Falungong's Challenge to China: Spiritual Practice or 'Evil Cult'*, New York: Akashic Books, 2001, p. 198. The case of Chen Zixu, which was later considered by the UN Committee on Torture, is but one example. Mrs Chen's daughter was unable to file a lawsuit to gain possession of her mother's body as no lawyer was willing to accept her case. For this item, 'A Deadly Exercise: Practicing Falun Gong Was a Right, Ms. Chen Said, to Her Last Day', *Wall Street Journal*, 20 March 2000 and other related human interest stories see Ian Johnson's Pulitzer Prize reporting at http://www.pulitzer.org/year/2001/international-reporting/works/falungong1.html

23 Peerenboom provides an informative analysis of the 5 November 1999 SPC 'Notice Concerning the Implementation of the 'Decision of the NPC Standing Committee on Banning Heretical Organizations and Preventing Heretical Activities', *China's Long March toward the Rule of Law*, pp. 99–101.

24 US State Department, Country Reports on Human Rights Practices-2000, February 2001, at http://www.state.gov/g/ddrl/rls/hrrpt/2000/eap/index.cfm?docid=684 (accessed March 2002), pp. 6, 10–11.

25 See 'Spokesman Criticizes US House Resolution on Falungong', Zhongguo Xinwenshe, Beijing, 19 November 1999 in FBIS-CHI-1999-1119, p. 1.

26 Li Hongzhi, 'Further Comments on Superstition', 13 July 1999, in Schechter, *Falungong's Challenge to China*, p. 267.

27 Julie Ching, 'The Falun Gong: Religious and Political Implications', *American Asian Review*, 1 January 2001, p. 2.

28 Julie Ching, 'The Falun Gong: Religious and Political Implications', p. 4.

29 Ian Adams, Riley Adams, and Rocco Galati, *Power of the Wheel: The Falun Gong Revolution*, Toronto: Stoddart Publishing, 2000, pp. 8, 29.

30 Bureau of Democracy, Human Rights and Labor, US Department of State, *International Religious Freedom Report*, China (Hong Kong and Macau), p. 1 at http://www.state.gov/g/drl/rls/irf/2001/5752.htm

31 US Commission on International Religious Freedom, *Recommendations for US Policy on China*, 13 February 2002, p. 2 at http://www.uscirf.gov/reports/13Feb02/chinaRecommendations.php3

32 Keith, *China's Struggle for the Rule of Law*, p. 14.

33 In a 26 September 1989 interview with R.C. Keith, Sun Guohua, a leading jurist, indicated that in his recent discussions with Jiang Zemin the latter endorsed 'rule of law' as an ethos which implies the limitation of the Party State in the supremacy of law. As cited in Keith, *China's Struggle for the Rule of Law*, p. 16.

34 See Ronald C. Keith and Zhiqiu Lin, *Law and Justice in China's New Marketplace*, London: Palgrave, 2001, p. 35.

35 Party Literature and Research Department, Central Committee, Communist Party of China, ed., Jiang Zemin, *On 'The Three Represents'*, Beijing: Foreign Languages Press, 2001, p. 162. The combination idea was in the mid-1980s

represented as especially appropriate to Chinese culture. See Keith, *China's Struggle for the Rule of Law*, pp. 15, 222–23.

36 Jiang Zemin, *On 'The Three Represents'*, p. 163.

37 During a Politburo meeting in December 2001, Jiang Zemin stressed the social contributions of religion and praised the role of the 'broad believing masses'. 'Giving China's Communist Party Some of that Old-Time Religion', *Globe and Mail*, 19 February 2002, p. A13.

38 A FLG press conference of 25 April 2001 claimed that Zhu had met with practitioners just outside the State Council and that as a result of his more moderate approach to the problem, Jiang forced him to do a 'self-criticism'. Jiang's strong-arm tactics against the FLG relate back to his apparently resolute role as Shanghai's mayor in suppressing the spread of demonstrations in that city in 1989. See Schechter, *Falungong's Challenge to China*, pp. 13, 29. If so, this would have come just after Jiang and Zhu had made strong common cause in favour of Zhu's April 1999 trip to Washington to advance the WTO negotiations. The disagreement may have focused on the nature of FLG organization rather than over whether the silent congregation around Zhongnanhai was detrimental to social stability as suggested in 'Handling the Falungong Case', trans. by Zong Haiwren from the Chinese, *Zhu Rongji zai 1999* (Zhu Rongji in 1999), in *Chinese Law and Government*, vol. 35, no. 1, January/February 2002, pp. 53–72.

39 Peerenboom, *China's Long March*, p. 98.

40 The US State Department cites the official government white paper that claims there are 200 million religious adherents, 3000 religious organizations, 300,000 clergy and 74 religious colleges. *Country Reports on Human Rights Practices 2000*, p. 24.

41 Abdelfattah Amor, January, 1998 report on the 'Elimination of All Forms of Intolerance of Discrimination Based on Religion or Belief', as cited and discussed by Peerenboom, chapter 3, *China's Long March*, p. 95.

42 For example see 'Text of [the] State Council Office Report "US Human Rights Record in 2002"', *Xinhua*, 3 April 2003 in FBIS-CHI-2003-0403, AFS Document No.: CPP200304030000132, p. 2.

43 'AFP: More on Falungong founder', AFP, Hong Kong, 23 July 1999, in FBIS-CHI-19999-0722. Also 'AFP: Falungong Founder "Shocked" by PRC Crackdown', AFP, Hong Kong, 22 July 1999 in FBIS-CHI-1999-0722, p. 1. Li Hongzhi told an AFP reporter that he was 'deeply worried that another June 4 bloodshed will take place.'

44 'Three Person Forum . . .', *Renmin Ribao* (People's Daily), Overseas edition, 19 August 1999, FBIS-CHI-1999-0901, p. 4.

45 For a view on the difference between religion and heretical cult see PRC Ministry of Justice, ed., *Yi fa qudi xiejiao xuzhi fangfan he chengzhi xiejiao huodong* (Taking Law to Ban Heretical Cult Organization and to Defend against and Punish Heretical Cult Movements), Beijing: Falu chubanshe, 1999, pp. 5–6.

46 'Spokeswomen Criticizes Rubin's Remarks on the Falungong', *Zhongguo Xinwenshe*, FBIS-CHI-1999-1028, 29 October 1999.

47 MacInnis, *Religion in China Today*, Mary Knoll, NY: Orbis Books, p. 2.

48 'A responsible person of the CCP CC Organization Department has issued a statement to *Renmin Ribao* reporters on CCP members practicing "Falun Dafu"', XinHuashe, Beijing, 23 July 1999, in FBIS-CHI-1999-0725, last page.

49 'Run the Country According to Law', *Renmin Ribao*, 31 October 1999 commentary in *Xinhua*, 30 October 1999, in FBIS-CHI-1999-1030, p. 2.

50 Xu Shengguo and Chang Ruxian, 'Swindler Plus Scoundrel – Record of Li Hongzhi's Denials Overseas', *Renmin Ribao*, 28 August 1999, p. 8 in FBIS-CHI-1999-0831, p. 5; and also Niu Aimin,' Organizing and Using Cults for Criminal Activities Must be Punished – Criminal Law Expert, Zhou Zhenxiang, on [the] Fanlungong's Cult Nature and Applicability of [the] Criminal Law', Beijing, Xinhuashe, 4 November 1999, in FBIS-CHI-1999-1108, p. 1. Zhou claimed: 'Throughout history, China always had laws to abide by when it had to ban cults.'

51 See the *Zhongguo Xinwenshe Series* on the FLG, in FBIS-CHI-1999-0820, 4 August 1999.

52 Xu Baokang and Wu Yingchun, 'States Do Not Tolerate Cults', *Renmin Ribao* (People's Daily), 8 November 1999, p. 6 in FBIS-CHI-1999-1112, p. 2. Also 'Run the Country According to Law, Sternly Punish Cults', *Renmin Ribao*, 31 October 1999, in FBIS-CHI-1999-1030, p. 2.

53 'CASS Official Xia Yong on Falungong, Rule of Law', *Xinwenshe*, Beijing, 3 August 1999 in FBIS-CHI-1999-0824, p. 1.

54 Central Television panel on the programme, 'Focus', Fang Hongjin, programme host, Zhuo Xinping, Director of and Research at the CASS Institute for World Religious Studies; Ye Xiaowen, Director, State Bureau of Religious Affairs, *Renmin Ribao* (Overseas), 19 August 1999 in FBIS-CHI-1999-0901, p. 3.

55 Xu Baokang and Wu Yingchun, 'States Do Not Tolerate Cults', p. 3.

56 'Absurd Heresy and Evil Motives – On Anti-Scientific, Anti-Mankind, Anti-Social and Anti-Government Essence of the Falungong', *Renmin Ribao*, 18 August 1999, p. 1 in FBIS-CHI-1999-0818, p. 4.

57 'Key Members on Organization, Motives of Falungong', *Xinhua*, 10 August 1999 in FBIS-CHI-1999-0810, p. 1.

58 Much of the regulation was brought together in the Ministry of Public Security publication, *Chajin qudi xiejiao zuzhi falu fagui* (Laws and Regulations Prohibiting and Banning Heretical Cult Organization), Beijing: Qunzhong chubanshe, 1999, *passim*.

59 'Falungong Ban Supported By Law', *Beijing Review*, vol. 42, no. 37, 13 September 1999, p. 9.

60 'New Law on Mass Rallies Took 10 Years of Effort', *China Daily*, 26 December 1989, p. 4.

61 'Commentary Views Public Organization Regulations', *Renmin Ribao*, 9 November 1999 in FBIS-CHI-89-230, 1 December 1989, p. 14.

62 *Minzhengbu youguan fuze ren zhichu quide Falun dafa yanjiushi yifa zouchude jueding* (Ministry of Civil Affairs Official Spokesperson Points Out that the Decision to Ban the Falun Da Research Society was Based in Law), *Renmin Ribao*, 24 July 1999.

63 Xiao Du, 'Faithfully Adhere to the Principles of the Constitution – Sidelights on How the NPCSC Examined and Discussed the Law Governing Assemblies, Parades and Demonstrations', *Renmin Ribao*, 1 November 1989, p. 2 in FBIS-CHI-89-214, 8 November 1989, p. 25.

64 In her analysis, Julie Ching argues the importance of the state constitutional guarantee of freedom of assembly, but she indicates: 'The government appears in the right when it describes the tight organization of the group which Li Hongzhi characterizes as spontaneous.' Ching, 'The Falun Gong: Religious and Political Implications', p. 4.

65 Text of 'The PRC Law Governing Assemblies, Parades and Demonstrations', in FBIS-CHI-89-210, 1 November 1989, p. 16.

66 Charles D. Paglee, 'Chinalaw Web-Regulations for the Implementation of the Law of Assembly, Procession and Demonstration', http://www.quis.net/chinalaw/prclaw113.html (accessed 23 June 2002).

67 Many of the Chinese texts of the central government and Party documentation on the case against the Falungong are provided in a single issue of *Xin
Hua yuebao* (New China Monthly), no. 8, 1999.
68 Zhang Qiang, ed., *Xuiding xingfa tiaowen shiyong jieshuo* (Explanations of the
Application of the Revised Criminal Law Articles), Beijing: Zhongguo jiancha
chubanshe, 1997, p. 388.
69 Zhou Daoluan, Shan Changzhong, Zhan Sihan *et al.*, *Xingfade xiugai yu shiyong* (The Revision and Application of the Criminal Law), Beijing: Renmin
fayuan chubanshe, 1997, p. 616.
70 Wang Lieming, 'Falungong Said to Disclose State Secrets', Xinhuashe, Beijing,
25 October 1999, in FBIS-CHI-1999-1027, p. 2.
71 Li Chun and Wang Shangxin, *et al.*, *Zhongguo xingfa xiudingde Beijing yu
shiyong* (The Background of Chinese Criminal Law Revision and its
Application), Beijing: Falu chubanshe, 1998, p. 395.
72 Charles D. Paglee, China Law Web-Regulations Governing Venues for
Religious Activities, http://www.lqis.net/chinalaw/prelaw110.html (accessed
23 June 2002).
73 'Guanyu quti xijiao zhuzhi, fangfan he chengzhi xiejiao huodongde jueding',
(NPCSC Decision on Eliminating Cult Organization, Preventing and
Punishing Cult Activity), 1 November 1999, *Renmin Ribao*.
74 'Zhu Rongji Discusses "Three Stresses" Campaign', Xinhuashe, Beijing,
19 August 1999, FBIS-CHI-1999-0819, p. 1.
75 'Guanyu banli zuzhi he liyong xiejiao fanzui anjian juti yingyong falu
ruogan wentide jieshi' (Interpretation of Several Questions in Law concerning
Criminal Cases or Organizing and Using Evil Cult Organization), *Renmin
Ribao*, 1 November 1999, p. 2.
76 See You Wei and Zhao Jianfeng, 'Lun woguo xingfa sifa jieshiquande guishu
wenti' (On the Issues Concerning the Power of Judicial Interpretation of our
Criminal Law), *Faxue yanjiu* (Studies in Law), no. 1, 1993, p. 58.
77 See Chen Sixi, 'Lun lifa jieshi wentide shiyu fei jiquita' (On Questions
Concerning Legislative Interpretation and other Issues), *Zhongguo faxue*
(Chinese Legal Science), no. 3, 1998, p. 63.
78 See Keith, *China's Struggle for the Rule of Law*, p. 82.
79 See, for example, Yin Yijun and Chan Jinzhao, 'Sifa jieshi lunxi' (Discussion
and Analysis of Judicial Interpretation), *Zhengfa luntan* (Law and Political
Science Forum), no. 1, 1994, p. 35.
80 Rather than using 'open-textured', Randall Peerenboom discusses 'thick' and
'thin' versions of the 'rule of law' and analyses how different constitutional
regimes including China can attempt to move towards the rule of law.
Peerenboom, *China's Long March to the Rule of Law*, pp. 5–6.

3 The criminal justice response to violence in the modern Chinese family

1 Ronald C. Keith, *China's Struggle for the Rule of Law*, London and New York:
Macmillan Ltd. and St. Martin's Press, 1994, p. 40.
2 Herlee Creel, *The Birth of China*, New York: Frederick Unger, 1979.
3 Fairbank, Reischauer, and Craig, *East Asia: Tradition and Transformation*,
Boston, MA: Houghton Mifflin Co., 1989, p. 230.
4 For discussion of these various examples see Geoffrey MacCormack, *The
Spirit of Traditional Chinese Law*, Athens and London: University of Georgia
Press, 1996, pp. 64, 67, 91, 96.
5 Ibid., p. 49.
6 Herlee Creel, *The Birth of China*, as cited from James Legge, vol. iv, p. 170.

7 Geoffrey MacCormack, *Traditional Chinese Penal Law*, Edinburgh: Edinburgh University Press, 1990, p. 161.

8 Ibid., p. 10.

9 Guo Jianmei *et al.* (eds), *Jiating baoli yu falu yuanzhu* (Domestic Violence and Legal Assistance), dual Chinese-English Text. Beijing: Zhongguo shehui kexue chubanshe, 2003, p. 193.

10 James Farrer and Sun Zhongxin, 'Extramarital Love in Shanghai', *The China Journal*, no. 50, July 2003, p. 19.

11 Bai Guimei, 'International Human Rights Law and the Elimination of Violence against Women: China's Theory and Practice', International Law Institute, Peking University, published paper, pp. 4–5.

12 The Centre for Women's Law Studies and Legal Services of Peking University, *Theory and Practice of Women's Rights and Interests in Contemporary China*, Beijing: Workers' Press, 2001, p. 414.

13 Ibid., p. 412.

14 Ibid., p. 413.

15 As cited and analysed in Ronald C. Keith, 'Legislating Women's and Children's "Rights and Interests" in the People's Republic of China', *The China Quarterly*, no. 149, March 1997, p. 48.

16 Discussion with Cui Min, Beijing, 15 October 2001.

17 See Ronald C. Keith and Zhiqiu Lin, *Law and Justice in China's New Marketplace*, London: Palgrave 2001, pp. 49–50, 55–57.

18 The 'humiliation' of women in this article refers to the crime of assembling 'a crowd to have brawls, stir up fights and cause trouble, humiliate women, or engage in other hooligan activities, undermining public order...' in NPC, PRC, *The Criminal Law and the Criminal Procedure Law of the People's Republic of China*, Beijing: Foreign Languages Press, 1984, p. 55. This kind of loose enumeration of crimes did not help to highlight the importance of violence against women.

19 This is Harold M. Tanner's analysis, 'The Offense of Hooliganism and the Moral Dimension of China's Pursuit of Modernity, 1979–96, *Twentieth-Century China*, vol. 26, no. 1, November 2000, p. 12.

20 Ibid., p. 13.

21 For related analysis see The Centre for Women's Law Studies and Legal Services, p. 416.

22 Ibid., p. 417.

23 Guo Jianmei *et al.* (eds), *Jiating baoli yu falu yuanzhu*, p. 183.

24 Allan Y. Jiao, 'Traditions and Changes of Police Culture: Organization, Operation, and Behavior of the Chinese Police', in Jianhong Liu *et al.* (eds), *Crime and Social Control in a Changing China*, Westport, CT and London: Greenwood Press, 2001, p. 173.

25 Guo Jianmei *et al.* (eds), *Jiating baoli yu falu yuanzhu*, p. 185.

26 NPC, PRC, *Zhonghua renmin gongheguo xingfa* (Criminal Law of the People's Republic of China), Chinese-English Edition, Beijing: Falu chubanshe, 2002, p. 183. For analysis of the 'object' in the crime of indecent sexual assault on women see Zhang Ying, 'Qiangzhi weixie funu zui lifa bijio he tezheng fenxi (A Comparative Analysis of Legislation on the Coercive Indecent Assault on Women), *Xiandai faxue* (Modern Law Science), vol. 22, no. 3, June 2000, pp. 73–77.

27 The Centre for Women's Law Studies and Legal Services, p. 473.

28 'Chinese Gynecologist Sentenced to Death for Sex Crimes', Hong Kong AFP, 14 February 2003, in *Daily Report*, FBIS, 1001.

29 Guo Jianmei *et al.* (eds), *Jiating baoli yu falu yuanzhu*, p. 159 and fn.1, p. 162.

30 Beijing discussions with Chen Mingxia and Huang Lie, October 2001.

31 'PRC Passes Changes to Marriage Law, Explicitly Bans Concubinage, Domestic Violence', *Xinhua*, 21 April 2001 in FBIS-CHI-2001-0428.
32 Beijing discussion with Xia Yinlan, October 2001.
33 For the reported opinion of a senior participant in the drafting process, Professor Wu Changshen, see in 'PRC Passes Changes to Marriage Law, Explicitly Bans Concubinage, Domestic Violence', *Xinhua*, 28 April 2001, in FBIS-CHI-2001-0428.
34 'NPC Standing Committee Members Discuss Amendments to Marriage Law, *Xinhua*, Beijing, 27 October 2000.
35 MacCormack, *The Spirit of Traditional Chinese Law*, p. 96.
36 Philip C. Huang, *Code, Custom, and Legal Practice in China: The Qing and the Republic Compared*, Stanford, CA: Stanford University Press, 2001, p. 186.
37 James Farrer and Sun Zhongxin, 'Extramarital Love in Shanghai', p. 2. These authors cite as their sources on the treatment of adultery Zha Bo and Geng Wenxiu, 'Sexuality in Urban China', *The Australian Journal of Chinese Affairs*, no. 28, July 1992 and Borge Bakken, *The Exemplary Society: Human Improvement, Social Control and the Dangers of Modernity*, Oxford: Oxford University Press, 2000.
38 'Survey Indicates Most Chinese Favor Sanctions Against Bigamy, Domestic Violence', Beijing, *Xinhua*, 2 August 2000, in FBIS-CHI-2000-0802, AFS Document No: CPP20000802000102, 3 August 2000.
39 'Li Peng Chairs NPC Meeting, Draft Marriage Law Revision Cited', *Xinhua*, 24 April 2001, in FBIS-CHI-2001-0424.
40 Beijing discussion with Wang Zuofu, October 2001.
41 Discussion with Xia Yinlan in Beijing, October 2001.
42 'Perfect Marriage and Family Laws, and Promote Social Civilization and Progress' (verbatim), *Xinhua*, 28 April 2001, in FBIS-CHI-2001-0429, p. 2.
43 'Survey Indicates Most Chinese Favor Sanctions Against Bigamy, Domestic Violence', Beijing, *Xinhua*, 2 August 2000, in FBIS-CHI-2000-0802, AFS Document No: CPP20000802000102, 3 August 2000.
44 For an explanation of this see The NPC Legal Work Committee and the Committee on Rights and Interests of the All-China Women's Federation, *Zhonghua renmin gongheguo jiehunfa shiyong shouce* (The Marriage Law of the People's Republic of China: A Practical Handbook), Beijing: Falu chubanshe, 2001, p. 58.
45 Xia Yinlan Beijing interview, October, 2001.
46 As translated and cited in Peking University's Centre for Legal Studies and Assistance for Women, *Jiating baoli yu falu huanzhu* (Domestic Violence and Legal Assistance), 2003.
47 Proferssor Bai Guimei of the Peking University Law Faculty discusses the UN Declaration's definitions in 'International Human Rights Law and the Elimination of Violence Against Women: China's Theory and Practice', in E.P. Mendes and A.-M. Traehold (eds), *Human Rights: Chinese and Canadian Perspectives*, The Human Rights and Education Centre, University of Ottawa, 1997, p. 586.
48 *Zhonghua renmin gongheguo xingfa* (Criminal Law of the People's Republic of China), Chinese-English edition, Beijing: Falu chubanshe, 2002, p. 183.
49 NPC Legal Work Committee, *Zhonghua renmin gongheguo jiehun fa: xiugai lifa ziliaoxuan* (The Marriage Law of the People's Republic of China: Selected Legislative Materials), Beijing: Falu chubanshe, 2001, pp. 351–53.
50 'Li Peng Joins NPC Group Discussion on Marriage Law Amendments', *Xinhua*, Beijing, 27 October 2000.
51 For the twin Chinese and English language texts of this law see People's Republic of China, *Law of Succession of the People's Republic of China; Adoption*

Law of the People's Republic of China; Marriage Law of the People's Republic of China, Beijing: Falu chubanshe, 2002. The Chinese version of the key Article 3 under 'General Provision' is on p. 78, the English on p. 79. The various amendments are discussed in 'PRC Decides on Revising Marriage Law', *Xinhua*, 28 April 2001, in FBI-CHI-2001-0429, pp. 1–7.

52 The Centre for Women's Law Studies and Legal Services, p. 468. Although most jurists are prepared to argue that forced sex within the marriage cannot be considered rape, some scholars are exploring whether rape might occur under highly selective circumstances such as a husband returning after many years of separation and 'raping' his wife, or such as forced sex during the period of divorce.

53 See, for example, Laio Wenli and Liu Yiping, 'Lun "hunnei qiangjian" fanzui yingdang huanxing' (On Postponing the Criminalization of 'Rape within Marriage', *Xingshi faxue* (Study of Criminal Law), no. 6, 2002, p. 55.

54 Reformers are at least at the stage of classifying different types of sexual harassment. Sun Xiaomei of the Chinese Women's College has conducted a survey of 4,000 urban women in Beijing, the Inner Mongolian Autonomous Region and Zhejiang and Hebei provinces. In 2000, her respondents identified the six most vexing forms of harassment as 'inappropriate sexual advances by male superiors in offices, ex-husbands' harassment of ex-wives, groping on buses, cat-calls on the street, and sexual misconduct by doctors to women patients and teachers to students.

55 See, for example, 'Xinhua Reports on Problems of Domestic Violence', *Xinhua*, 25 November 2003. This report indicated: 'Jurists with the Law School of Beijing University say the new Marriage Law, which clearly prohibits domestic violence, doesn't specify related judicial procedures, which leaves too large room [*sic*] for free judgment.'

56 *Marriage Law of the People's Republic of China*, pp. 98–99.

57 As explained in October 2001 discussions with CASS Law Professor, Yan Xilan, in Beijing.

58 *Marriage Law of the People's Republic of China*, pp. 97–99.

59 Ibid., pp. 98–99.

60 'PRC Lawmaker: Items Against "Family Violence" Urged in Marriage Law Amendment', *Xinhua*, 26 April 2001, in FBIS-CHI-2001-0426, p. 1.

61 Ibid., p. 1.

62 For a detailed analysis of one such case concerning the victim's refusal to disclose assault and the offender's claim that 'rape' was, in fact, a dispute between lovers see Pu Yaxin, 'Falu yu xisuzhi jiande xingbie yinsu' (Gender Relations Between Law and Customs), *Funu yanjiu luncong* (Collection of Women's Studies), no. 9, September 2002, pp. 16–23.

63 *Zhonghua renmin gongheguo xingfa*, p. 63.

64 Guo Jianmei *et al.* (eds), *Jiating baoli yu falu yuanzhu*, p. 207.

65 For the text of this Interpretation see Ma Yuan (ed.), *Xin jiehunfa ji sifa jiesi shiyong zhunan* (Practical Guidelines on the Interpretation of the New Marriage Law), Beijing: Zhongguo shehui kexue chubanshe, 2002, p. 410.

66 Guo Jianmei *et al.* (eds), *Jiating baoli yu falu yuanzhu*, p. 207.

67 Ibid., pp. 208–09.

68 Ibid., p. 212.

69 Kang Shuhuai and Wei Xinwen, *Youzuzhi fanzui toushi* (An Examination of Organized Crime), Beijing: Beijing daxue chubanshe, 2001, p. 227.

70 'Ministry Official on Women, Children Abductions' Beijing, *Xinhua* in English, 13 November 98, FBIS-CHI-98-317, 17 November 1998.

71 Kang Shuhuai and Wei Xinwen, *Youzuzhi fanzui toushi*, p. 227.

72 Ye Gaofeng and Liu Defa (eds), *Jiyuan fanzui duice yanjiu* (Study on Countermeasures against Organized Crime Groups), Beijing: Zhongguo jiancha chubanshe, 2000, p. 340.

73 Ye Gaofeng and Liu Defa (eds), *Jiyuan fanzui duice yanjiu*, p. 342. 'Ministry Official on Women, Children Abductions', Beijing, *Xinhua* in English, 13 November 98, FBIS-CHI-98-317, 17 November 1998.

74 'Ministry Official on Women, Children Abductions', Beijing, *Xinhua*.

75 Ye Gaofeng and Liu Defa (eds), *Jiyuan fanzui duice yanjiu*, p. 348.

76 The Centre for Women's Law Studies and Legal Services, p. 439.

77 'Ministry Official on Women, Children Abduction', Beijing, *Xinhua*.

78 'PRC Political Bureau Member Luo Gan Urges Crackdown on Women, Children Abduction', Beijing, Xinhua Domestic Service in Chinese, 26 May 2000, translated from a report by *Renmin Ribao* reporter Liu Xiaosen and Xinhua reporter Wang Leiming 'Luo Gan Stresses the Need to Conscientiously Study General Secretary Jiang's Important Concept of "Three Represents" and Effectively Carry out Special Struggle to "Crack down on Abducting and Trafficking in Women, Children" ', FBIS-CHI-2000-0526, 8 June 2000.

79 'PRC Security Ministry to Help Resettle Women, Children Rescued From Abductors', Beijing, *Xinhua*, in English, 22 June 2000. FBIS-CHI-2000-0622, 27 June 2000.

80 Zhao Bingzhi and He Xingwang, *Xin Xingfadian de chuangzhi* (The Making of the New Chinese Criminal Code), Beijing: Falu chubanshe, 1997, p. 310.

81 The Centre for Women's Law Studies and Legal Services, p. 441.

82 The texts for the 'Decision' and the 'Answers' are available on line at Guangzhou Lawman Network Information Limited, http://www.lawman.com.cn (accessed 23 July 2003).

83 Zhao Bingzhi and He Xingwang, *Xin xingfadiande chuangzhi*, pp. 310–15.

84 Ou Jinxiong, Li Lan, Qing zhuwen, Liu Yuanhua, and Wu Daxian, '*Guaimai funu, ertongzui ji xiangguan fanzuide lifa quexian yu wanshan*' (On the Legislative Flaws and Improvement of [the] Crime of Abducting and Selling Women and Children and Other [Related Crimes]), *Guangxi zhengfa guanli ganbu xueyuan xuebao* (Journal of the Guangxi Institue of Law and Politics for Cadre Administration), vol. 16, no. 2, June 2001, p. 22.

85 The Centre for Women's Law Studies and Legal Services, pp. 421–22.

86 A recent survey found that 50 per cent of rural females, who have been subject to a beating by their spouse, are likely to go to relatives for mediation, and another 33 per cent responded by taking violent revenge. Only 7 per cent went to law enforcement agencies for assistance. See 'Xinhua Reports on Problems of Domestic Violence in China', *Xinhua*, 23 November 2003.

87 For related discussion of organizational strategies such as top-down 'comprehensive management of public order' and bottom-up 'comprehensive community intervention' see Ronald C. Keith and Zhiqiu Lin, 'The Making of a Chinese NGO: The Research and Intervention Project on Domestic Violence', *Problems of Post-Communism*, vol. 50, no. 6, November–December 2003, pp. 46–48.

88 'China Tackles Domestic Violence at Community Level', Tianjin, 7 March 2003.

4 'Organized crime', politics, and the law

1 For example, refer to R.J. Kelly, Lo-Lin Chin, and J.A. Gangan, 'The Dragon Breathes Fire: Chinese Organized Crime in New York City', *Crime, Law and Social Change*, vol. 19, 1993, pp. 245–69; W.H. Myers III, 'The Emerging Threat

of Transnational Organized Crime from the East', *Crime, Law and Social Change*, vol. 24, 1996, pp. 181–222; and John Huey-Lond Song and John Dombrink, 'Asian Emerging Crime Groups: Examining the Definition of Organized Crime', *Criminal Justice Review*, vol. 19, no. 1, Autumn 1994, pp. 228–43.

2 After an extensive search in the social sciences, political science, sociology and criminology abstracts and citation indices for the past fifteen years, no single item was found concerning Chinese jurist discussion on 'criminal organization'.

3 See Ye Gaofeng and Liu Defa (eds), *Jituan fanzui duice yanjiu* (The Study of Countermeasures against Crime by Criminal Organization), Beijing: Zhongguo jiancha chubanshe, 2000, pp. 13–20.

4 Ye Gaofeng and Liu Defa (eds), *Jiytuan fanzui duice yanjiu*, p. 175.

5 Gao Mingxuan (ed.), *Xingfa xue* (Criminal Law Science), Beijing: Falu chubanshe, 1981, pp. 72–90.

6 Ye Gaofeng and Liu Defa (eds), *Jituan fanzui duice yanjiu*, pp. 53–77.

7 Ibid., p. 57.

8 The city authorities also complained about other problems associated with the inflow of rural surplus labour, such as serious housing shortages, congested transportation systems, inability to implement birth control policies and programmes, and rising urban unemployment due to state-enterprise reform. For more discussion on migrant rural labour and its effects on urban communities, see Ye Gaofeng and Liu Defa (eds), *Jituan fanzui duice yanjiu*, p. 207.

9 *The Criminal Law and the Criminal Procedure Law of China*, dual English-Chinese texts, Beijing: Foreign Languages Press, 1980.

10 See Articles 22–26 of the CL 79.

11 Yu Zhigang (eds), *Redian fanzui falu yinan wenti jiexi* (Analysis and Explanations of Difficult Legal Issues Concerning Hotly Debated Crimes), p. 23.

12 Zhao Bingzhi and He Xingwang, *'Lun tebie xingfa he xingfa xiugai'* (On Special Criminal Law and the Revision of the Criminal Code), *Zhongguo faxue* (Chinese Legal Science), no. 4, 1996, pp. 15–23.

13 Ye Gaofeng, 'Introduction to Organized Crimes', in Ye Gaofeng and Liu Defa (eds), *Jiyuan fanzui duice yanjiu*, p. 38.

14 Ye Gaofeng, 'Introduction to Organized Crimes', p. 38; for a detailed study on Chinese criminal gangs before 1997, see Lening Zhang, S. Messner, Zhou Lu, and Xiaogang Deng, 'Gang Crime and its Punishment in China', *Journal of Criminal Justice*, vol. 24, no. 4, 1997, pp. 289–302.

15 The Chinese version of this 'Opinion' can be found in *Xingshi fagui huibian* (Compilation of Criminal Legislation), Harbin: Heilongjiang renmin chuban-she, 1990, pp. 862–64.

16 See Michael D. Maltz, 'On Defining "Organized Crime": The Development of a Definition and a Typology', *Crime and Delinquency*, vol. 22, July 1976, p. 19.

17 Ibid.

18 For an excellent selection of key articles by Western scholars on organized crimes, see Noks Passas (ed.), *Organized Crime*, Sydney: Dartmouth, 1995.

19 Yu Zhigang, *Redian fanzui falu yinan wenti jiexi*, p. 175.

20 Ye Gaofeng and Liu Defa (eds), *Jituan fanzui duice yanjiu*, p. 76.

21 Zhao Bingzhi and He Xingwang, *Xin Xingfadian de chuangzhi* (The Making of the New Chinese Criminal Code), Beijing: Falu chubanshe, 1997, p. 64.

22 Ye Gaofeng and Liu Defa (eds), *Jituan fanzui duice yanjiu*, p. 75; Zhao Bingzhi (ed.), *Xin xingfadian de chuangzhi* (The Making of the New Criminal Code), Beijing: Falu chubanshe, 1997, p. 380.

23 Ni Ruiping, Cheng Peilang, and Ke Gezhuang, '*Heishehui xingzhi zuzhi fanzui he fangzhi duice*' (Crimes Committed by Organizations with a Triad Nature and Prevention Strategies), *Xingshi faxue* (Criminal Law), no. 3, 1997, p. 61.
24 Gao Jinghong, 'Article Defines "Triad Crimes"', Beijing, *Renmin Ribao*, Overseas Edition in Chinese, 16 August 1997, p. 5; Article from the 'Outline of Criminal Law' column by Gao Jinghong entitled 'Crimes of a Triad Nature', FBIS-CHI-97-246, 9 April 1997.
25 Liu Shoufen and Wang Xiaoming, '*Lun heishehui zuzhi fanzui yu woguo xingshi lifa de wanshan*' (On the Crime of Black Society and the Perfection of Criminal Legislation in China), in Gao Mingxuan Zhao Bingzhi and Hu Yunting (eds) *Xingfa xiugai jianyi wenji* (Collection of Articles Concerning the Suggestions for Chinese Criminal Law Revision), Beijing: Zhongguo renmin daxue chubanshe, 1997, p. 711.
26 Yuan Fanmin, '*Qiantan heishehui zuzhizui de rending*' (Preliminary Discussions on the Identification of Organization with a Triad Nature), *Xingshi faxue* (Criminal Law), no. 5, 1998, p. 65.
27 Chan Minghua and Guo Xiaoming, '*Luelun heishehui zuzhi fanzui de jige weni*' (Brief Discussions of Several Issues Concerning the Crime of Underground Societies), in Gao Mingxuan Zhao Bingzhi and Hu Yunteng (eds), *Xingfa xiugai jianyi wenji* p. 702.
28 Ibid., p. 700.
29 Liu Shoufen and Wang Xiaoming, 'Lun heishehui zuzhi fanzui yu woguo xingshi lifa de wanshan' p. 11.
30 Li Wenyan and Tian Hongjie, '*Dahei chue*': xingshi falu shiyong jieshuo (Eliminating Underworld and Evil Forces: Explaining the Application of Criminal Legislation), Beijing: Qunzhong chubanshe, 2001, p. 49.
31 Gao Jinghong, 'Article Defines "Triad crimes"'.
32 Yuan Fangmin, '*Qiantan heishehui zuzhizui de rending*', 1998, p. 65.
33 Article 69 of the 1997 CL; Zhu Erjun, ' "Guanyu shenli heishehui xingzhi zuzhi fanzui de anjian juti yingyong falu ruogan wenti de jieshi" de lijie yu shiyong' (Understanding and Application of 'The Interpretation of Several Issues concerning the Application of Law in Adjudicating Cases Concerning the Crimes of Organization with a Triad Nature'), *Xingshi shenpan cankao* (Reference Materials for Criminal Trials), 2001, no. 2, p. 73.
34 Ibid.
35 Ibid., Article 3 of the 'Explanations'.
36 Ibid., Article 4 of the 'Explanations'.
37 Zhu Erjun, 'Guanyu shenli heishehui xingzhi zuzhi fanzui de anjian juti yingyong falu ruogan wenti de jieshi de lijie yu shiyong' p. 73.
38 Shong Xiaoming, '*Shixi youzuzhi fanzui fenzi dui guojia gongzuo renyuande huilu fushi yiqi duice*' (Preliminary Analysis of the Bribery of State Functionaries by Organized Criminal Elements), *Xingshi faxue* (Criminal Law), no. 1, 1998, p. 64.
39 See 'China Redefines Criminal Syndicates, Misappropriating Public Funds', Beijing, *Xinhua*, 24 April 2002, from *China News Digest*, http://www.cnd.org/Global/02/04/020424-91.html (accessed 24 October 2003).
40 Article 67 of PRC 1982 Constitution, Beijing: Renmin chubanshe, 2004.
41 The Chinese version of this new legislative interpretation is available at http://www.news.xinhuanet.com/zh . . ./content_376894.ht (accessed 19 October 2003).
42 NPC *Zhonghua renmin gongheguo xingfa* (PRC Criminal Law), Beijing: Renmin chubanshe, 2004.

43 For a basic understanding of this distinction see Wang Nanling, 'Tianjingshi heishehui xingzhi zuzhi fanzui de xianzhuang, yuanyin ji zhencha duice sikao' (Reflections on the Current Situation and Causes, and Strategies of Investigation of Organizations with a Triad Nature), *Xingshi faxue* (Criminal Law), no. 3, 1998, p. 79.

44 Li Wenyan and Tian Hongjie, '*Dahei chue': Xingshi falu shiyong jieshuo*, p. 71.

45 Ibid., p. 49.

46 Guo Jiangan, 'Lianheguo yufang fanzui he xingshi sifa weiyuanhui diwujie huiyi zongshu' (Overview of the Fifth Meeting of the UN Crime Prevention and Criminal Justice Committee), *Xingshi faxue* (Criminal Law), no. 3, 1997, p. 53.

47 Zhao Bingzhi and He Xingwang, *Xin xingfadian de chuangzhi* (The Making of the New Chinese Criminal Code), Beijing: Falu chubanshe, 1997, p. 167.

48 Ye Gaofeng and Liu Defa (eds), *Jituan fanzui duice yanjiu*, p. 379.

49 John Z. Wang, 'The Eastern Turkistan Islamic Movement: A Case Study of a New Terrorist Organization in China', *International Journal of Offender Therapy and Comparative Criminology*, vol. 47, no. 5, 2003, p. 576.

50 For an extensive discussion of Chinese viewpoint on the role of motivation and purpose in determining crime in Chinese criminal justice see Ronald C. Keith and Zhiqiu Lin, 'To Revise or not to Revise China's Law on Counterrevolution', *China Information*, vol. 5, no. 4, Spring 1991, pp. 24–41.

51 Ou Yongtao, Wekejian, and Liu Ranwen, *Zhonghua renmin gongheguo xin xingfa zhushi yu shiyong* (Interpretation and Application of the PRC Criminal Law), Beijing: Renmin fayuan chubanshe, 1997, p. 231.

52 The Chinese version of the NPC Standing Committee Revision can be located in http://news.xinhuannet.com/zh.../content_218520.ht (accessed 27 September 2003).

53 Mo Hongxian and Wang Mingxing, '*Woguo dui kongbu zuyi fanzui de xingfa kongzhi ji lifa wanshan*' (Improving China's Criminal Law Control over and Legislative Improvement of Terrorist Crime), *Xingshi faxue* (Criminal Law), no.2, 2004, pp. 59–65.

54 Denny Roy, 'China and the War on Terrorism', *Orbis*, Summer 2002, p. 511.

55 Ibid., p. 514.

56 Ibid., p. 517.

57 Liu Shoufen, Wang Minglang, and Huang Shaoze, 'Heishehui (xingzhi) zuzhi fanzui duice yanjiu' (Studies on the Prevention Strategies against Criminal Organizations with a Triad Nature and their Crimes), *Zhongguo Jiancha* (Chinese Prosecution), vol. 1, 2002, p. 157.

58 Kang Shuhuai and Wei Xinwen, *Youzuzhi fanzui toushi* (An Examination of Organized Crime), Beijing: Beijing daxue chubanshe, 2001; for a detailed account of organized crimes concerning the manufacture and distribution of counterfeit goods, see Daniel C.K. Chow, 'Organized Crime, Local Protectionism, and the Trade in Counterfeit Goods in China', *China Economic Review*, vol. 14, 2003, pp. 473–84.

59 'Guangdong Police Crack Down on Drug Abuse', 26 June 2000, Guangzhou, *Xinhua*, FBIS-CHI-2000-0626, 29 June 2000; Lan Xinzhen, 'Saying No to Drugs', *Beijing Review*, vol. 47, no. 26, 1 July 2004, pp. 20–23.

60 Lan Xinzhen, 'Saying No to Drugs', pp. 20–23. Also see Randall Peerenboom, 'Out of the Pan and into the Fire: Well-Intentioned but Misguided Recommendations to Eliminate all Forms of Administrative Detention in China', *Northwestern University Law Review*, vol. 98, no. 3., pp. 1002–03, 1087, 1102.

61 These laws and regulations are primarily concerned with the procedures for use, storage, and transportation of narcotics and other psychotropic substances. Such law and regulation includes the 1984 PRC 'Law on the

Management of Medicines and Chemical Agents'; the 1987 State Council 'Procedures for Narcotic Drug Control', and the 1988 State Council 'Procedures for Psychotropic Substances'; the 1995 State Council 'Procedures for Compulsory Drug Addiction Rehabilitation'; and the 1995 Ministry of Health 'Procedures for the Administration of Pharmaceuticals for Drug Addiction Treatment'. For more detail on these laws and regulations, see 'PRC White Paper on Narcotics Control', Beijing, *Xinhua*, 26 June 2000, FBIS-CHI-2000-0626, *Daily Report*, China, 29 June 2000.

62 These include the legislative organs of Yunnan, Guizhou, Sichuan, Guangdong, Gansu, Shaanxi, Heilongjiang and Jiangsu provinces, the Guangxi Zhuang and Ningxia Hui Autonomous Regions, see 'PRC White Paper on Narcotics Control', 26 June 2000.

63 Gao Mingxuan, *Zhonghua renmin gongheguo xingfa de yunyu he dansheng* (The Embryo and Birth of the Criminal Code of the People's Republic of China), Beijing: Falu chubanshe, 1980, p. 231.

64 Lan Xinzhen, 'Saying No to Drugs', pp. 20–23.

65 Kang Shuhuai and Wei Xinwen, *Youzuzhi fanzui toushi*, p. 229.

66 *The Criminal Law and the Criminal Procedure Law of China*, Beijing: Foreign Languages Press, 1980, p. 229.

67 The NPC Standing Committee's Decision on Drug Control in Chinese can be located in Wang Yongcheng *et al.* (eds) *Daji dupin fanzui shiyong* (Handbook for Fighting Drug-Related Crime), Beijing: Renmin fayuan chubanshe, 1992, pp. 2–6, 17.

68 Zhao Bingzhi and He Xingwang, *Xin xingfadiande chuangzhi*, p. 439.

69 Supreme People's Court, '*Guanyu yange zhixing (guanyu jindu de jueding) yancheng dupin fanzui fenzi de tongzhi*' (1991 Notice regarding Implementation of the NPCSC 'Decision on Drug Control' and the Punishment of Drug-Related Criminal Elements) in Wang Yongcheng *et al.* (eds), *Daji dupin fanzui shiyong*, 1992, p. 18.

70 Wang Yongcheng *et al.* (eds), *Daji dupin fanzui shiyong*, pp. 2–6.

71 '*Quanguo fayuan shenli dupin fanzui anjian gongzhuo zuotan hui jiyao*' (Selected Minutes of the National Law Court Working Conference on Adjudicating Drug-Related Criminal Cases), *Xingshi shenpan cankao*, (Reference to Criminal Trial), 2000, no. 3, p. 74.

72 Zhao Bingzhi and He Xingwang, *Xin xingfadiande chuangzhi*, p. 453.

73 '*Quanguo fayuan shenli dupin fanzui anjian gongzhuo zuotan hui jiyao*' (Selected Minutes of National Law Court Working Conference on Adjudicating Drug-Related Criminal Cases), *Xingshi shenpan cankao*, p. 77.

74 Deng Zhenlin *et al.*, 'Drug Trafficking and Consumption in China: Two Case Studies', *International Social Science Journal* (A Special Issue on Drug Trafficking: Economic and Social Dimensions), vol. 53, no. 169, September 2001, p. 417.

75 Ibid.

76 Zhao Bingzhi and He Xingwang, *Xin xingfadiande chungzhi*, p. 440.

77 'China Executed 12 Drug Dealers, Burns Two Tons of Confiscated Narcotics', Beijing, *Xinhua*, 26 June 2000, FBIS-CHI-2000-0626, 29 June 2000.

78 Wu Zongzhi, 'Striking "Border Sneaking" ', *Beijing Review*, 29 April 2004, pp. 26–27.

79 For David Kyle and Rey Koslowski's discussion on human smuggling in the other Asian countries, see David Kyle and Rey Koslowski (eds), *Global Human Smuggling: Comparative Perspectives*, Baltimore, MD: The Johns Hopkins University Press, 2001.

80 Zai Liang and Wenzhen Te, 'From Fujian to New York: Understanding the New Chinese Immigration' in David Kyle and Rey Koslowski (eds), *Global*

Human Smuggling: Comparative Perspectives; Andrea Schloenhardt, 'Trafficking in Migrants: Illegal Migration and Organized Crime in Australia and the Asia Pacific Region', *International Journal of the Sociology of Law*, vol. 29, 2001, pp. 331–78; John Z. Wang, 'Illegal Chinese Immigration Into the United States: A Preliminary Factor Analysis', *International Journal of Offenders Therapy and Comparative Criminology*, vol. 45, no. 3, 2001, pp. 345–55.

81 'Report on Efforts to Prevent Illegal Emigration' Beijing, Xinhua Domestic Services in Chinese, 14 January 1995, FBIS-CHI-95-014, 19 November 1995.

82 Kong Xiaoning, '*Daji toudu chu zhongquan*' (Fighting Illegal Border Crossing by Sea with Powerful Fists), *Renmin Ribao* (People's Daily), Overseas edition, 26 April 2002, p. 1.

83 Wu Zongzhi, 'Striking "Border Sneaking" ', *Beijing Review*, 29 April 2004, pp. 26–27.

84 John Wang, 'Illegal Chinese Immigration into the United States: A Preliminary Factor Analysis', *International Journal of Offender Therapy and Comparative Criminology*, vol. 45, no. 3, 2001, p. 147.

85 Zai Liang and Wenzhen Te, 'From Fujian to New York: Understanding the New Chinese Immigration', p. 194.

86 Liu Jiachen, *Xingfa fenze ji peitao guiding xinshi xinjie* (New Interpretation of Criminal Law and Other Related Regulations), Beijing: Renmin fayuan chubanshe, 2000, vol. 2, p. 2291.

87 Ko-lin Chin, 'The Social Organization of Chinese Human Smuggling', in David Kyle and Rey Koslowski (eds), *Global Human Smuggling: Comparative Perspective*, pp. 224–25.

88 Kong Xiaoning, '*Daji toudu chu zhongquan*' (Fighting Illegal Border Crossing by Sea with Powerful Fists), p. 1.

89 For a general discussion on Chinese comprehensive management strategy as a means of crime control, Ronald C. Keith and Zhiqiu Lin, 2001, *Law and Justice in China's New Market Place*, London: Palgrave, 2001, pp. 61, 79, 89.

90 For a discussion of hooliganism and its deletion from the CL 97, see Ronald C. Keith and Zhiqiu Lin, *China Information*, pp. 211–12.

5 Crime and human rights in cyber-space

1 Cai Xiuying, 'Xin zhendi, xin tiaozhan, xin duice' (New Fronts, New Challenges, New Countermeasures), *Yunmeng jikan*, no. 4, July 2002, p. 91.

2 For a discussion of the dilemma faced by the leadership in the other Asian authoritarian states because of the development of the internet, see Nina Hachigian, 'The Internet and Power in One-Party East Asian States', *The Washington Quarterly*, vol. 25, no. 3, Summer 2002, p. 41.

3 Cai Xiuying, 'Xinzhendi, xintiaozhan, xinduice', p. 90.

4 'China NPC, CPPCC Discussions Focus on the IT Industry', *Xinhua*, Beijing, 13 March 2001, in FBIS-CHI-2001-0313, 13 March 2001, p. 1.

5 Full report is available at: http://www.state.gov/g/drl/rls/hrrpt/2002 (accessed 23 August 2003).

6 Richard Spencer, 'Chinese Web Police Hacked', *Calgary Herald*, 4 September 2004, p. A16.

7 For more information on the earlier development of the Internet in China, see Eric Harwit and Duncan Clark, 'Shaping the Internet in China', *Asian Survey*, vol. 41, no. 3, May/June 2001, pp. 377–408.

8 Yang Guangliang, 'Paying Attention to Information Security', Beijing, *Liaowang* (Outlook), 4 June 2001, no. 23, pp. 37–38; FBIS-CHI-2001-0612, *Daily Report*, China, 4 June 2001; and 'Safeguarding Internet Security in Accordance

with Law and Promoting Comprehensive Social Progress, *Renmin Ribao* (People's Daily) (Internet Version), 30 December 2000, p. 3, FBIS-CHI-2001-0103, *Daily Report*, China, 2 April 2000.

9 'Quanguo wangmin shuliang yida 6800 wan' (China's Internet Users have Already Reached 68 Millions), *Renmin Ribao* (People's Daily) (Overseas Edition), 25 July 2003, p. 1.

10 Yang Guangliang, 'Paying Attention to Information Security'.

11 'Internet, A New Way for Chinese to Participate in Decision Making', *Xinhua*, Beijing, 5 June 2001, in FBIS-CHI-2001-0605, pp. 1–2.

12 'PRC Internet Users Flock Online to Follow NPC, CPPCC Sessions, Voice Opinions', FBIS-CHI-2002-0308, *Daily Report*, China. Beijing *Xinhua*, 8 March 2002.

13 Zhao Bingzhi and Yu Zhigang, 'Jisuanji fanzui jiqi lifa he lilun zhi huiying', (Computer Crime Legislation and its Theoretical Responses) in Gao Mingxuan and Zhao Bingzhi (eds), *21shiji xingfaxue xinwenti yantao* (Studies of the New Criminal Law Issues Emerging in the 21st Century), Beijing: Zhongguo jiancha chubanshe, 2001, p. 818.

14 Yu Zhigang (ed.), *Jisuanji fanzui yinan wenti sifa duice* (Strategies in Dealing with Difficult Issues in the Administration of Law concerning Computer Related Crime), Jilin: Jilin chubanshe, 2001, pp. 61, 121.

15 Zhao Bingzhi and Yu Zhigang, 'Jisuanji fanzui jiqi lifa he lilun zhi huiying', p. 818.

16 Digital Freedom Network's 1 May 2002 online discussion with David Sheff at www.dfn.org/voices/china/sheffchat.htm, p. 3.

17 'PRC Financial Website Attacked by Hackers', Beijing, *Xinhua*, FBIS-CHI-2000-0323, China, *Daily Report*, 23 March 2000.

18 The context of these attacks related to the China–US plane collision incident in South China Sea which had occurred in the previous April. Mu Qiao, 'Both "Red Hackers" and "Black Hackers" Are Distrupting Web Order', Beijing, *Renmin Ribao* (Internet Version), FBIS-CHI-2001-0507, *Daily Report*, China, 5 May 2001; 'Websites in Fujian, White House Hit in "Cyberwar" '. Hong Kong *Ta Kung Pao* (Worker's Daily), 7 May 2001, p. 2, FBIS-CHI-2001-0507, *Daily Report*, China, 7 May 2001; Li Jialu, 'PRC Computer Security Official Interviewed on Hackers' Activities', Beijing, Xinhua Domestic Service, FBIS-CHI-2001-0503, *Daily Report*, China, 3 May 2001.

19 'AFP Cites PRC Government Survey Reporting Hackers Attack 40 Per cent of Chinese Websites', Beijing, *Xinhua*, FBIS-CHI-2000-0404, China, *Daily report*, 4 April 2000.

20 Yang Guangliang, 'Paying Attention to Information Security', Beijing, *Liaowang*, 4 June 2001, no. 23, pp. 37–38 in FBIS-CHI-2001-0612, *Daily Report*, China, June 4 2001; 'Nearly 100 Hacker Cases in PRC Reported in 1998', Beijing, *Xinhua*, FBIS-CHI-99-006, *Daily Report*, China, 6 January 1999.

21 'Chinese Academy of Sciences Establishes Anti-hacking Force', Hongkong Zhongguo Tongguo Tongxun She, FBIS-CHI-2000-0822, China, *Daily Report*, 22 August 2000.

22 Si Lian, 'China Adopts Positive Measures to Guard against Computer Network Invasion by Hackers', Hong Kong Zhongguo Tongguo Tongxun She, FBIS-CHI-2000-0217, *Daily Report*, China, 17 February 2000; Li Shuangqi, *Wangluo fanzui fangkong duice* (The Strategies in Prevention and Control of Internet Crimes), Beijing: Qunzhong chubanshe, 2001, pp. 170–74; and Si Liang, 'Chinese Strengthens the Protection of Network and Information Security', Hongkong Zhongguo Tongguo Tongxun She, FBIS-CHI-1999-0829, *Daily Report*, China, 13 August 1999.

23 'Wu Jichuan Says China to Build National Information Security System', Beijing, *Renmin Ribao* (Internet Version), 12 October 2000, FBIS-CHI-2000-1012, *Daily Report*, China, 12 October 2000; 'FM Spokesman: PRC Stance Against Computer Crime Clear', Beijing, *Xinhua*, FBIS-CHI-2000-0215, *Daily Report*, China, 15 February, 2000; Xia Jinyao, *Jisuanji fanzui wenti de diaocha fenxi yu fangfan* (Investigation and Prevention of Computer-Related Crime), Beijing: Zhongguo gongan daxue chubanshe, 2001, p. 70.

24 Yu Zhigang (ed.), *Jisuanji fanzui yinan wenti sifa duice*, p. 52; for the full text of these provisions in Chinese, see Li Shuangqi, *Wangluo fanzui fangkong duice* (The Strategies in Prevention and Control of Internet Crime), Beijing: Qunzhong chubanshe, 2001, pp. 441–44.

25 See Articles 6 and 7 of the provisions. Full text of the provisions in Chinese is available in the Legal Committee of the Standing Committee of the NPC, *Jisuanji ji wangluo falu fagui* (Law and Regulations on Computer and Computer Networks), Beijing: Falu chubanshe, 1998.

26 For more discussions on the reasons and extent of the revision, see chapter 5: 'Balancing Society and the Individual in Judicial Justice' of Ronald C. Keith and Zhiqiu Lin, *Law and Justice in China's New Marketplace*, London: Palgrave, 2001.

27 Yu Zhigang, *Jisuanji fanzui yinan wenti sifa duice*, p. 54.

28 Zhao Yanguang, Zhu Huaci, and Pi Yong, *Jisuanji fanzui de dingzui yu liangxing* (Determining Computer-Related Crime and Punishment), Beijing: Renmin fayuan chubanshe, 2000. p. 126.

29 Yu Zhigang (ed.), *Jisuanji fanzui yinan wenti sifa duice*, p. 87; Zhao Yanguang, Zhu Huaci, and Pi Yong, *Jisuanji fanzui*, p. 161.

30 Ibid., p. 109.

31 Liu Jiachen, *Xingfa fenze ji peitao guiding xinshi xinjie* (New Interpretations of the Special Provisions of the Criminal Law and Related Regulations) Beijing: Renmin fayuan chubanshe, 2000, vol. 2, p. 2023.

32 Zhao Yanguang, Zhu Huaci, and Pi Yong, *Jisuanji fanzui de dingzui yu liangxing* (Determining Computer-Related Crime and Punishment), Beijing: Renmin fayang chubanshe, 2000, p. 162; and Yu Zhigang, *Jisuanji fanzui yinan wenti sifa duice*, p. 109.

33 Zhao Yanguang, Zhu Huaci, and Pi Yong, *Jisuanji fanzui yinan wenti sifa duice*, p. 162.

34 Author's italics. Criminal Law Research Unit, the Legal Work Committee of the NPCSC, *Zhonghua renmin gongheguo xingfa shiyi* (Interpretation of PRC Criminal Law), Beijing: Falun chubanshe, 1997, pp. 404–06.

35 For an extensive discussion on the debate in the mid-1990s, see Ronald C. Keith, *China's Struggle for the Rule of Law*, London: Macmillan, 1994, pp. 93–96.

36 Yu Zhigang (ed.), *Jisuanji fanzui yinan wenti sifa duice*, p. 96.

37 Ibid., p. 160.

38 Ibid., p. 95.

39 Yu Zhigang (ed.), *Jisuanji fanzui yinan wenti sifa duice*, pp. 107–10; Wang Shizhou, *'Lun Zhongguo jisuanji xingshi lifa yu sifa de wanshan wenti'* (On the Issues Concerning the Perfection of Chinese Criminal Legislation on Computer Crime), in Gao Mingxuan and Zhao Bingzhi (eds), *Shiji xingfaxue xinwenfi yanta*, p. 85.

40 'China to Boost Effects Against Crimes Jeopardizing Network Security', Beijing, Xinhua Domestic Service, FBIS-CHI-2001-0827, 27 August 2001.

41 The full Chinese text of both 'Notices' are available at http://www. chinacourt.org/Newlaw2002/SLC/SLC.asp?Db=chl&Grid=32109

42 'HK Paper: PRC Public Security Ministry Calls for Strict Control over Internet', Hong Kong *Ming* Pao, FBIS-CHI-2002-0118, *Daily Report*, China, 18 November 2002, World News Connection.

43 'China to Boost Effects Against Crimes Jeopardizing Network Security', Beijing, Xinhua Domestic Service, FBIS-CHI-2001-0827, 27 August 2001; Si Lian, 'China Adopts Positive Measures to Guard against Computer Network Invasion by Hackers', Hong Kong Zhongguo Tongxun She, FBIS-CHI-2000-0217, China, *Daily Report*, 17 February 2000.

44 Hu Jian and Wang Leiming, 'China to Institute Grading System for Security Protection for Computer Information Systems', Beijing, Xinhua Domestic Service, FBIS-Chi-2000-0405, China, *Daily Report*, 2 April 2000.

45 Jian Ping, *Jisuanji fanzui wenti yanjiu* (Researching the Problems of Computer Related Crime), Beijing: Shangwu chubanshe, 2000, p. 321.

46 'PRC Decisions to Safeguard Internet Safety', FBIS-CHI-2000-1228, China, *Daily Report*, Beijing, Xinhua Domestic Service in Chinese, 28 December 2000, World News Connection.

47 Philip Sohmen, 'Taming the Dragon: China's Efforts to Regulate the Internet, *Stanford Journal of East Asian Affairs*, Spring 2001, vol. 1, p. 19.

48 See the Legal Committee of the Standing Committee of the NPC, *Jisuanji ji wangluo falu fagui* (Law and Regulations on Computer and Computer Networks), Beijing: Falu chubanshe, 1998.

49 Full text of the Decision in Chinese is available at http://www. chinacourt.org/Newlaw2002/SLC/SLC.asp?Db=chl&Grid=32109

50 Luisetta Mudie, 'AFP: PRC Net-Surfers Shrug Off Cyber-Dissident Sentence', FBIS Transcribed Text No.: OW2001115099, Hong Kong AFP, China, 20 January 1999.

51 Human Rights Watch, World Report 2001: China at www.hrw.org/press/2001/02/huangqi0208.htm

52 Cindy Sui, 'AFP: China Jails First Cyber-Dissident for Pro-Democracy Essay', FBIS Transcribed Text, Number: CPP20010427000108, Hong Kong AFP, China, 27 April 2001.

53 'AFP: Chinese Court Turns Down Appeals of Four Internet Dissidents' FBIS-CHI-2003-1110, Hong Kong AFP, *Daily Report*, China, 10 November 2003, World News Connection. For other examples see 'Attacks on the Internet in China: Internet-Related Legal Actions and Site Shutdowns since January 2000', Digital Freedom Network at www.dfn.org/focus/china/ shutdown.htm

54 'AFP: Rights Group Says China Formally Arrested Internet Dissident for Subversion' FBIS-CHI-2003-0924, Hong Kong AFP, *Daily Report*, China, 25 September 2003. World News Connection.

55 Nina Hachigian, 'China's Cyber-Strategy', *Foreign Affairs*, March/April 2001, vol. 80, no. 2. http://www.rand.org/nsrd/capp/cyberstrategy.htm (accessed 26 March 2003); 'AFP Cites Rand Report: China Winning Internet War Against Dissidents For Now', FBIS Transcribed Text, No. CPP20020829000059, Hong Kong AFP, China, 29 August 2002. For an extensive discussion of the political implications of Internet usage in China, see Nina Hachigian and Lily Wu, '*The Information Revolution in Asia*', http://www.rang.org/publications/MR/MR1719 (accessed 26 March 2003).

56 Philip Sohmen, 'Taming the Dragon: China's Efforts to Regulate the Internet', *Stanford Journal of East Asian Affairs*, Spring 2001, vol. 1, pp. 17–26, p. 24.

57 'China To Regulate Online News "To Ensure Healthy Growth"', FBIS Transcribed Text, no.: CPP20000517000017, Beijing *Xinhua*, China, 17 May 2000.

58 Full text of this regulation in Chinese is available at http://law.chinalawinfo. com/Newlaw2002

59 'Xinhua Article Views Issues Relating to Internet Use in PRC', FBIS Transcribed Text, no.: CPP20020628000018, Beijing, *Xinhua*, China, 28 June 2002.
60 Ibid.
61 Full text of the Notice in Chinese is at http://www.chinacourt.org/flwk/show1.php?_id=37062&strl=%BB%A5% C1%AA%CD (accessed 3 May 2003).
62 Philip Sohmen, 'Taming the Dragon: China's Efforts to Regulate the Internet', p. 21.
63 Full text of the Charter in Chinese is available: http://www.chinacourt.org/flwk/show1.php?file_id=37424&str1=%BB%A5%C1%AA%CD (accessed 24 May 2003).
64 The Chinese text of the Covenant can be found at http://www.chinacourt. org/flwk/show1.php?file_id=38696&str1=%BB% A5%C1%AA%CD (accessed 24 May 2003).
65 Zhou Qizochun, 'PRC: Hechi People's Congress Vetoes City Work Report on Internet Café Rectification', FBIS Transcribed Text, No.: CPP20020111000085, Beijing, *Xinhua*, China, 11 January 2002.
66 'Xinhua Article Views Issues Relating to Internet Use in PRC', FBIS Transcribed Text, No.: CPP20020628000018, Beijing, *Xinhua*, China, 28 June 2002.
67 Luisetta Mudie, 'AFP: PRC Orders all Internet Cafes to Install Software to Block Foreign Websites' FBIS-Lat-2002-0626, *Daily Report*, China, Hong Kong AFP, 28 June 2002; 'FP: PRC Net-Surfers Shrug Off Cyber-Dissident Sentence', FBIS Transcribed Text, no. OW2001115099, Hong Kong AFP, China, 20 January 1999; Hsiao Peng. 'Central Propaganda Department Blocks Media Reporting of Yuanhua Corruption Case', FBIS Translated Text, no. CPP20000904000020, Hong Kong, *Sing Tao Jih Pao*, China, 3 September 2000.
68 Full Chinese text of 'The Provisions for Managing Business Providing Internet Service' can be located at http://law.chinalawinfo.com/Newlaw2002 (accessed 23 May 2003).
69 Philip Sohmen, 'Taming the Dragon: China's Efforts to Regulate the Internet', p. 17.
70 Richard Spencer, 'Chinese Web Police Hacked', *Calgary Herald*, 4 September 2004, p. A16.
71 The full text of the Management Methods in Chinese is available at http://law.chinalawinfo.com/Newlaw2002/SLC.asp?Db=chl&Gid=31477 (accessed 25 April 2003).
72 Refer to Article 5 of the Provisions as cited in 'PRC To Revoke Websites' Rights To Release Information', FBIS Translated Text, no.: OW1601144600, Hong Kong, *Ming Pao*, China, 14 January 2000; the full text of this regulation in Chinese is available at http://www.chinacourt.org/flwk/show1.php?file_id=36231&str1=%BB%A5%C1%AA%CD
73 'PRC To Revoke Websites' Rights To Release Information', FBIS Translated Text, no.: OW1601144600, Hong Kong, *Ming Pao*, China, 14 January 2000.
74 Ibid.
75 Ibid.
76 'Xinhua "Roundup" on PRC Internet Publication', FBIS Transcribed Text, no.: CPP20000721000132, Beijing, *Xinhua*, 21 July 2000; Yang Zhenwu, Lu Xinning, and Zhu Huaxin, '*Renmin Ribao* on Drive of Eliminating Pornography, Cracking Illegal Publications', FBIS Translated Text, no.: CPP20000614000060, Beijing, *Renmin Ribao* WWW, China, 14 June 2000. The Ministry of Information Industry was created out of the former Ministry of Posts and Telecommunications and Ministry of Electronic Industry in March 1998. Apparently, the Ministry is the primary government organization responsible for the development of the internet. For more details on the role of the

Ministry in the development of the internet in China, see Eric Harwit and Duncan Clark, 'Shaping the Internet in China', *Asian Survey*, vol. 41, no. 3, May/June 2001, p. 384.

77 The full text of the Provisional Regulations is available at http://www.chinacourt.org/ flwk/show1.php?file_id=36231&str1=%BB%A5%C1% AA%CD

78 Wang Yi, 'Confusion of three freedoms: A critique of *"Provisional Regulations on the Management of Online Publications"* ', http://article.chinalawinfo.com/ article/user/article_display.asp?Articleid=20284 (accessed 27 April 2003).

79 Yang Zhenwu, Lu Xinning, and Zhu Huaxin, *'Renmin Ribao* on Drive of Eliminating Pornography, Cracking Illegal Publications', FBIS Translated Text, no.: CPP20000614000060, Beijing, *Renmin Ribao* WWW, China, 14 June 2000.

80 'PRC Official Warns of [the] Pornographic "Peril" of Internet', FBIS Transcribed Text, no.: CPP20000425000161, Beijing, *Xinhua*, 25 April 2000.

81 Yang Zhenwu, Lu Xinning, and Zhu Huaxin, *'Renmin Ribao* on Drive of Eliminating Pornography, Cracking Illegal Publications'.

82 'AFP Cites Rand Report: China Winning Internet War Against Dissidents For Now', FBIS Transcribed Text, no.: CPP20020829000059, Hong Kong AFP, China, 29 August 2002.

83 The BBS (bulletin board system) is a computer or an application designed for the sharing or exchange of messages, or other files on a network.

84 'AFP Cites Rand Report: China Winning Internet War Against Dissidents For Now'.

85 Philip Sohmen, 'Taming the Dragon: China's Efforts to Regulate the Internet', *Stanford Journal of East Asian Affairs*, Spring 2001, vol. 1, p. 21.

86 Gan Weishu, 'Xinxi wangluo lifa chuyi' (On Internet Legislation), *Journal of National Procurators College*, vol. 10, no. 3, July 2002, p. 105.

87 Philip Sohmen, 'Taming the Dragon: China's Efforts to Regulate the Internet', p. 19.

88 Nina Hachigian, 'China's Cyber-Strategy', *Foreign Affairs*, March/April 2001, vol, 80, no. 2. http://www.rand.org/nsrd/capp/cyberstrategy.html (accessed 3 May 2005); Harwit and Clark also point out that the high degree of government control over foreign web access is inconsistent and has not yet materialized. Harwit and Clark, 'Shaping the Internet in China', p. 398.

89 Philip Sohmen, 'Taming the Draging: China's Efforts to Regulate the Internet', p. 21.

90 'PRC Foreign Ministry Official: US Media Websites Unblocked for APEC; BBC, Other Sites Still Blocked', FBIS Transcribed Text, no.: CPP20011016000143, Hong Kong AFP, China, 16 October 2001.

91 Luo Chunhua and Wu Yingchun, 'PRC WTO Institute Director Calls For System Reform, Freer Information Access', FBIS Translated Text, no.: CPP20020116000083, Beijing, *Renmin Wang* (People's Outlook), WWW-Text, China, 15 January 2002.

6 Squaring the circles of criminal justice reform?

1 'China: Justice Minister on Criminal Law', *Xinhua*, 14 March 1997 in FBIS-CHI-97-079, 23 March 1997, p. 2.

2 See Mao Zedong's 20 March 1958 talk at the Chengdu Party conference in Stuart R. Schram (ed.), *Mao Zedong Unrehearsed*, Harmondsworth, UK: Penguin Books, 1974, p. 109. Perhaps it is a great irony that at a time when he was in the midst of the Great Leap Forward Mao thought that 'haste' must be transformed into 'deliberation' and vice versa.

3 PRC, State Council, Information Office, *Progress in China's Human Rights Cause in 2003*, 2003, pp. 15–17.

4 For discussion of the reform issues surrounding extended custody and related compensation see Fang Baoguo, '*Chaoqi jiya xingshi peichangede ruogan wenti*' (Several Issues Concerning Criminal Compensation for Extended Custody), *Zhengfa luntan* (Tribune of Political Science and Law), no. 1, 2004, pp. 158–64.

5 Chen Xingliang's arguments are drawn from discussions with him on 11 June 2004 at the Law School of Peking University.

6 Chen Xingliang *et al.* (eds), *Fazhide yanshuo* (Discussions on the Rule of Law), Beijing: Falu chubanshe, 2004, p. 2.

7 Ibid.

8 11 June 2004 discussion with Wang Zuofu at the Law School of People's University.

9 In his 11 June 2004 discussion with the authors at the People's University Law School, Wang Zuofu reviewed the options for dealing with logjams in the system of interpretation. Wang also discussed 'extended interpretation' by the SPC. Wang seemed lukewarm towards colleagues' advocacy of the circulation of case law through the gazettes of the SPC and SPP as a new means of achieving rational flexibility.

10 '*Youzuzhi fanzuizhi duice yanjiu*' (Research on the Countermeasures against Organized Crime), *Xingshi faxue* (Criminal Law), no. 11, 2003, p. 72.

11 See 'Step Up Comprehensive Management, Do a Good Job in Public Order', *Liaowang* (Outlook), 16 April 2001, p. 1 in *Daily Report*, China, FBIS-CHI-2001-0426.

12 For analysis of this problem see You Wei and Xie Xiwei, '*Fanzuihua yuanze he Woguode "yanda" zhengce*' (The Principles of Criminalization and China's Strike Hard Policy), *Xingshi faxue* (Criminal Law), no. 5, 2003, p. 9.

13 'Step Up Comprehensive Management, Do a Good Job in Public Order', p. 1.

14 Ibid., p. 2.

15 'Various Localities Develop in Depth the Struggle to "Strike Hard" and Sort Things Out', Beijing, *Xinhua*, 2 May 2001 in *Daily Report* in FBIS-CHI-2001-0502, p. 2.

16 *Zhonghua renmin gongheguo xingshi susongfa* (Criminal Procedure Law of the People's Republic of China), Beijing: Falu chubanshe, 2002, p. 95.

17 Ibid., p. 97, authors' italics.

18 Zhang Xu would disagree with this analysis. He provides an example of an argument that attempts to square 'strike hard' with human rights protection. Zhang Xu, '*Yanda: Bixu chulihao sige guanxi*' ('Strike Hard': The Four Relations Must be Properly Handled), *Xingshi faxue* (Criminal Law), no. 3, 2002, p. 59. In Zhang's view, 'strike hard' incorporates the spirit of human rights protection and it requires that conviction and punishment should take place in strict accordance with the stipulations of the criminal law.

19 As cited in Jianhong Lu *et al.*, *Crime and Social Control in a Changing China*, Westport, CT and London: Greenwood Press, 2001, pp. 128–29.

20 'China's Top Judge "Under Fire" Over Human Rights, Legal Standards', AFP, Hong Kong, 12 March 2001.

21 15 June 2004 discussion with Professor Dan Wei at the International Association for Friendship with Foreign Countries, Beijing.

22 For further analysis refer to Ronald C. Keith, *China's Struggle for the Rule of Law*, London and New York: Macmillan and St. Martin's, 1994, p. 12.

23 Liu Yanhong has researched how the application of the criminal law has become the application of judicial explanation. See Liu Yanhong, '*Xingfa*

leixinghua gannian yu fazhiguo yuanzezhi zheli' (Conceptualizing the Criminal Law and the Theoretical Principles of a Rule of Law Country), *Xingshi faxue* (Criminal Law), no. 9, 2003, pp. 23–38.

24 June 11th discussion with Chen Xingliang. Chen argued that the gap between changing criminal activity and the legislative agenda could be filled with more judicial interpretation and with the development of case law.

25 Song Yinghui, *'Bubi ziwo guizui yuanze yu rushi chenshu yi wu'* (The Principle of Non-self-Incrimination and the Obligation to State the Truth), *Faxue yanjiu* (CASS Journal of Law), no. 5, 1998, p. 142.

26 Information Office, State Council, PRC, *Progress in China's Human Rights Cause in 2003*, p. 16.

27 Chen Guangzhong and Zheng Xu, 'Xingshi susong faxue ershi nian' (Twenty Years of the Science of Criminal Procedural Law), *Zhongguo faxue* (Chinese Legal Science), no. 4, 1998, p. 17.

28 As cited in David Hsieh, 'China Executes Willful SARS Spreaders', *The Straits Times Interactive*, 16 May 2003, http:/straitstimes.asia1.com.su/sars/story/o,4395,189291,00.html (accessed 3 August 2004).

29 Lu Qinzhong, *'Lun chuanranbing fanzhi fanzuide lifa wanshan'* (Perfecting Legislation on Crime Concerning the Prevention of Infectious Disease), *Xingshi faxue* (Criminal Law), 2003, p. 28.

30 See the full Chinese text for the 1989 PRC Law on Infectious Disease Prevention and Control at http:/www.chinacourt.org/flwk/show1.php?file_id=8774 (accessed 3 August 2004).

31 *Zhonghua renmin gongheguo xingfa* (Criminal Law of the People's Republic of China), Chinese-English edition, Beijing: Falu chubanshe, 2002, p. 73.

32 Ou Yangtao, Wekejian, and Liu Ranwen (eds), *Zhonghua renmin gongheguo xingfa: zhushi yu shiyong* (The Criminal Law of the People's Republic of China: Interpretation and Application), Beijing: Renmen fayuan chubanshe, 1997, p. 630.

33 For the Chinese text of the Explanations see http:/www.chinacourt.org/flwk/show1.php?file_id=85196=%BF%D6%B2%Co (accessed 4 August 2004).

34 See the discussion of Professor Wang Shunan, Chinese University of Politics and Law, in David Hsieh, 'China Executes Willful SARS Spreaders', 16 May 2001.

35 For example, see Xin Wen, 'Methods Used by the "Falungong" to Trample on Human Nature, Infringe on Human Rights', *Xinhua*, 12 June 2000, in *Daily Report*, China, FBIS-CHI-2000-0613.

36 'Commentary Condemning Falungong Cult for Hindering SARS Control', *Xinhua*, 11 June 2003, in *Daily Report*, China, FBIS-CHI-2003-0609, p. 1.

37 'The "Falungong" Cult is Totally Unconscionable', *Xinhua*, 9 June 2003, in *Daily Report*, China, FBIS-CHI-2003-0611, p. 1.

38 See 'Shanghai Issues Methods for AIDS Prevention', Hong Kong, Zhongguo Tongshun She, 11 May 1999 in FBIS-CHI-1999-0518, 19 May 1999, and also 'Health Ministry Urges Rights Protection for AIDS Patients' Beijing, *Xinhua*, in English, 20 May 1999 in FBIS-CHI1999-0520, 21 May 1999.

39 'Legislator Calls for Law on AIDS Control', *Xinhua*, 11 March 2004, AFS Document, no.: CPP20040311000024.

40 'CNA: Revised Version of Sars Prevention and Relief Statute Passed', Central News Agency, 5 June 2003 in FBIS-CHI-2003-0605, p. 1.

41 Li Jing, 'Epidemic Control to Enter National Plan', *China Daily*, 23 June 2004, in APFC, Asia News, 23 June 2004.

42 Chen Guangzhong, 'Xinshi susongfa zaixiugaizhi jiben jinian – Jianji ruogan jiben yuanzezhi xiugai' (The Fundamental Concept for Re-amending the Criminal

Procedure Law – The Amendment of Several Basic Principles), *Zhengfa luntan* (Tribune of Political Science and Law), no. 3, 2004, p. 4.

43 Chen Guangzhong, '*Xinshi susongfa zaixiugaizhi jiben jinian*', *Zhengfa luntan*, no. 3, 2004, p. 8.

44 Chen Guangzhong and Zheng Xu, '*Xingshi susong faxue ershi nian*' (Twenty Years of the Science of Criminal Procedural Law), *Zhongguo faxue* (Chinese Legal Science), no. 4, 1998, p. 16.

45 Bian Jianlin and Li Jingjing, '*Cong Woguo xingshi fating shezhi kan xingshi shen-pan gouzaode wanshan*' (The Perfection of Criminal Trial Structure as Seen from the Design of the Chinese Criminal Tribunal), *Faxue yanjiu* (Chinese Legal Studies), no. 3, 2004, pp. 82–93.

46 Discussion with Wang Minyuan, CASS Institute of Law, 15 June 2004.

47 ' "Two Laws" Protect Citizen's Legitimate Rights', *Wen Wei Po*, Hong Kong, 12 March 1996, p. A2 in FBIS-CHI-96-061, 28 March 1996, p. 17.

48 Discussion with Song Yinghui on the reform of the CPL767 on 8 June 2004.

49 Zhu Yuling and Si Liantao, '*Meiguo bianhu jiaoyi zhiduzhi lilun tanxi*' (A Theoretical Analysis of the American System of Plea Bargaining), *Susong faxue, sifa zhidu* (Procedural Law and Judicial System), vol. 8, 2004, p. 83.

50 'Further on NPC Adopting Amendments to China's Constitution', *Xinhua*, 14 March 2004, AFS Document, no.: CPP2004031400004, 15 March 2004.

51 During our 11 June 2004 discussion with Wang Zuofu in Beijing, Wang referred to the urgent demands for CPL revision and also to his satisfaction with the post-1997 process of selected amendment to the CL97. For an argument favouring selected amendment see Jiang Xihui, '*Moshi chonggou yu jiben pingjia – Guanyu xingfa gaijinde jige wenti*' (The Model for Reconstruction and Basic Evaluation – Several Problems Relating to Criminal Law Amendment), *Xingshi faxue* (Criminal Law), no. 4, 2003, p. 51.

52 8 June 2004 Beijing discussions with Song Yinghui, Executive Deputy Director, Procedural Law Research Center of the Chinese University of Politics and Law.

53 For example, see Chen Xingliang, '*Wei bianhuquan bianhu: Xingshi fazhi shiye zhongde bianhuquan*' (Defending the Right to Defence: The Right to Defence in View of the Criminal Law's Rule of Law), *Susongfaxue, sifazhidu* (Procedural Law and Judicial System), no. 5, 2004, p. 10.

54 Chen Guangzhong and Song Yinghui, '*Guanyu xingshi susongfa zai xiugaide jidian sikao*' (Thoughts on the Re-Amendment of the Criminal Procedural Law', *Susongfaxue, sifazhidu* (Procedural Law and Judicial System), no. 1, 2004, p. 28.

55 Zhao Bingzhi, 'Discussion on the Gradual Abolition of [the] Death Penalty for Non-Violent Crimes', in Zhao Bingzhi, Chief Editor, *The Road of Abolition of the Death Penalty in China* (English-Chinese), Beijiing: Press of [the] Chinese People's Public Security University of China, 2004, p. 3.

56 Ibid., pp. 4–6.

57 This at least was the view of Chen Xingliang during Beijing discussions on 11 June 2004.

58 11 June 2004 Beijing discussion with Chen Xingliang, Deputy Dean, Law School, Peking University.

59 'Highlights: PRC Legal, Judicial Developments Cite Zhang Fusen, Xiao Yang, Jia Chunweng', FBIS 26 April 2004, AFS Document, no.: CPP20040504000057, FBIS-CHI-2004-0504, pp. 6–7.

60 As reported in Randall Peerenboom, 'Out of the Pan and into the Fire: Well-Intentioned but Misguided Recommendations to Eliminate all Forms of Administrative Detention in China', *Northwestern University Law Review*, vol. 98, no. 3, pp. 1025–26.

61 Fan Peigen, '*Woguo buyi yizhi "Meishi" feifa zhengju paichu guize*' (China Cannot Transplant 'American Rules' concerning the Exclusion of Evidence), *Susong faxue, sifazhidu* (Procedural Law and Judicial System), no. 8, 2002, p. 65.
62 8 June 2004 discussions with Song Yinghui.
63 *Zhonghua renmin gongheguo xingshi susongfa*, p. 99.
64 8 June 2004 Beijing discussions with Song Yinghui.
65 Randall Peerenboom, 'Out of the Pan and into the Fire: Well-Intentioned by Misguided Recommendations to Eliminate all Forms of Administrative Detention in China', *Northwestern University Law Review*, vol. 98, no. 3, 2004, p. 997.
66 Pitman Potter compares and contrasts the recently published viewpoints of Lubman and Peerenboom. See Pitman Potter, 'Legal Reform in China: Institutions, Culture and Selective Adaptation', *Law and Social Inquiry*, vol. 29, no. 2, Spring 2004, pp. 465–95.

References

Selected reference materials in Chinese and English

Criminal Law Research Unit, the Legal Work Committee of the NPCSC, *Zhonghua renmin gongheguo xingfa shiyi* (Interpretation of PRC Criminal Law), Beijing: Falu chubanshe, 1997.

Heilongjiang Politics and Law Management College, Comp., 'Guanyu chuli fandong huidaomen gongzuozhong youguan wentide tongzhi' (Circular Regarding Issues in the Handling of Counterrevolutionary Secret Society), *Xingshi fagui huibian* (Collection of Criminal Law Regulations and Law), Harbin: Heilongjiang chubanshe, 1990.

Information Office, State Council of the People's Republic of China, *Progress in China's Human Rights Cause in 2003*, 2003.

Ministry of Justice, PRC (ed.), *Yi fa qudi xiejiao xuzhi fangfan he chengzhi xiejiao huodong* (Taking Law to Ban Heretical Cult Organization and to Defend against and Punish Heretical Cult Movements), Beijing: Falu chubanshe, 1999.

Ministry of Public Security, PRC, *Chajin qudi xiejiao zuzhi falu fagui* (Laws and Regulations Prohibiting and Banning Heretical Cult Organization), Beijing: Qunzhong chubanshe, 1999.

NPC, PRC, *Zhonghua renmin gongheguo xianfa* (Constitution of the People's Republic of China), Beijing: Renmin chubanshe, 1975.

NPC, PRC, *The Constitution of the People's Republic of China*, Beijing: Foreign Languages Press, 1978.

NPC, PRC, *The Constitution of the People's Republic of China*, Beijing: Foreign Languages Press, 1983.

NPC, PRC, *The Criminal Law and the Criminal Procedure Law of the People's Republic of China*, Beijing: Foreign Languages Press, 1984.

NPC, PRC, *Xingshi fagui huibian* (Compilation of Criminal Legislation), Harbin: Heilongjiang renmin chubanshe, 1990.

NPC, PRC, *Penal Regulations of the PRC for the Comprehensive Management of Public Order*, Beijing: Zhongguo fazhi chubanshe, 1997.

NPC, PRC, *Law of Succession of the People's Republic of China*, Beijing: Falu chubanshe, 2002.

NPC, PRC, *Marriage Law of the People's Republic of China*, Beijing: Falu chubanshe, 2002.

NPC, PRC, *Zhonghua renmin gongheguo xingfa* (Criminal Law of the People's Republic of China), Chinese-English Edition, Beijing: Falu chubanshe, 2002.

NPC, PRC, *Zhonghua renmin gongheguo xingshi susongfa* (Criminal Procedure Law of the People's Republic of China), Beijing: Falu chubanshe, 2002.

NPC Legal Work Committee, *Jisuanji ji wangluo falu fagui* (Law and Regulations on Computer and Computer Networks), Beijing: Falu chubanshe, 1998.

NPC Legal Work Committee, *Zhonghua renmin gongheguo jiehun fa: xiugai lifa ziliaoxuan* (The Marriage Law of the People's Republic of China: Selected Legislative Materials), Chinese-English Edition, Beijing: Falu chubanshe, 2001.

NPC Legal Work Committee and the Committee on Rights and Interests of the All-China Women's Federation, *Zhonghua renmin gongheguo jiehunfa shiyong shouce* (The Marriage Law of the People's Republic of China: A Practical Handbook), Beijing: Falu chubanshe, 2001.

Peking University's Centre for Law Studies and Legal Services for Women, *Jiating baoli yu falu huanzhu* (Domestic Violence and Legal Assistance), 2003.

Peking University's Centre for Law Studies and Services for Women, Research Report of the Legal Aid Cases Undertaken by the Center for Women's Law Studies and Legal Services Under the Law School of Peking University (1996–2000), unpublished manuscript, n.d.

Shanghai tanhuang wenhua yanjiuhui (ed.), *Fazhi yu dezhi* (Rule of Law and Rule of Virtue), Beijing: Zhongguo jiancha chubanshe, 2001.

US Commission on International Religious Freedoms, *Recommendations for U.S. Policy on China*, 2002. Available Online at: http://www.uscirf.gov/reports/13Feb02/chinarecommendations.php3 (accessed 15 September 2004).

US Department of State, 'China Chapter', *Country Reports on Human Rights Practices*, 1999. Available Online at: http://www.state.gov/global/human_rights/1999/hhrp_report/china/html (accessed 10 July 2004).

US Department of State, *Country Reports on Human Rights Practices–2000*, 2001. Available Online at: http://www.state.gov/g/ddrl/rls/hrrpt/2000/eap/index.cfm?docid=684 (accessed 15 February 2004).

US Department of State, *Country Reports on Human Rights Practices – 2002*, 2003. Available Online at: http://www.state.gov/g/drl/rls/hrrpt/2002 (accessed 14 May 2003).

US Department of State, Bureau of Democracy, Human Rights and Labor, *International Religious Freedom Report: China (Hong Kong and Macau)*, 2001. Available Online at: http://www.state.gov/g/drl/rls/irf/2001/5752.htm (accessed 10 July 2004).

Chinese newspapers and legal and political journals

Note: The titles of journals are cited herein. Detail regarding all of the specifically cited articles are given in full in the chapter notes.

Agence France Presse, Hong Kong

Falixue, fashixue (Jurisprudence and the History of Laws)

Faxue yanjiu (Chinese Journal of Law, CASS)

Funu yanjiu luncong (Collection of Women's Studies)

Guangxi zhengfa guanli ganbu xueyuan xuebo (Journal of the Guangxi Institute of Law and Politics for Cadre Administration)

Liaowang (Outlook)

Ming Pao, Hong Kong

Renmin Ribao (People's Daily)
Renmin Wang (People's Outlook)
Susong faxue, sifa zhidu (Procedural Law and Judicial System)
Ta Kung Pao (Worker's Daily)
Xiandai faxue (Modern Law Science)
Xin Hua yuebao (New China Monthly)
Xingshi faxue (Criminal Law Science)
Xingshi shenpan chankao (Reference to Criminal Trials)
Xingshifa pinglun (Criminal Law Review)
Zhengfa luntan (Tribune of Political Science and Law)
Zhongguo faxue (Chinese Legal Science)
Zhongguo jiancha (Chinese Prosecution)
Zhonghua nuzi Xueyuan xuebao (Journal of National Women's University of China)
Zhongwai faxue (Peking University Law Journal)

Chinese books

Cai Xiuying, 'Xin Zhendi, Xin tiaozhan, Xin duice' (New Fronts, New Challenges, New Countermeasures), Yunmeng jikan, no. 4, July 2002, pp. 91–93.
Chan Minghua and Guo Xiaoming, 'Luelun heishehui zuzhi fanzui de jige wenti' (Brief Discussions of Several Issues Concerning Crime in Underground Societies), in Gao Mingxuan, Zhao Bingzhi, and Hu Yunteng (eds), *Xingfa xiugai jianyi wenji* (Collection of Articles Concerning Suggestions for Chinese Criminal Law Revisions), Beijing: Zhongguo renmin daxue chubanshe, 1997.
Chen Mingxia *et al.* (eds), *Jiating baoli duice yanjiu yu ganyu* (Research and Advances in Countermeasures against Domestic Violence), Beijing: Zhongguo shehuikexue chubanshe, 2003.
Chen Xingliang *et al.* (eds), *Fazhide yanshuo* (Discussions on the Rule of Law), Beijing: Falu chubanshe, 2004.
Gao Mingxuan, *Zhonghua renmin gongheguo xingfa de yunyu he dansheng* (The Conception and Birth of the Criminal Code of the People's Republic of China), Beijing: Falu chubanshe, 1980.
Gao Mingxuan (ed.), *Xingfa xue* (Criminal Law Science), Beijing: Falu chubanshe, 1984.
Gao Mingxuan and Zhao Bingzhi (eds), *Xin Zhongguo xing faxue wushi nian* (Fifty Years of New China's Criminal Law Studies), vol. 1, Beijing: Zhongguo fangzheng chubanshe, 2000.
Gao Mingxuan and Zhao Bingzhi (eds), *21shiji xingfaxue xinwenti yantao* (Studies of the New Criminal Law Issues Emerging in the 21st Century), Beijing: Zhongguo renmin gongan daxue chubanshe, 2001.
Gao Mingxuan, Zhao Bingzhi, and Hu Yunteng (eds), *Xingfa xiugai jianyi wenji* (Collection of Articles Concerning Suggestions for Chinese Criminal Law Revisions), Beijing: Zhongguo renmin daxue chubanshe, 1997.
Guo Jianmei *et al.* (eds), *Jiating baoli yu falu yuanzhu* (Domestic Violence and Legal Assistance), dual Chinese-English Text, Beijing: Zhongguo shehui kexue chubanshe, 2003.
Jian Ping, *Jisuanji fanzui wenti yanjiu* (Researching the Problems of Computer Related Crime), Beijing: Shangwu chubanshe, 2000.

Jiang Zemin, *On the 'Three Represents'*, Beijing: Foreign Languages Press, 2001.

Kang Damin, *Gongan lun* (On Public Security), Beijing: Qunchong chubanshe, 1998.

Kang Shuhuai and Wei Xinwen, *Youzuzhi fanzui toushi* (An Examination of Organized Crime), Beijing: Beijing daxue chubanshe, 2001.

Li Chun and Wang Shangxin *et al.*, *Zhongguo xingfa xiudingde beijing yu shiyong* (The Background of Chinese Criminal Law Revision and its Application), Beijing: Falu chubanshe, 1998.

Li Shuangqi, *Wangluo fanzui fangkong duice* (The Strategies in Prevention and Control of Internet Crimes), Beijing: Qunzhong chubanshe, 2001.

Li Wenyan and Tian Hongjie, *Dahei chue: xingshi falu shiyong jieshuo* (Eliminating Underworld and Evil Forces: Explaining the Application of Criminal Legislation), Beijing: Qunzhong chubanshe, 2001.

Liu Jiachen, *Xingfa fenze ji peitao guiding xinshi xinjie* (New Interpretations of Special Provisions of the Criminal Law and Related Regulations), vol. 2, Beijing: Renmin fayuan chubanshe, 2000.

Liu Shoufen and Wang Xiaoming, *'Lun heishehui zuzhi fanzui yu woguo xingshi lifa de wanshan'* (On Crime of the Black Society and the Perfection of Criminal Legislation in Our Country), in Gao Mingxuan, Zhao Bingzhi, and Hu Yunteng (eds), *Xingfa xiugai jianyi wenji* (Collection of Articles Concerning Suggestions for Chinese, Criminal Law Revisions), Beijing: Zhongguo renmin daxue chubanshe, 1997.

Ma Yuan (ed.), *Xin jiehunfa ji sifa jiesi shiyong zhunan* (Practical Guidelines on the Interpretation of the New Marriage Law), Beijing: Zhongguo shehui kexue chubanshe, 2002.

Ou Yongtao, Wei Kejian, and Liu Ranwen, *Zhonghua renmin gongheguo xin xingfa zhushi yu shiyong* (Interpretation and Application of the PRC Criminal Law), Beijing: Renmin fayuan chubanshe, 1997.

Tian Pingan *et al.*, *Dangdai fa chexue yanjiu yu shensuo* (Research and Inquiry on the Contemporary Philosophy of Law), Beijing: Falu chubanshe, 2000.

Wang Taixian and Ai Ming, *Fazhide linian yu fanglue* (The Concept and Summary of Nomocracy), Beijing: Zhongguo jingcha chubanshe, 2001.

Wang Yongcheng *et al.* (eds), *Daji dupin fanzui shiyong* (Handbook of Fighting Drug-Related Crimes), Beijing: Renmin fayuan chubanshe, 1992.

Xia Jinyao, *Jisuanji fanzui wenti de diaocha fenxi yu fangfan* (Investigation and Prevention of Computer-Related Crime), Beijing: Zhongguo gongan daxue chubanshe, 2001.

Xu Famin, *Fawenhua yu xingfa xiandaihua yanjiu* (The Study of Legal Culture and the Modernization of the Criminal Law), Beijing: Zhongguo fangzheng chubanshe, 2001.

Ye Gaofeng and Liu Defa (eds), *Jiyuan fanzui duice yanjiu* (The Study of Countermeasures against Organized Crime Groups), Beijing: Zhongguo jiancha chubanshe, 2000.

Yu Zhigang (ed.), *Jisuanji fanzui yinan wenti sifa duice* (Strategies in Dealing with Difficult Issues in the Administration of Law Concerning Computer-Related Crime), Jilin: Jilin chubanshe, 2001.

Yu Zhigang, *Redian fanzui falu yinan wenti jiexi* (Analysis and Explanations of Difficult Legal Issues Concerning Hotly Debated Crimes), vol. 1, Beijing: Zhongguo renmin gongan daxue chubanshe, 2001.

Zhang Qiang (ed.), *Xuiding xingfa tiaowen shiyong jieshuo* (Explanations of the Application of the Revised Criminal Law Articles); Beijing: Zhongguo jiancha chubanshe, 1997.

Zhao Bingzhi (ed.), *The Road of Abolition of the Death Penalty in China*, English-Chinese Edition, Beijing: Chinese People's Public Security University of China Press, 2004.

Zhao Bingzhi and He Xingwang, *Xin xingfadiande chuangzhi* (The Making of the New Criminal Code), Beijing: Falu chubanshe, 1997.

Zhao Yanguang, Zhu Huaci, and Pi Yong, *Jisuanji fanzui de dingzui yu liangxing* (Determining Computer-Related Crime and Punishment), Beijing: Renmin fayan chubanshe, 2000.

Zhou Daoluan, Shan Changzhong, Zhan Sihan *et al.*, *Xingfade xiugai yu shiyong* (The Revision and Application of the Criminal Law), Beijing: Renmin fayuan chubanshe, 1997.

Zuo Zeyuan, *Fazhi fanlun* (On the Rule of Law), vol. 2, Beijing: Falu chubanshe, 2001.

Articles, books, and documentation in English

Adams, I., Adams, R., and Galati, R., *Power of the Wheel: The Falun Gong Revolution*, Toronto: Stoddart Publishing, 2000.

Bai Guimei, 'International Human Rights Law and the Elimination of Violence against Women: China's Theory and Practice', in Errol Mendes and Anne-Marie Traeholt (eds), *Human Rights: Chinese and Canadian Perspectives*, Ottawa: Human Rights Research and Education Centre, University of Ottawa, 1997, pp. 581–95.

Bakken, B., *The Exemplary Society: Human Improvement, Social Control, and the Dangers of Modernity*, Oxford: Oxford University Press, 2000.

Benjamin, G., 'Review of Carlos Wing-hung Lo, China's Legal Awakening: Legal Theories and Criminal Justice in Deng's Era', *Review of Central and East European Law*, vol. 23, no. 2, 1997, pp. 165–72.

Bo, Z. and Wenxiu, G., 'Sexuality in Urban China', *The Australian Journal of Chinese Affairs*, no. 28, 1992, pp. 1–20.

Bodde, D. and Morris, C., *Law in Imperial China*, Philadelphia, PA: University of Pennsylvania, 1973.

Centre for Women's Law Studies and Legal Services of Peking University, *Theory and Practice of Women's Rights and Interests in Contemporary China*, Beijing: Workers' Press, 2001.

Chen, Theodore H.E. (ed.), *The Chinese Communist Regime: Documents and Commentary*, New York: Frederick A. Praeger Publishers, 1976, p. 294.

Ching, J., 'The Falun Gong: Religious and Political Implications', *American Asian Review*, 1 January 2001.

Chow, D.C.K., 'Organized Crime, Local Protectionism, and the Trade in Counterfeit Goods in China', *China Economic Review*, vol. 14, 2003, pp. 473–84.

Clark, D., 'Shaping the Internet in China', *Asian Survey*, vol. 41, no. 3, 2001, pp. 377–408.

Clarke, D.C. and Feinerman, J., 'Antagonistic Contradictions: Criminal Law and Human Rights in China', *China Quarterly*, no. 141, 1995, pp. 135–54.

Creel, H., *The Birth of China*, New York: Frederick Unger, 1979.

Deng Xiaoping, *Selected Works of Deng Xiaoping (1975–82)*, Beijing: Foreign Languages Press, 1984.

Deng Xiaoping, *Fundamental Issues in Present-Day China*, Beijing: Foreign Languages Press, 1987.

Deng Zhenlai *et al.*, 'Drug Trafficking and Consumption in China: Two Case Studies', *International Social Science Journal* (Special Issue on Drug Trafficking: Economic and Social Dimensions), vol. 53, no. 169, 2001, pp. 415–20.

Dobinson, I., 'The Criminal Law of the People's Republic of China (1997): Real Change or Rhetoric', *Pacific Rim Law and Policy Journal*, vol. 11, no. 1, 2002, p. 4.

Fairbank, J.K., Reischauer, E.O., and Craig, A.M., *East Asia: Tradition and Transformation*, Boston, MA: Houghton Mifflin Co., 1989.

Farrer, J. and Zhongxin, S., 'Extramarital Love in Shanghai', *The China Journal*, no. 50, 2003, pp. 1–36.

Gelatt, T., *Criminal Justice with Chinese Characteristics*, New York: Lawyers Committee for Human Rights, 1993.

Hachigian, N., 'China's Cyber-Strategy', *Foreign Affairs*, vol. 80, no. 2, 2001, pp. 118–33.

Hachigian, N., 'The Internet and Power in One-Party East Asian States', *The Washington Quarterly*, vol. 25, no. 3, 2002, pp. 41–58.

Hachigian, N. and Wu, L., *The Information Revolution in Asia*, 2003. Available Online at: http://www.rand.org/publications/MR/MR1719 (accessed 26 March 2003).

Haiwren, Z. (trans.), 'Handling the Falun Gong Case', from the Chinese, '*Zhu Rongji zai 1999*' *Chinese Law and Government*, vol. 35, no. 1, 2002, pp. 53–72.

Harwit, E. and Clark, D., 'Shaping the Internet in China', *Asian Survey*, vol. 41, no. 3, 2001, pp. 377–408.

Hecht, J., *Opening to Reform? An Analysis of China's Revised Criminal Procedure Law*, New York: Lawyers Committee for Human Rights, 1996.

Hecht, J., 'Can Legal Reform Foster Respect for Human Rights in China?', Testimony before the Congressional Executive Commission on China, 11 April 2002.

Hsieh, D., 'China Executes Willful SARS Spreaders', *The Straits Times Interactive*. Available Online at: http://straitstimes.asia1.com.su/sars/story/o,4395, 189291,00.html (accessed 16 May 2003).

Huang, P.C., *Code, Custom, and Legal Practice in China: The Qing and the Republic Compared*, Stanford, CA: Stanford University Press, 2001.

Human Rights in China, 'Human Rights Situation in China and the Dialogue on Human Rights', 2000. Available Online at: http://iso.hrichina.org (p. 3) (accessed 29 July 2000).

Human Rights in China, 'Empty Promises: Human Rights Protections and China's Criminal Procedure Law in Practice', 2001. Available Online at: http://iso.hrichina.org,p.2 (accessed 30 March 2001).

Human Rights Watch (1999), 'China Uses "Rule of Law" to Justify Falun Gong Crackdown', *Human Rights Watch World Report*. Available Online at: http://www.hrw.org/press/1999/nov/china1109.htm,p1

Jiao, A.Y., 'Traditions and Changes of Police Culture: Organization, Operation, and Behaviour of the Chinese Police', in J. Liu, L. Zhang, and S.F. Messner, (eds), *Crime and Social Control in a Changing China*, Westport, CT and London: Greenwood Press, 2001.

Johnson, I., 'A Deadly Exercise: Practicing Falun Gong was a Right, Ms. Chen Said, to Her Last Day', *Wall Street Journal*, 20 March 2000. Available

Online at: http://www.pulitzer.org/year/2001/internationalreporting/works/falungong1.html

Jordan, Ann D., 'Human Rights, Violence against Women, and Economic Development (The People's Republic of China Experience)', *Columbia Journal of Gender and Law*, vol. 5, no. 2, 1996, pp. 217–72.

Keith, R.C., *China's Struggle for the Rule of Law*, London and New York: Macmillan Ltd. and St. Martin's Press, 1994.

Keith, R.C., 'Legislating Women's and Children's "Rights and Interests" in the People's Republic of China', *The China Quarterly*, no. 149, March 1997, pp. 29–55.

Keith, R.C., ' "Internationalization" and "Localization" in the Chinese Pursuit of Human Justice', in S. Ismael (ed.), *Globalization, Policies, Challenges, and Responses*, Calgary: Detselig, 1999, pp. 143–67.

Keith, R.C. and Lin, Z., 'To Revise or not to Revise China's Law on Counterrevolution', *China Information*, vol. 5, no. 4, Spring 1991, pp. 24–41.

Keith, R.C. and Lin, Z., 'The Changing Substantine Principles of Chinese Criminal Law', *China Information*, vol. xiii, no. 1, Summer 1998, pp. 77–105.

Keith, R.C. and Lin, Z., *Law and Justice in China's New Marketplace*, London: Palgrave, 2001.

Keith, R.C. and Lin, Z., ' "Falungong Problem": Politics and the Struggle for the Rule of Law in China', *The China Quarterly*, no. 175, September 2003, pp. 623–42.

Keith, R.C. and Lin, Z., 'The Making of a Chinese NGO: The Research and Intervention Project on Domestic Violence', *Problems of Post-Communism*, vol. 50, no. 6, November–December 2003, pp. 46–48.

Kelly, R.J., Chin, K.-L., and Gagan, J.A., 'The Dragon Breathes Fire: Chinese Organized Crime in New York City', *Crime, Law and Social Change*, vol. 19, 1993, pp. 245–69.

Kyle, D. and Koslowski, R. (eds), *Global Human Smuggling: Comparative Perspectives*, Baltimore, MD: The Johns Hopkins University Press, 2001.

Lan Xinzhen, 'Saying No to Drugs', *Beijing Review*, vol. 47, no. 26, 1 July 2004, pp. 20–23.

Lanham, D., 'The Chinese Criminal Procedure Law – A Comparative Review', *Global Journal on Crime and Criminal Law*, vol. 4, no. 1, 1997, pp. 37–48.

Leng, S. and Hong, D.C., *Criminal Justice in Post-Mao China: Analysis and Documents*, Albany, NY: State University of New York Press, 1985.

Li, L.C., 'The "Rule of Law" Policy in Guangdong: Continuity or Departure? Meaning, Significance, and Processes', *The China Quarterly*, no. 161, March 2000, pp. 193–220.

Liang, Z. and Te, W. (2001), 'From Fujian to New York: Understanding the New Chinese Immigration', in D. Kyle and R. Koslowski (eds), *Global Human Smuggling: Comparative Perspectives*, Baltimore, MD: The Johns Hopkins University Press, 2001, pp. 187–215.

Lo, C.W., *Legal Awakening: Legal Theory and Criminal Justice in Deng's Era*, Hong Kong: Hong Kong University Press, 1999.

Lu, J., Zhang, L., and Messner, S.F., *Crime and Social Control in a Changing China*, Westport, CT and London: Greenwood Press, 2001.

Lubman, S., *Bird in a Cage: Legal Reform in China After Mao*, Stanford, CA: Stanford University Press, 1999.

Lubman, S., 'Introduction', in P. Pitman (ed.), *Domestic Law Reforms in Post-Mao China*, Armonck, NY: M.E. Sharpe, 1999, pp. 3–16.

Lubman, S., 'Prospects for the Rule of Law in China After Accession to the WTO'. Available Online at: http://www.law.berkely.edu/institutes/csis/lubmanpaper.doc (accessed 3 June 2004).

MacCormack, G., *Traditional Chinese Penal Law*, Edinburgh: Edinburgh University Press, 1990.

MacCormack, G., *The Spirit of Traditional Chinese Law*, Athens and London: University of Georgia Press, 1996.

Mac Innis, D.E., *Religion in China Today*, Mary Knoll, NY: Orbis Books, 1989.

Maltz, M.D., 'On Defining "Organized Crime": The Development of a Definition and a Typology', *Crime and Delinquency*, vol. 22, 1976, pp. 338–46.

Mao Zedong, 'The Chinese Revolution and the Communist Party', *Selected Works of Mao Zedong*, vol. 11, Beijing: Foreign Languages Press, 1965, p. 308.

Mendes, E.P. and Traehold, A.-M., *Human Rights: Chinese and Canadian Perspectives*, Ottawa: The Human Rights Research and Education Centre, University of Ottawa, 1997.

Myers, W.H. III, 'The Emerging Threat of Transnational Organized Crime from the East', *Crime, Law and Social Change*, vol. 24, 1996, pp. 181–222.

Paglee, C.D., 'Chinalaw Web-Regulations for the Implementation of the Law of Assembly, Procession and Demonstration'. Available Online at: http://www.quis.net/chinalaw/prclaw113.html (accessed 15 March 2002).

Paglee, C.D., 'Chinalaw Web-Regulations Governing Venues for Religious Activities'. Available Online at: http://www.quis.net/chinalaw/ prclaw110.html (accessed 23 June 2002).

Passas, N. (ed.), *Organized Crime*, Sydney: Dartmouth, 1995.

Peerenboom, R., *China's Long March to the Rule of Law*, Cambridge: Cambridge University Press, 2002.

Peerenboom, R., 'Competing Conceptions of the Rule of Law in China', in R. Peerenboom (ed.), *Asian Discourses of Rule of Law*, London and New York: Routledge, Taylor & Francis Group, 2004.

Peerenboom, R., 'Out of the Pan and into the Fire: Well-Intentioned but Misguided Recommendations to Eliminate All Forms of Administrative Detention in China', *Northwestern University Law Review*, vol. 98, no. 3, 2004, pp. 991–1104.

Pomfret, J., 'China Voids Rule on Jailing Vagrants', *Washington Post*, 19 June 2003.

Potter, P., *The Chinese Legal System: Globalization and Local Legal Culture*, London and New York: Routledge, 2001.

Potter, P., 'Legal Reform in China: Institutions, Culture, and Selective Adaptation', *Law and Social Inquiry*, vol. 29, no. 2, 2004, pp. 465–96.

Roy, D., 'China and the War on Terrorism', *Orbis*, Summer 2002, pp. 511–21.

Schechter, D., *Falungong's Challenge to China: Spiritual Practice or 'Evil Cult'*, New York: Akashic Books, 2001.

Scholenhardt, A., 'Trafficking in Migrants: Illegal Migration and Organized Crime in Australia and the Asia Pacific Region', *International Journal of the Sociology of Law*, vol. 29, 2001, pp. 331–78.

Schram, S.R. (ed.), *Mao Zedong Unrehearsed*, Harmondsworth, UK: Penguin Books, 1974.

Seay, P., 'Law, Crime and Punishment in the People's Republic of China: A Comparative Introduction to the Criminal Justice and Legal System of the PRC', *Indiana International and Comparative Law*, vol. 9, no. 1, 1998, pp. 143–54.

Sheff, D., Online Discussion, Digital Freedom Network, 1 May 2002. Available Online at: http://www.dfn.org/voices/china/sheffchat.htm (accessed 31 July 2002).

Sohmen, P., 'Taming the Dragon: China's Efforts to Regulate the Internet', *Stanford Journal of East Asian Affairs*, vol. 1, pp. 17–26.

Song, J.H.-L. and Dombrink, J., 'Asian Emerging Crime Groups: Examining the Definition of Organized Crime', *Criminal Justice Review*, vol. 19, no. 1, 1994, pp. 228–43.

Tanner, H.M., 'The Offense of Hooliganism and the Moral Dimension of China's Pursuit of Modernity, 1979–1996', *Twentieth Century China*, vol. 26, no. 1, November 2000, pp. 1–40.

Vogel, E., *Canton Under Communism: Programs and Politics in a Provincial Capital, 1949–1968*, New York: Harper & Row, Harper Torchbooks, 1970, p. 65.

Wang, J.Z., 'Illegal Chinese Immigration Into the United States: A Preliminary Factor Analysis', *International Journal of Offender Therapy and Comparative Criminology*, vol. 45, no. 3, 2001, pp. 345–55.

Wang, J.Z., 'Eastern Turkistan Islamic Movement: A Case Study of a New Terrorist Organization in China', *International Journal of Offender Therapy and Comparative Criminology*, vol. 47, no. 5, 2003, pp. 568–84.

Wu Zhongzhi, 'Striking "Border Sneaking",' *Beijing Review*, 29 April 2004, pp. 26–27.

Xin Ren, *Tradition of the Law and Law of Tradition: Law, State and Social Control in China*, Westport, CT and London: Greenwood Press, 1997.

Zhang, L., Messner, S., Lu, Z., and Deng, X., 'Gang Crime and its Punishment in China', *Journal of Criminal Justice*, vol. 24, no. 4, 1997, pp. 289–302.

Index

A Xi 17
'act according to law' 13, 29, 51
administrative detention: 'custody for
   investigation' 26, 143, 153, 166;
   'custody for repatriation' 26–27, 45,
   143, 153, 166; 'extended detention'
   142, 153–54; 'Measures for Assisting
   and Managing Urban Vagrants and
   Beggars with no Means of
   Livelihood' 153
adultery 32, 73; military and civilian
   74, 86
All China Women's Federation 32, 73;
   2000 Guangdong survey 32, 74, 76
Amnesty International 27
analogy 8, 12–13, 19, 22, 150, 152, 154;
   computer related crime 123, 133, 155;
   'other social purposes of terrorist
   organization' 105; see also 'flexibility'

'balance of values' 5, 7, 16, 19, 28,
   49, 62, 88, 118, 120, 141, 147;
   criminal justice reform 167–68;
   cyber-crime 136; death penalty 163;
   synthesis of internationalization
   and localization 153; women's
   personal rights 68
Bank of China 107
baojia 64
'big baskets' 4, 68
'black societies' 6, 98
'blind Westernization' 2, 5, 7, 8, 16, 17,
   18, 49, 71; see also
   'internationalization'; 'localization'
Bu Xinghua 138

Catholic Church 41
'causing death by negligence' 68, 74;
   and 2001 Marriage Law 75

Central Commission for the
   Comprehensive Management of
   Public Order 14
Centre for Intervention and Research
   Against Domestic Violence 68,
   77, 79, 87
Centre for Women's Law Studies and
   Legal Services, Peking University
   66, 70
Chan Minghua 100
Chen Guangzhong 154, 159–60, 162
Chen Guizun 32
Chen Sixi 59
Chen Xingliang 144–45
Cheng Jianhong 21
Chin Kelin 114
CHINA VD and HIV/AIDS Control
   Association 158
Chinese Communist Party 1, 5, 27;
   20 May 1963 resolutions 42;
   Central Commission for
   Discipline Inspection 11; Central
   Committee Law and Politics
   Committee 82; Falungong 16, 38,
   61; Propaganda Department 29;
   proper leadership 149
Ching, Julie 46
Clarke, Donald 22
'community intervention' 87
'compensation for injury' 80
'comprehensive management of public
   order' 12, 13, 16, 18, 28, 66, 86, 115,
   167–68; 2000 circular on drug use
   108; and Falungong 58, 144; internet
   security 126, 139; national plan 14,
   29; strike hard 149
'comprehensive stipulation' see
   'flexibility'
'compulsory drug treatment' 108

'computer-related conventional crime' 35, 119, 143

concubines 32, 73, 119

'Confucianization of the law' 8

counterrevolutionary crime 12, 35, 37, 43, 45, 49, 54, 56; 1951 regulations 40, 42; 1952 measures 40; political crime 121; as 'unscientific' 44

crime: 'balance of crime, criminal liability, and criminal punishment' 20; definition 20; minor crime or misdemeanours 25; *see also* 'organized crime'; 'social harm'

'crime committed by a work unit' 98–99

'crime committed by organized populace' 98

'crime endangering state security' 35

'crime of intentional injury' 68

'criminal gang': distinguished from 'criminal organization' 95

Criminal Law: 1997 Criminal Law 1–2, 4, 23; as basic law 1; CL79 version 4, 10, 12, 13, 24, 32, 42, 57, 82, 113–14, 155; CL97 Article 115 'other dangerous means' 156; CL97 Article 300 45, 56–58, 60, 62; CL97 Article 357 on amount of drugs 111; CL97 Articles 285, 286 and 287 on computer network crime 123–25, 128; CL97 Articles 318–21 on illegal border crossings 114; CL97 Articles 330–37 on public health 155–56

criminal liabilities 4, 13, 16, 18, 56, 115, 161; cyber-crime 118, 120, 124, 140; and family violence 66; obstructed rescue 85

'criminal organization with a triad nature' 33, 91, 100–05; 2000 SPC 'Explanations for the Application of Laws Concerning the Adjudication of Cases involving Criminal Organization with a Triad Nature' 102–03; CL97 Article 294 102–03

Criminal Procedure Law 1996: application 2; equal status with Criminal Law 15, 19; major revision 162, 167; subordinated to criminal law 3, 160; 'timely and accurate ascertainment of the facts' 149;

'using facts as the basis and the law as the yardstick' 149; *see also* equality before the law

criminal responsibilities *see* criminal liabilities

cultural relativism 2, 7, 9, 28, 31, 49, 85–86

'custody for investigation' *see* administrative detention

'custody for repatriation' *see* administrative detention

'cyber-crime': 'computer-related conventional crime' 120; definition 119; 'pure computer crime' 119

Dai Xinglie 70

Dan Wei 150

death penalty 32, 44, 70; abduction and sale of human beings 82; CL97 Article 115 and public health crisis 156–57; CL97 chapters 2 and 6 125; drug-related crime 32, 109–11; and economic crime 21; potential revision 162–64; under-age youth 164

Deng Xiaoping 10, 11, 16, 43–44, 48, 55; and comprehensive stipulation 13, 115, 154; on severe punishment 43–44; 'sixteen-character policy' 13; southern tour theory 14; and Tiananmen Square 47

Deng Zhenlai 111

domestic violence 5, 32, 64, 74–80, 86, 88; as 'crime' 32, 76; crimes of injury and abuse 68; first reference, National Program for Women's Development 68; Liaoning regulations 75, 150; as physical, sexual and psychological violence 75, 77, 80, 167

drug trafficking 108–12

'dual purposes theory' 19

equality before the law 3, 37, 64, 141, 149, 161; different definitions 159; plea-bargaining 161

evidentiary principles 21, 164–65

'evil cult' 5, 6, 27, 28, 38–40, 45, 51, 55, 137; definition 58, 133; organization 50, 60

'extended judicial interpretation' 22, 141, 143, 152, 154

Falungong 16, 24, 27, 31–32, 37–62, 86, 118, 143–44, 152, 167; Document 19 and foreign religious groups 51; re-education through labour 45; SARS crimes 157–58; *see also* Chinese Communist Party; counterrevolutionary crime; 'evil cult'
Farrar, James 65
Feinerman, James 22
Feng Shuliang 149
'flexibility' 3, 11, 12, 19, 35, 37, 44, 58, 85, 91, 95, 166–68; 2000 SPC Minutes 110; computer crime 124, 127–32, 141; good and bad 152; moral struggle 139; SARS 154, 157; state publication regulation 137–38; 'suit measures according to local conditions' 150–51; versus comprehensive stipulation 3, 20, 22, 88, 141, 143, 151–52, 167
'floating population' (*liudong renkou*) 14, 26–27, 82, 115; *mangliu* as the pejorative term 93
Ford Foundation 87
'four haves' 17

Gao Jinghong 99, 100
Gao Mingxuan 21, 39, 43, 94
Gao Pan 164
'globalization' *see* 'internationalization'
'good person politics' 17
Green Gang 92
Guo Qinghai 130
Guo Xiaoming 100

habeas corpus 3, 160
Hachigian, Nina 131, 139
He Xingwang 99, 105, 111
'heavy penalty-ism' 10, 21, 27, 108, 116, 160, 166; 'as for leniency and severity, take severity as primary' 21; non-violent crime 163–64; protection of computer systems 124–25, 132
Hecht, Jonathan 22
Heindrich Boell Foundation 87
'heretical cult' *see* 'evil cult'
'hooliganism': CL79 Articles 160, 169 and 1982 67, 70; 'hooligan criminal organization' 95, 115; 'hooligan gangs' 95; 'Opinion on How to Identify and Adjudicate Hooligan

Criminal Organization' 96; 'organized hooligan activities' 95
Hou Zongbin 30
Hu Jintao 27
Hu Kangsheng 103
Huang Qi 130
'human rights protection' 15, 44
Hung Dahchiu 10

'independent purposes theory' 19
'institutionalized management' 29–30
'Interim Provisions on the Registration of Public Organization' 55
International Covenant of Civil and Political Rights 3
International Religious Freedom Act 46
'internationalization' 2, 5, 31, 67, 87, 89, 108, 129, 140, 152, 160, 162, 164–68
internet: Cybercafe Rectification Campaign 135; e-governance 119; great firewall 118, 140; self censorship 134–35
Internet Society of China 134–35

Jiang Zemin 6; on internet 119, 138; and 'public feeling' 7, 147, 148; on rule of law 16, 17, 47
judicial independence 37
'judicial integration' 161
judicial interpretation 62, 111, 151, 159; versus legislative interpretation 58–60

Kang Shuhuai 108
Keith, Ronald 19, 22
Kong Xiaoning 114, 115

Lanham, David 23
Law on the Protection of Minors 150
Law on the Protection of Women's Rights and Interests: Article 3 67–68, 75
'legalization' 11, 28, 44, 55
Leng Shao-chuan 10
Li Baoku 55
Li Chun 57
Li Hongzhi 45, 46, 50, 55–56; 'theory on uselessness of the law' 53–54
Li, Linda Chelan 23
Li Wenyan 104
Li Zhi 130
Lin Hai 130

Lin Zhiqiu 19, 22
Liu Defa 81, 92
Liu Jiachen 124
Liu Shaoqi 41
Liu Yong 145
Lo, Carlos 22
'local protectionism' 82, 150
'localization' 2, 5, 18, 31, 35, 67, 85–86,
    152, 161–62, 165–68; distinguished
    from 'localism' 112, 150; 'social
    harm' 129
Lubman, Stanley 22, 23, 167
Luo Gan 14, 82

MacCormack, Geoffrey 9
'maltreatment' 33, 74, 78
Maltz, Michael 97
Mao Zedong 165; dialectics 142; mass
    line and crime prevention 149; and
    peasant revolt 39
Marriage Law: 2001 revision 32, 70,
    73, 74, 76, 78, 167; as 'localization'
    74; 'right to request' 79
'Methods for the Prevention of
    AIDS' 157
Ministry of Civil Affairs 25, 27, 56
Ministry of Information Industry:
    'Management Methods concerning
    Internet Service Providers on
    Business Premises' 134
Ministry of Justice 29, 43, 45, 59;
    human rights 144; Institute for
    Crime Prevention 149
Ministry of Personnel: 'Notice on
    Website Management for the
    Purpose of Preventing Incidence of
    Releasing Confidential Information
    on the Internet' 126
Ministry of Post and
    Telecommunications 122
Ministry of Public Security 43; 1996
    'Notice on Strengthening the
    Security of International Computer
    Network Connections' 128; 1997
    'Provisions for the Security,
    Protection and Management of
    Computer Networks and
    International Networks' 126; 2000
    'Guidelines for Assessing Security
    Protection of Computer Information
    Systems' 126; adversarial trial
    format 144; arrest of Li Hongzhi 56;
    Computer Management and
    Inspection Bureau 122; June 2000

Notice 82; 'Notice on the
    Strict Enforcement of the Criminal
    Procedure Law and on the
    Conscientious Prevention
    and Correction of Extended
    Detention' 153; opposition to
    2000 SPC Explanations 103;
    'Proposal on Crimes Endangering
    Computer Information System'
    Security 123

National People's Congress: 1982–83
    NPCSC Decisions 43, 59, 82–83, 94,
    109; 1989 'Law on Infectious Disease
    Prevention and Control' 155–56;
    1992 'Decision on the Prohibition of
    Prostitution' 34; 1994 'Decision on
    Severe Punishment for Organizing
    and Transporting People Across
    State Borders' 34, 113; 2000
    'Decision on Safeguarding Internet
    Security' 127–29; bans Falungong
    58; Committee for Internal and
    Judicial Affairs 30; Fifteenth
    Congress 51; human rights and
    2004 constitutional amendment 162;
    Legal Work Committee 57, 59, 73,
    124; legislative interpretation
    58–59, 104, 145; NPCS 1990
    'Decision on Drug Control' 109–10;
    NPCSC 'Supplementary Decision
    Regarding the Punishment of
    Smuggling' 109; rejects SPC 2000
    Explanations 103, 116
Nei Li 78
'no crime without a law' 3, 19, 23,
    31, 43, 59, 60, 62, 71, 119, 120, 127,
    140, 152
'no punishment without a law' 24, 31,
    43, 60, 62, 71, 119, 120, 127, 140, 152,
    160, 161
'non-penalization' 21

'organized abduction and sale of
    human beings' 95
'organized crime' 32, 95, 147; Chinese
    definition 33, 90, 96, 97; CL97
    distinctions between 'ordinary
    criminal organization', 'criminal
    organization with a triad nature'
    and 'terrorist organization' 97–98,
    101–04, 116; Western definition 97;
    see also 'criminal organization with
    a triad nature'

Peerenboom, Randall 26, 48, 149,
   165, 167
Peking University Law School 145
People's University Research Center
   of Criminal Jurisprudence 163
plea-bargaining 161
'policy is the soul of law' 8, 37
pornography 33, 57, 72; internet 134;
   Party viewpoint 137
Potter, P. 2, 4–5, 22
PRC Law Governing Assemblies,
   Parades and Demonstrations 55
presumption of innocence 162
principle of legality 3
prostitution 34; 1992 NPC decision
   32; organized crime 91; UN
   Declaration 80
'protection of society' 15, 62
'punish crime and protect human
   rights' 159
'punishment and no stipulation' 19
'punishment must fit the crime' 20, 88,
   108, 111, 137, 141, 160, 161, 164, 166
'pure computer crime' 35, 119, 143
'purpose' (*mudi*) 40, 44, 50, 106

rape: and adultery 73; CL97 Articles
   236, 237 on 'indecent sexual acts'
   70; distinguished from 'illicit sexual
   intercourse' 64; in marriage 77,
   86, 152
're-education through labour' 25, 108
'Regulations Governing Venues for
   Religious Purposes' 58
'Regulations on Administrative
   Penalties for Public Security' 54, 70
'Regulations on Governing Public
   Order and Security' 54, 56
religious freedom 41, 47
'right to defence' 165
'right to remain silent' 165
'rights and interests' 2, 15, 29, 68;
   women's 74
Robinson, Mary 107
'rule of law' 1, 13, 16, 19, 44, 50, 60, 61,
   71, 90; in criminal law 26;
   Falungong 50–51; heresy 61, *see also*
   Jiang Zemin; and market 15, 38;
   'nomocracy' 28; public order and
   human rights 1, 5, 35, 37, 141, 142,
   158, 168, *see also* 'balance of values';
   in public security 6; and rule of
   man 16–18, 47, 71; and rule of
   virtue 5, 7, 8, 9, 16–18, 20, 28–31, 47,

66, 71, 73, 85, 118, 141; and socialist
   spiritual civilization 13, 17; and
   state constitution 1999 revision 15,
   16, 18, 129
'rule of virtue' *see* 'rule of law'

sanwu population 93
Seay, Pamela 22
secret societies *see* 'heretical cult'
Severe Acute Respiratory Syndrome
   36, 154–59
'severe punishment' 21; *see also*
   'heavy penalty-ism'
'Severe Punishment for Organizing
   and Transporting People Across
   State Borders' 34
sexual harassment 32
Shan Changzhong 56
Sheff, David 121
Shi Yan'an 5
Shu Haide 79
Si Lantao 161
'smuggling of illegal immigrants'
   112–15; 2003 strike hard campaign
   103
'social harm' 20–21, 32, 33, 35, 161;
   computer-related crime 125, 132–33;
   Falungong 50–52; illegal border
   crossings 114; infectious disease
   156; organized crime 116; state
   functionaries 102
Sohmen, Philip 131, 136, 140
Song Xiaoming 103
Song Yonghui 153, 162
'spirit of the leader' 13, 37, 71
State Bureau of Religious Affairs 49, 53
State Council 58, 59; 1992 white paper
   on criminal law 25; 1994 'PRC
   Provisions on the Protection of
   Computer Information Security
   Systems' 122; 2000 'Methods for
   Managing Website Content
   Providers' 137; 2000 'Methods of
   Managing Internet Service
   Providing Businesses' 133; 2001
   'Notice on Strengthening the
   Management of Internet Service
   Providers on Business Premises'
   134; 2002 'Provisions for the
   Management of Internet Service
   Providing Businesses' 136–37; 2003
   human rights reporting 142;
   'Emergency Provisions in Dealing
   with Public Health Crises' 156

State Environmental Protection
  Agency 119
State Press and Publication
  Administration Bureau: 'Provisional
  Regulations on the Management of
  Online Publications' 137–38
State Secrecy Bureau: 'Provisional
  Regulations on the Management of
  State Secrets on Computer
  Information Networks' 126
State Sports Administration 46
'stipulation and less punishment' 19
'strike hard' 12, 20, 95, 115; 1980–5
  campaigns 92; 2001 campaign
  147–48; Xinjiang separatists 107
'substituting words for law' 54
Sun Yat-sen 91
Sun Zhigang 27
Sun Zhongxin 65
superstition and witchcraft 43
supremacy of law 37, 62, 148
Supreme People's Court 22, 42; 1992
  'Answers on Abduction' 83; 2000
  Minutes regarding drug purity
  110–11; 2002 'Explanations for the
  Application of Laws in Adjudicating
  Cases of the Organizing,
  Transporting of Others for the
  Illegal Crossing of Borders' 114;
  and analogy 12, 13; 'Explanations
  concerning the Issues in the
  Application of Law Regarding
  Criminal Cases on the Prevention
  and Control of Outbreaks of
  Infectious Disease' 156–57;
  interpretation of 2001 Marriage Law
  150; interpretation of CL97 Article
  300; Liu Yong case 145
Supreme People's Procuratorate 22,
  43, 58; compared to the SPC 146;
  Research Institute of Procuratorial
  Theory 150; *see also* Supreme
  People's Court

Taiwan: SARS legislation 159
Tanner, Harold 68
'ten abominations' 9, 64
terrorism 86, 91; 2001 NPC revision of
  CL97 on terrorism 106; CL97 Article
  120 105, 107; definition of purpose
  106; FBI's definition 105; as
  'organized crime' 28, 105
'third parties' *see* adultery
'three evils' 107

'three represents' 14, 147
'three stresses' 58
Tian Hongjie 104
Tong Lihua 164
'triangular model' 160

'umbrella model' 160
'uncontrollable media' 117
United Nations Convention on Civil
  and Political Rights 160
United Nations Declaration on the
  Elimination of Violence Against
  Women 66, 75, 80
United States Anti-Terrorism Law 49
United States Constitution: First
  Amendment 53
United States House of
  Representatives 46
United States State Department:
  Falungong 45; human rights
  reporting in 1999 and 2000 24;
  human rights reporting 2003 118

'vanishing case(s)' 79, 86
Vogel, Ezra 40

Wang Hanbin 2, 33, 100, 106
Wang Shangxin 57
Wang Yi 137–38
Wang Zuofu 3, 155
Wen Jiabao 154
Wen Xiaoli 17
World Health Organization 157
World Trade Organization 6, 30, 140

Xia Yong 52
Xiao Yang 2, 142, 150
Xin Ren 8

Ye Gaofeng 81, 92, 95
Ye Xiaowen 49, 53
Yu Rongheng 121
Yu Wei 21
Yu Zhigang 94, 98, 120, 124–26
Yuan Fanmin 100, 101

Zhang Chunsheng 17
Zhang Fengge 3
Zhang Kong 157
Zhang Qiyue 51
Zhang Shihan 56
Zhao Bingzhi 99, 105, 111, 120, 163
Zhao Tingguan 20
Zhao Yanguang 123

Zhao Zuojun 106
zhengfa system 4, 11, 12, 16, 22–25, 35, 37–38, 59, 90–91, 115–16, 118, 128, 139, 143, 160, 165–68; public order 152; separation of powers 151

Zhou Daoluan 56
Zhu Erjun 101
Zhu Rongji 48
Zhu Yantao 81
Zhu Yuling 161